TIME TO DE

CW01081115

An innovative new
Project Management approach revealed

Yaniv Shor

TIME TO DELIVER

YANIV SHOR

Copyright © 2017 by Project Map LTD.

All rights reserved.

No part of this publication may be reproduced, stored in a retrieval system, or transmitted, in any form or by any means, electronic, mechanical, photocopying, recording or otherwise, without the prior written permission of the copyright owner.

ISBN-13: 978-1983936777

ISBN-10: 1983936774

Editor: Amichai Shalev
Cover Design: Studio Dor Cohen
Design & Formatting: Socciones Editoira Digitale

Published by
Project Map LTD.
Hataas 23, Kfar Saba, Israel
info@progg.io

Contents

Introduction

Twenty years have passed since I managed my first project. Back then, project management was based on the Theory of Constraints methods, supported by Gantt charts and concepts such as "Critical Chains" and "Bottlenecks" were endemic.

The Critical Chain was not invented twenty years ago; it was first developed along with PERT diagrams by the United States Navy in the early 1950s. The Gantt chart came even earlier, going back to the beginning of the twentieth century. Despite the vast changes in organizational environments over the last one hundred years, project managers are still using outdated Gantt charts as a central tool to show activity in a schedule. In fact, almost all project management tools rely on them to some extent or another.

Like many others, I too planned with the help of Gantt charts and I used associated concepts, even before I knew anything about the background of TOC. Concepts such as "Bottlenecks," "Constraints," "Buffers," and "Critical Paths" were part of my routine. I made every effort to manage my projects "right" with the tools and methods used in the industry, but time and time again I realized that Gantt charts and methods taken from production line management were not enough for the modern environment. I learned that there were other, no less important aspects that had to be addressed in project management.

Moreover, changes in business environments and communications habits in the workplace and elsewhere were also affecting project management. Projects have become shorter and more exposed to change; specialization is an increasing need and every project now involves dozens of parties. At the same time, the marketplace is becoming more sophisticated. Competition is stiffer; customers now spanning the whole globe, are more demanding and online information is accessible to one and all. In the absence of orderly principles for project management under such challenging conditions, these phenomena have made project management an art.

Additionally, use of the limited tools available to project managers has backfired. Project managers are finding themselves doing a mechanical job, preoccupied with enormous charts nobody wants to see, and forsaking their natural, desirable place as project leaders. This is keeping many people with extraordinary management skills out of the profession.

Over the years, I developed project management tools that can restore the occupation to its rightful place as a sophisticated, advanced management profession. After close to twenty years of managing many different projects for international companies, I decided to document the method presented herein, a method I call "The Project Map." At the end of the book, readers will find an appendix of basic project management terms.

I hope I shall succeed in showing you that project management is indeed an art, but it is a highly structured art that can be learned by taking an in-depth view of the organization's reality while using advanced tools and excellent communication. Along the way, I hope you will also enjoy the story for its own sake.

Chapter One

The Project

1

I stood outside the building waiting for Lisa to give me the sign to enter. For some reason, I was too blasé. I suppose you could say we'd already failed, and I therefore had nothing to lose. I would try to do what I'd planned, nothing more. Still, something in me refused to accept failure. Somehow, I still believed there was hope, that it was still possible to make a change, that this meeting was not a waste of time, perhaps even contained the seeds of a new beginning.

I saw my reflection in the building's transparent glass cladding: I was wearing a smartly pressed, three-piece suit and a starched white shirt. I kept unbuttoning and rebuttoning the top and second buttons of my shirt, indecisive about leaving them open or closed.

Suddenly it started to rain.

I waited in the building's busy lobby, impatient to see Lisa. She still hadn't shown up. Was everything all right? I felt a stab of concern.

The conference was taking place exactly three years after the project started. I had tried to postpone the gathering using diplomatic and not-so-diplomatic means, until I realized that was a dead end. It simply couldn't be ignored or bypassed. It was stuck there, like a giant wall blotting out the future. I knew it was right in front of me and that I would crash into it; I had no choice. I was only hoping the pain would be endurable.

So why was Lisa late? She should have been here to meet me already. What the hell was holding her up?

Just as I decided to go ahead without her, she appeared wearing a tight blue dress and elegant heels. She had short blond hair, metallic blue eyes, and an odd habit of gesticulating as she spoke. Most people use their hands to speak, but Lisa's gestures were unlike any I had seen. She'd speak while making strange circular motions with one hand that would force the attention of her audience away from what she was saying. She knew it, but could not control this tic.

"Are you OK?" she asked.

I shrugged. "Does it make a difference if I'm not?"

She smiled at me with understanding, and proceeded quickly towards the conference hall. The hubbub coming from the room made it clear that the number of participants exceeded expectations. For if a catastrophe was about to occur, why not have a ring-side seat?

But actually, I told myself, there is no catastrophe. The failure is already behind us, though not entirely. We were now dealing with the wreckage, and it was my job to collect the pieces and reassemble them into something entirely new.

Lisa marched towards the podium. She was a member of my team. Before that, she'd been involved in internet projects, and for a time had worked as a project manager in a large production company. When I took the job, and met her for the first time, she'd been full of self-confidence; she'd made the impression that the job was tailor-made for her. Despite the project's failure, I had nothing against her. Without her, the situation would have been much worse; of that, I was certain.

Lisa and the other managers were all professionals. They had mastered the fields they managed, and I couldn't point to a single significant mistake any of them had made – the same way I couldn't understand where I myself had gone wrong. So, what happened? The truth was that I no longer had the energy to think about it.

As I was waiting for Lisa's hands and her opening remarks, I continued to repeat my mantra; praise the work done to date, stress the project's importance and define clear goals that can be attained in the future. But how would I manage to speak about each of these points for fifteen minutes, without mentioning a single concrete task or deadline?

I was no longer sure if there was any point to this whole exercise, but with one hundred members of the project group, crammed into a space designed for eighty, it seemed too late to retreat. The wall was right in front of me. For a second, I thought of myself as a superhero who'd manage to smash through it.

Lisa signaled me to step up and take the microphone.

The silence was complete. I heard it descend on every corner. The gazes coming my way were getting darker. It seemed as if one enormous, dumb-struck eye were looking at me; I was facing a gigantic pixelated storm cloud. I took a deep breath. Lisa sent me a piercing glance, as if asking me if I was all right, but afraid to be overheard. My hand made a calming motion in her direction, to say that everything was under control.

I took another deep breath, cleared my throat, and started speaking in the most confident voice I could muster.

"To all of you – welcome. I am very happy to be here with you. You must be asking yourselves why you were invited here today and what is so important to share in this setting. And, you know what? You're right.

"We've come a long way, but we've reached a difficult point. Some would describe it as failure. I hate that word. As do you, don't you? And, maybe you're asking yourselves how we got to where we are and what role each of us played. It's hard to avoid these questions. Believe me, I'm asking them too. Along with many other questions. But I suddenly find myself saying; why ask? And even if I had answers, what good would they do?

"In any case, the reason I asked you to come here today is essential, and has nothing to do with what is past. It concerns what will be.

"What do I mean? I'll get to that in just a moment, all right?"

I took another deep breath. The storm cloud dissolved into familiar human faces. I took a moment to look at each one, if only for a fraction of a second. Instead of the heavy sense of despair that had been my constant companion this whole time, I felt something else – a kind of transcendence of spirit, a feeling that perhaps, after all, with all of the resourcefulness and talent packed into this room, it was still possible to do something and save this project.

2

Four days earlier, at the end of March, I had returned from yet another meeting with George Madison, our major donor. We used to meet with George and his people at the end of every month for a day or two to present the state of the project. Sometimes we met face-to-face, and sometimes by conference calls. This time, it was just George and me; each of my team members had half an hour by phone to present the month's progress, the major achievements and key challenges still to be met.

In the past, there had been some unpleasant meetings with George and his team, but this was the worst yet. I had the feeling George was sick of our presentations, or more accurately, sick of our excuses. Which was understandable. After all, he had given us tens of millions of dollars, waiting to see his name emblazoned on the new wing of the maternity ward at the end of two years. But it was now three years later, and the end was nowhere in sight.

In the first few months, it was easy to present progress in the form of walls going up, one floor being finished, another emerging, until the new four-story wing was complete. We had the sense of making great strides, right on schedule. We received many compliments. But over time, our presentations became increasingly ill-defined.

In hindsight, I can say perfectly honestly that we did nothing. Construction was the responsibility of a contractor, who had been selected by tender and had to show incremental progress in order to get paid, which is precisely what he did. Throughout that period, which lasted around eighteen months, we observed a great deal of impressive action, but we weren't planning for the day when the building would be delivered to us and we would have to get it ready to fulfill its function.

And, in fact, after a year and a half of construction, we took possession of the building as planned, ushering in the stage considered simpler; bringing in and installing the new systems and getting them ready for a trial run. This stage, which was supposed to have lasted all of six months, was dragging on and on a year and a half later.

Gradually, we realized that almost all our operating assumptions had been too optimistic. Although everyone was working very hard, progress was painfully slow, and I couldn't find a way to speed it up. As if that weren't enough, suppliers failed to meet their deadlines, holding us up for long stretches and blaming us for the delays, leading us to distrust our own plans and forecasts, which we had to postpone over and over again.

George was a wealthy and extraordinarily generous man. He was at least seventy-years-old, but he still had a full head of salt-and-pepper hair. He dressed well, but casually, in a way that didn't hint at his great riches. Aside from his philanthropic activities, I think he also owned some baseball team, but I wasn't sure. I didn't feel comfortable asking him, because I knew less than nothing about the sport. I didn't know any of the teams; in fact, without fail, baseball induced in me nothing but stupendous boredom.

As far as our project was concerned, he was the perfect donor, expecting us only to use his money well. During the last year, we made sure to thank him at every opportunity and apologize for the many delays, but George's patience was running out.

Four days ago, at our last meeting, he was furious. He said he had completely lost faith in our ability to complete this project, and even hinted that we were deliberately misleading him. Worse still, after realizing where matters stood, he turned his brown eyes on me and said:

"You know there is a clause in the contract that says I can withdraw my donation if the project is not completed in four years? I see you know and as far as I can tell, that's exactly what's going to happen!"

A slight tremble started climbing up my legs, and the room seemed to grow dark. I opened my mouth to answer, but all I managed was some hesitant stammering. I really didn't know what to say. Should I promise to have the project done on time? I had to promise, but did I believe in it myself?

George's words were like an ice-bath. To my great embarrassment, I couldn't contradict him from my heart. I knew that, given the current situation, there was an excellent chance this could drag on for four years. When the construction phase ended, I really thought we'd be able to complete the project in six months. I never imagined that we'd be where we were at the end of the third year. I did my best to reassure George, promising we would do everything possible to improve the situation.

"Give us one last chance," I was close to begging. He dismissed me with a noncommittal grunt. He wouldn't act on the clause in the contract, at least not yet, but the threat was hanging over our heads like a gloomy, menacing shadow. The rifle had been introduced in the first act, and it was set to be fired in the third. A clear and present danger.

The meeting ended because there was nothing left to say. I walked towards the door, feeling as though I was losing my balance. Someone saw me and sent me a questioning look; I think she wanted to ask me if I was all right, if I needed some water. I quickly looked down and hurried out.

Just outside the building, I stood as if the ground beneath my feet was shaking. My mouth was ashy, and for a moment I lost all sense of time and place. I had no idea where I was supposed to go now, what I was supposed to do. Just then, my wife tried to reach me on my cell phone. I rejected the call, but she called again. When I answered, she spoke for a while. I'm sure I listened but whatever she said made no impression. In that moment, I couldn't think at all. I mumbled something into the phone and walked away from the glittering office tower into a plaza, filled with artificial trees, SUVs, and glass windows reflecting blinding light in every direction. When I reached my rental car, I realized I had no idea where to go now. I was supposed to be meeting George for dinner later on, a dinner scheduled before the blow-up of the meeting. How could I get through a meal with him after what had happened? And how was I supposed to pass the time until then? I was hoping he would call to cancel.

I started the car and took a deep breath. "I'm OK, everything will be OK," I muttered as I started driving. I didn't believe my own words.

The next few hours were hazy. George didn't cancel our dinner plans, and I think I went back to the hotel. I probably checked my emails and talked with some of my colleagues on the phone; I know I called my wife to see what she wanted earlier. She asked me if everything was all right; of course, I said everything was fine, but I knew that she realized something was off.

I kept looking at my watch. I wasn't sure if time was slowing down or speeding up. What the hell was I supposed to talk about? I tried to reach Lisa, Fabian and Laura, but all I got was recorded messages saying they'd get back to me, which only stretched my nerves even thinner.

I thought about project managers and how alone they are, especially when everything goes wrong and everyone else is trying to distance themselves from the failure. When one of them finally called me back, I didn't pick up. I was incapable of speech. I had to concentrate, put something together right away, but nothing came to mind.

At dinner, I sat down next to George. He looked relaxed, as if our earlier conversation were a distant dream. He drank more than a couple of glasses of wine, told some funny stories, and praised the spaghetti alle vongole, as if the dish were a classic work of art.

Then, a lull in the conversation. Like a hawk, I swooped down on the opportunity and asked a smiling George for three more months before he acted on his threat and withdrew his donation and support. I swore to him that we would regroup and present a different state of affairs next month. Virtually begging, I asked him not to do anything drastic till then.

I had no idea what I was going to do, but I must have been desperate enough and pitiful enough for George to decide to wait. He finished the dregs of his wine, looked at me again with his steady brown eyes, and said:

"It's your last chance. Afterwards, we pack up what's left and go home." He put the glass down on the table, got up, and left.

* * *

The next day, we cut out the meetings we had planned with George as the gist had already been said the day before; there was no point in making presentations if the entire project was now on ice. The cancellations left me with plenty of time on my hands until my flight home, scheduled for noon the next day. Looking for a place to sit down and think about what had happened in the last twenty-four hours, I decided to go into the city. Maybe seeing the water and the bridges would cheer me up.

I got out of the cab somewhere near the Golden Gate Bridge. I looked at the big store windows, fancy restaurants, souvenir shops and never-ending stream of foot traffic, the cars whizzing past like futuristic vehicles, all clean and metallic, looking as if untethered to the ground and about to take off for the sky and the stars.

At some point, it started to rain but I just continued walking down the street, overcome by an enormous sense of failure. I felt trapped, and so intense was my gloom that I didn't notice I was without an umbrella, until I realized I was wet to my skin.

I ducked into a small neighborhood bar. It was relatively quiet and tastefully furnished, the walls covered in murals done by graffiti artists. The large television screens were showing different sports channels. Despite the odd juxtaposition between the graffiti and the digital screens, the designer had managed to create a welcoming ambience.

The indoor heating helped dry the worst of my soaking. I hung up my jacket and sat down on one of the comfortably padded barstools at the horseshoe-shaped bar. The barman placed the menu in front of me and immediately started reciting the list of cocktails he assured me matched my mood. I must have looked truly miserable, but I still opted for a Belgian beer, whose only advantage over its competitors was its unusually high ten percent alcohol contents. At that point, this was the only thing I cared about.

Music was playing softly. I recognized Nirvana's "All Apologies." The song mirrored my state of mind so perfectly I almost burst out laughing.

8

I sipped my beer slowly. My mind kept churning over the situation. I tried to find a sequential line of thinking that would lead me out of the corner I was backed into. The barman sent me a look of understanding, and started to talk. At first, I didn't realize he was talking to me, but once I caught on I tried to pay attention, even though the last thing I wanted to do was engage in pointless small talk.

I gathered that the murals had been done by a well-known artist and had even been photographed and featured in an art magazine. I nodded with feigned enthusiasm and asked how long it had taken to paint. I must have touched a sore spot, because the barman switched gears and embarked on a long saga he had obviously recited dozens of times before, complaining about the many months the project took and how the bar opening had to be postponed because of the delay in the artist's work.

At least I'm not alone, I thought. If the opening of a thirty-square-meter bar is delayed, no wonder it's tough to add eight hundred square meters to every floor of a major hospital's maternity wing based on a far-reaching technological vision, new systems, and many suppliers.

"So how long did it take you to build this place?" I asked, trying to shift the burden to speaking to him. Maybe I didn't want him to start asking me questions about my own story; I feared the moment I would have to open up about it.

He told me about the old space he had bought at an outrageous price, the three months of renovations, followed by three unscheduled months of mural painting. I smiled and said that I understood him more than he could imagine. He tilted his head to one side and raised his eyebrows, as if asking me to explain. In answer, I told him I was in charge of building a new hospital wing, including buying equipment and getting it ready for use, adding that the project's completion had already been postponed by a year and the end was not yet in sight. I thought this would finish our conversation; maybe a customer at the other end of the bar was trying to catch his attention, and I sighed in relief that he didn't ask any in-depth follow-up questions. I sipped the last of my beer and got ready to leave. There had to be a better way to pass the time.

"Why was it postponed?" I suddenly heard another voice coming from behind my right shoulder. I turned my head and saw a balding man of about fifty, smiling at me. He must have overheard everything.

"Pardon me for butting in," he apologized but again asked, "but why was it postponed?"

I smiled back and said: "I wish I knew."

He was clearly unsatisfied. He shook his head and said, "Tell me more."

I took a deep breath and looked at him more closely. He was built broadly, like a wrestler. He was wearing black slacks and a button-down shirt, whose tails he had pulled free as one would after a hard day of work. Yet he didn't seem exhausted or even particularly tired. On the contrary, he seemed relaxed and energetic, as if he were only just gearing up for the day.

In any case, something in him exuded calmness, and he seemed genuinely interested in the story. It may, I thought, be good to share it. Maybe I would suddenly be struck by a new angle, shout "eureka," and run outside like a madman. Besides, the beer was making itself felt. My speech suddenly felt lighter. Nirvana's *In Utero* notes also helped put me in a pleasant twilight state.

I started telling him about the decision to expand the maternity ward and the technological vision. I described how we spent years trying to identify a donor, and once he was found, how we messed up the project so that its very existence now hung in the balance. With a wry smile and in broad strokes, I told him about yesterday's awful meeting and how I suddenly had a free day because I was such a rock-star. "So maybe there's nothing to do but have another beer," I joked, but the stranger didn't laugh.

I expected the fellow to say something like, "I'm sorry for your troubles," and perhaps add how he was sure things would get better, the type of statements used to frame a conversation and allow it to move on to other topics and superficial chatter. Instead, he leaned forward, pulled his chair a little closer, and said:

"OK. Now you've really got my attention. What happened? And what was your role in all of it?"

Who does this guy think he is? I asked myself. Why does he think that small talking at a bar entitles him to know the finer details of a failure I intend to forget? And why does he care? Is he working on something similar? Is this some kind of industrial espionage?

I needed to decide if I wanted to continue the conversation. So I stalled, and said: "I'm Gary, I'm a project manager at a hospital. I have a small team, but I am personally responsible for this fiasco, which I'm still managing. Who are you, sir, and if I may ask – why are you so interested?"

This may have been brusque, but it didn't faze him. He provided a cheerful answer: He was an experienced project manager, though he had recently been spending most of his time consulting for various institutions and large project managers.

I felt my lips curling into a bitter smile. There were too many project managers running around in the world in general and in San Francisco in particular. They look like everyone else, dress in corporate clothes, carry on normal conversations, and go for a beer at the local watering hole. Nothing I didn't know already.

I also knew all about so-called consultants who troll business district bars, dropping in ostensibly by chance, to sink their hooks into the next sap, desperate for someone to extricate him from a mess with their "expertise." All of San Francisco was a pond full of fish, and these types walked around with their transparent nets. I remember Fabian telling me about one such type who pestered him like a black fly. It took him a long time to get rid of him, and the resulting irritation lasted months.

I despised consultants. Even the best, who really had the experience and had managed many successful projects, were generally only engaging in Monday morning quarterbacking. I felt that without the heavy responsibility, that in practice weighs on project managers' shoulders, it was really hard to be of any help in decision-making. The consulting process always seemed promising at first, but would invariably end up being pointless, though time-consuming and costly. The last thing I needed right now was another consultant who would scatter about pearls of wisdom and feel-good insights about perfect project management.

"I'm not interested in consulting services at the moment. And whatever we discussed here must remain confidential." I was sorry to have gotten sucked into the conversation, sorry about the beer, my irresponsible meandering when I was supposed to be solving serious problems. The sound system had by now segued into bland country music, which was grating on my nerves. My plan was to excuse myself with a smile, pay for the beer, and leave. "And any case, I'm flying home tomorrow," I added.

To my surprise, he continued looking at me in a friendly, cheerful way, and said with undisguised confidence that he was not looking for a consulting position and had no intention of offering me his services for a fee. I was stymied. Was this a new trick of the trade?

"The bottom line is," he continued, "that your hospital story strikes me as interesting. Seeing that fate threw us together, I'm curious about the project's circumstances."

I looked at him wordlessly. I had no idea what to say.

"Look. Years ago, I cracked the code of project management and made myself a tidy little sum. I expect I will continue to make money off it in the future too. So, the last thing I want is to offer you a service you don't want, certainly not for money."

"I understand, but not really. Forgive me for being frank, but what *do* you want?"

He opened his mouth and let out a loud guffaw. "Listen, till your flight tomorrow, I can show you some simple principles that will help you down the line, but if you want to continue spending your working hours in bars, that's fine with me."

He turned to the barman and said: "Put his beer on my tab and let us have another round."

The barman served us new beers. We clinked our glasses and after a small sip, which became a rather larger one than I'd intended, I said to him: "OK. You win. Now I'm curious. What can you teach me by tomorrow?"

"It's really simple," he answered. "I'm going to give you two assignments and see if you can carry them out. If you can, you're on the right track, and we'll take it from there. What do you say?"

"Sounds great," I said. "But don't you want to hear a little about the project I'm managing? How it's structured? What's been done, and what's left to do?"

"At this point, it's best that I don't know," he said with absolute confidence. "Just describe the project in a few words, tell me what your role is, how many people are involved in it and how many report to you directly and indirectly. Also, who is the worst employee without whom the entire project would advance faster?"

The worst employee? I thought, and started to laugh. It really was an interesting thought, and my mind immediately started going through all the bad people in the project. They bubbled to the surface and disappeared without leaving a trace.

"All right," I said. "As I mentioned, the project is the expansion of the hospital's maternity wing. The building is up. What's left essentially is to bring in the equipment and systems, install them, test-run them, and get the space ready for use.

"I report to the hospital's development and operations manager, and occasionally also to the hospital director. My title is general project manager and I have three project managers under me. Each of them is responsible for a particular piece of the project. That means that I directly supervise only three people. Indirectly, there are about two hundred professionals and team members, as well as service and goods providers."

"And who is the worst performing?"

"I can think of one person in particular. I can hardly deal with him," I said with a grim smile. "He manages the hospital's integration group. When we install new computer systems, he's supposed to test them and link them up with the hospital's existing systems. Every conversation with him becomes an argument, and every single assignment I give him is late. Sometimes I feel like giving him a good swift kick in the pants and getting rid of him."

"OK," he answered.

"Is that enough data for you?"

"Actually, it's way more than I needed. In fact, I only wanted to know the number of people involved in the project and the worst performer, but I figured that if I only asked those two details you'd insist on telling me about the project as a whole. All right, what you told me about your job and the structure of the team is typical of almost every project in the world. Let's get started."

I'd finished my beer and was feeling a little logy, but was still focused. The barman had finally turned the country music off and was now playing something lighter with a good beat, a piece I couldn't place. A cluster of people entered the bar just then. I looked at the bald guy in front of me and thought, assignments? He's going to give me assignments? Is that all that's missing from my life at this moment? More assignments?

In any case, the beer in my brain and pleasant surroundings dispelled all resistance. "Fine," I said, "assignments it is. What have I got to lose?"

"Please note," he said in a serious tone of voice, his eyes suddenly larger than before, "the first assignment is to prepare a forty-five-minute speech you're going to give to all the people involved in the project. Later on, I'll help you get all the people together in the most effective way possible.

"The speech itself should be divided into three parts. In the first, you'll describe the amazing work that's been done to date. In the second, you'll emphasize the project's importance. And in the third, you'll define clear goals that can be achieved in the future."

"Are you kidding me? I've done this more times than I can count," I protested.

"Wait, I'm not finished."

"Yeah?"

"Yeah. Your speech cannot contain a single negative statement whatsoever! It also cannot refer to any specific assignment or specific goal."

I mulled that over for a couple of seconds before responding: "Let's say I can talk about failure in a positive way for fifteen minutes. Most of the people know the background as well as I do, so we can skip those fifteen minutes. And defining goals that can be achieved – doesn't this require one to relate to specific tasks and targets and deadlines?"

"Look," he said, "I can't explain everything right away. For now, you're just going to have to trust me. But I will say this: You're experiencing a problem every project manager faces. Everyone tries to move the project in the right direction, on time, along with the various parties – the managers, the personnel, the suppliers – to achieve the same goal.

"This is a complex problem, but the solution is simple, and it begins with people. I have just given you your first step. After you take it, I'll tell you more about its purpose. Shall we go on to the second assignment?"

"Fine."

"Do you have a GPS or some type of navigation app on your phone?"

"Yeah, I have an app based on driver information and other traffic data."

"Excellent," he said, glancing at his watch. "It's almost two o'clock. I want you to leave at five and head into town and drive to Eric's Place. Just put that into your app. Every app knows it."

"All right, but what exactly will I find there, and why do I have to go there at five? What am I supposed to do there?"

"Nothing special. Just show up and gather some impressions. We'll talk about it tomorrow morning over breakfast. Where are you staying?"

"At the new hotel near the university."

"Outstanding! I know it. When is your flight?"

"At three in the afternoon."

"Which means you have to be at the airport at one. I'll pop over to your hotel at eight in the morning, if that's all right with you. We'll have some time to go over your speech and talk about your impressions of Eric's Place. And now, if you'll excuse me, I have to run."

"Wait! If you're such an expert, could you take a look at our plans tomorrow? I have a pretty detailed Gantt chart with close to six hundred lines that Lisa, one of my project managers, maintains. I think this Gantt gives an excellent picture of what we planned to do compared to what actually got done in practice."

"Uh-mazing!" he answered, with an amused look on his face. "When I say 'uh-mazing,' I mean that it's quite a product, that Gantt of yours! If it has six hundred lines, I'll bet it has at least a thousand six hundred links. I'm really sorry that you guys worked so hard on it, because it's not going to do us a lot of good at this point."

"Yeah, it's pretty complex, but how can you say it's not going to work without even looking at it?"

"Listen," he said, pausing for a moment to consider his next words, "to succeed, you have to understand that every project is a dynamic, social and human event long before it becomes an engineering or operational challenge. I'm sure that your Gantt contains a brilliant analysis of the project, but you have to admit that it hasn't really helped you so far. Don't worry, we'll be getting back to this. But now I really have to go. See you tomorrow at eight."

He put a fifty-dollar bill on the bar and hurried out the door.

* * *

I stayed put, trying to understand what exactly I'd done and why I'd agreed to the stranger's scheme. Eric's Place? What is he trying to get out of this or teach me? What's waiting for me there? Should I be wasting my time on this instead of trying to understand how to dig myself out of the hole I'm in?

Maybe George Madison was right after all. Maybe there was no chance of completion by the end of the fourth year if the project manager was gallivanting around the city like a pilgrim, looking for the Holy Grail, instead of working nonstop.

But I had no choice. I'd agreed to meet him over breakfast and didn't have his phone number. Suddenly it dawned on me: I didn't even know his name! If I tried to tell anyone about this, they'd think I'd lost my mind and had been talking with a ghost.

Come on, man, pull yourself together, I told myself. Given the state I was in, I had nothing to lose. I'd followed my principles and experience, and look where those had gotten me.

I considered the sentence the stranger tossed out at the end, about a project being a social event. Any endeavor involving people is a social event, but what did this mean in the context of this project? I hoped things would get clearer with time. Now it was time to head to the hotel. I used the opportunity to call home and speak with my wife and kids.

I told her about the lousy meeting with George and the cancellation of the other appointments. Anna wasn't particularly surprised, because she had experienced the gradual worsening of our relationship with George Madison and his team of consultant together with me. When she asked how I was going to pass the time till my flight, I said something vague about going into town, and a breakfast meeting tomorrow with a consultant I'd met in a bar.

I knew that, at some point, I'd have to tell her exactly what I'd done, and I was suddenly disconcerted. I could already hear her grilling me: You did *what*? You met some lunatic in a bar who gave you an assignment to go someplace you've never heard of? For real? What's wrong with you?

Instead of being with her and the children, in the little down-time that I had, reading Sean a story or helping Marianna study for a test, I'm chasing my own tail in another city. And she and I have grown so distant. We hardly talk anymore. Eric's Place? What's happening to me?

17

I'll make it up to her, I promised myself. When it's all over, I'll take a vacation and make it up to her.

But when would it all be over? And how?

3

I got into my rental and set up my navigation app. It found Eric's Place right away and steered me into the heart of the city's financial district. It has to be a restaurant or a bar, I thought. It was only twenty-five miles away, but for some reason the app was giving me a drive-time of ninety minutes.

I didn't pay much attention to this oddity, and assumed the app would find the best route to the destination. I was off. For a second I considered calling Anna, but changed my mind. Not now. This wasn't a good time.

The first part of the journey was routine. For the first twenty-five miles or so, the navigation app took me down the highway, heading to the city, with no hint of what was to come. Although only thirteen more miles were left, the app continued to insist on the time lag, indicating I had another seventy minutes of travel ahead of me.

As if I'd made no progress to date.

I tried to battle the nerves that were starting to seize me, especially as I saw the app calculating and recalculating the route. There must be a traffic jam up ahead. Great, more time down the drain.

For a second, I considered making a U-turn, and telling the smiling fellow tomorrow that I was grateful for his willingness to guide me, but really – wasting my entire afternoon stuck in traffic was not exactly my idea of help.

But, deep within, I knew it was already too late.

At exactly the twelve-mile mark, the navigation app instructed me to exit the highway, which is when I realized the reason for the extended time it was showing. It was about half past five, and, in the city's financial district, thousands of brokers, account managers, office assistants, and investment advisors were hurrying home. It was rush-hour, and travel was reduced to a virtual crawl. Was this a test of the limits of my patience? Was that the whole story?

I tried to move the map on the screen to see where I was supposed to go next, but it was baffling. Eric's Place nestled in a tangle of tiny side streets, and it seemed that there were dozens of possible approaches.

The app struggled to find the shortest route. It would change its directions after I'd already entered an intersection. The first time it did that, I had just enough time to switch lanes, though I did see jumpy drivers cursing me on all sides. The second time, I had no opening to move; to my horror, I saw the app adding another ten minutes to my arrival time. Wonderful. If the man at the bar wanted to show me how much was out of my hands, how much I was dependent on other people and outside factors, he should have found a different method.

After a while, I started cursing the navigation app, the bald guy whose name I didn't know, the hospital, George Madison, and my life in general. I decided to try to figure out how to get to Eric's Place on my own, and I stopped listening to the app. I slowed down to ask passersby for directions, but everyone shrugged and indicated they didn't know it.

After driving for an hour, I was only a mile and a half away, but then I realized that Eric's Place was located near the local football stadium where a game was starting at seven. Better and better. I found myself caught amongst cars painted green and white, surrounded by fans on foot, who were moving faster to the stadium than the cars in the street. The app, which had earlier advised many turns in an apparent attempt to keep me away from the stadium, chose this moment to come back to life. I followed its new directions and left the river of fans behind. At last I was driving at a normal speed.

The journey is close to its end, I thought. Another turn or two, a stubborn red light, a short delay in trying to find the entrance to the parking lot, and voila – here I was, in front of my destination, after eighty minutes of driving.

The Holy Grail, I thought, almost laughing out loud in despair and relief.

The place was set higher than the parking area, which was almost empty. Judging by its size, the place attracted many visitors. An ostentatious neon sign with the name and a bottle of wine flickered fitfully. The entrance wasn't immediately visible, so I got out of the car and walked around the building looking for the door.

Finally, I found a wide staircase that led to a set of wide double doors. I pushed on one, but it was locked. I could see inside and clearly saw light and movement, so I decided to knock. Almost immediately, I heard a shout: "Just a moment please." I waited by the door. As far as I could remember, the bald fellow hadn't told me what I was supposed to do here, other than register my impressions.

"Hello!" I heard a friendly voice greeting me through the crack of the barely open door. "Are you the electrician?"

I was momentarily confused, but answered: "No, I'm not the electrician."

"Oh, so how may I help you?"

"I wanted to come in and see the place. Are you open?"

"Not right now. But come by later, around eleven tonight."

"Sorry, but I won't be in the area that late. Couldn't you just let me in now?"

The door opened a little wider to reveal a handsome Latino, whose body language indicated he was not about to let me in. In fact, he seemed to be hiding the space behind him on purpose.

"I'm sorry, sir, but we're closed. There's nothing to see. But if you come back at eleven, I promise you'll have a good time."

"Couldn't I just take a peek? Someone asked me to stop by and have a look at this place and express my opinion."

"Sir, you do understand that none of the ladies has arrived yet? There's nothing to see. I'm going to have to ask you to leave."

"What do you mean 'none of the ladies has arrived yet'?"

"Just that. None of the ladies are here. This is a strip club, sir. Please go away. I have work to do." He didn't wait for my answer before slamming the door in my face.

I stood in front of the double-doors. I could feel my sense of outrage radiating from my chest and spreading down to the tips of my fingers. A strip club? What kind of a sick joke was this? What was I supposed to tell Anna?

I looked right and left to make sure I was alone. I felt more mortified that I had ever felt in my life. I wanted the earth to open up beneath me and swallow me whole.

I started walking, almost running back to the car, while trying to set my thoughts in order. How did I allow a man, I don't know at all, lead me astray like this? How did I fall into this trap? He was surely sitting someplace laughing his head off, planning to tell his buddies about the senior manager he sent on a wild goose chase to a closed strip club at rush hour.

All those people I stopped to ask for directions – what could they have been thinking? I was lucky nobody here knew me. When I see him in the morning, if I see him at all, I thought, I don't know if I'll be able to contain myself. You're such an idiot, I told myself, you and him both. What an incredible waste of time.

I got into the car feeling angry and ashamed. My phone screen showed I'd missed a call from Lisa. She'd left a text message asking me where I was. What was I supposed to answer? That I fell prey to some crook whose name I hadn't even bothered asking for? I decided to keep the whole thing to myself. Better that no one knows, better to forget how low I'd sunk.

I turned the navigation app back on, but turned it off at once. Furious, I decided I'd figure it out on my own, no matter how long it took me.

The road was clear now that the game was under way; the fans were gone from the streets. Within half an hour, I was back at my hotel. I decided to skip dinner as I had no appetite left. All I wanted to do was end this day as fast and simply as possible and get under the covers.

I parked in the lot facing the lobby and walked in, receiving a friendly greeting from Michelle at reception. After three years of monthly meetings, I knew almost all the staff at the hotel.

"Good evening, Mr. Balder. How are you?"

"Great," I lied. "And you?"

"Just fine, thanks. I have a letter for you. It came about an hour ago, and then we had a call from Mr. Hamilton who personally asked me to make sure you got it."

"Who is Mr. Hamilton?"

"Oh, I thought you knew him. He said you'd met today in town."

"So, Hamilton's his name. I see. Do you know that clown?"

"Sure, everyone does. He's a regular at the academic center nearby. He's very partial to our Burgundy Suite."

Michelle handed me the letter. For some reason, I couldn't meet her eye. I felt that she was able to read the humiliation in my face. I regretted having called him a clown. I thanked her, took the envelope, and headed for the elevator.

The Burgundy Suite occupied the entire top floor of the hotel and was reserved for special guests and VIPs only. Assuming Michelle was right, someone like that would not have misled me in such a degrading way. So, what was going on?

I sat down on one of the lobby sofas and opened the envelope:

Gary,

Please allow me to apologize for the rough ride you endured this afternoon. Tomorrow morning, I'll explain why I asked you to go there. I know you're feeling tricked, but that wasn't the intention. Try to find the humor in the situation, and meet me for breakfast as planned.

As for the first assignment, I'm attaching a link you can use during our meeting.

I'm curious about your situation, and look forward to staying in touch. I've handled projects for many years, but it isn't every day one runs

22

into projects such as yours. This is an opportunity for us both. I hope to see you at eight. I'll be waiting in the dining room.

Your friend

Michael Hamilton

Chapter Two

Overly Optimistic and Cognitively Biased

1

The next day, I headed to breakfast looking forward to my meeting with that Michael Hamilton.

"Good morning," he called out in a confident voice. The expression on his face said he hadn't doubted I'd show up. Apparently, neither had I.

He was already seated, an empty coffee cup in front of him and a rumpled newspaper on the seat next to him. A faint scent of aftershave in the air mingled with the aromas of scrambled eggs and croissants fresh out of the oven.

"Shall we hit the buffet? I'm starving!" he said.

While exchanging the required pleasantries, we walked over to the laden tables to collect cheese, vegetables, and omelets to order. Business hotels tend to serve breakfasts of remarkable similarity, as if following an identical script. Nonetheless, there is a kind of pleasure in the selection process at the end of which you end up with exactly the same plate as you had last time, but have the feeling you're eating exactly what you want.

When we reached the bread table, I could no longer resist: "Listen, I have to ask you, why did you send me to Eric's Place? I mean, why a strip club, of all places?"

He smiled. He opened his mouth to answer, but just then a heavyset man of about sixty and his white-haired wife appeared, greeted Michael, and started chatting. I took my full tray back to the table, sat down, and started eating mechanically. Doubt coursed through my body once again.

A few minutes later, Michael joined me, bringing a breakfast the same as mine.

"All right then," he caught his breath, "we have lots of work and not a lot of time till your flight."

He started cutting into his omelet, started at me hard, and asked: "Did you check out the link I sent you?" Without waiting for an answer, he asked, "Well, what did you think? I want to hear what you intend to tell the people involved in your project."

"Michael, if you don't mind," I said while struggling with a stubborn tomato, "first of all, I found out your name is Michael Hamilton." He smiled and motioned me to continue. "And that you're a sought-after speaker on project management and management in general. I therefore want you to know that I really appreciate the fact that you're spending time with me."

I abandoned the tomato and focused my attention of the cooling coffee. "But still, we met less than twelve hours ago. And in this short relationship, there are too many holes. So, before we go on, I want to clarify some things. OK?"

"OK," he smiled, and continued to eat heartily. "You want to know what I think of Eric's Place."

"Yeah, that would be great. But it's important that I know why you want to help me, and why it was so important that I get stuck in a horrid traffic jam to reach a strip club that wasn't even open. Which was just as well. Had it been open, it might have been even more embarrassing."

Michael had polished off his omelet and was nibbling a multi-grain roll like a bunny rabbit. He put it down and said: "Fair enough. We can start there. But it means introducing you to some concepts I assume you're not familiar with. All right?"

"All right."

Michael sipped some coffee and continued: "As for your first question, I have no clear answer. Yesterday was the first I heard of your project, and it just grabbed my imagination. I've never been involved in a hospital expansion before. Had you said this was a construction project, I probably wouldn't have pursued it, because construction is almost entirely out of your hands. At most stages of construction, you are more client than project manager.

"In your case, because the building is already up, you have to manage all the rest of the work, which, before it's all over, will involve development and coordination among many different parties. It's exactly the type of project that interests me."

His coffee was gone. He stopped speaking for a second, his hand patting the small potbelly that poked out above his brown wool pants, and then said: "You still hungry?"

I shook my head. In truth, I wasn't full, but the excess of vegetables, cheeses, eggs, breads, and the people, and the noise – all put a damper on my appetite.

"I'm having another coffee," he said. We approached the drinks table and I pushed the button for an espresso, while Michael put together precisely the same plate he'd had earlier. With some reluctance, I too helped myself to seconds. I snorted. He looked like a kid in a candy shop. He was staring at the croissants and fresh fruit. I thought he'd go back to our corner with his second omelet and extra bread, but suddenly he cleared his tray and loaded it instead with grapes, melon, and papaya. His face beamed with satisfaction.

He put the tray down, picked up a piece of fruit, and went on: "Look, at the base of the method I've developed lies the assumption that the right use of my method can benefit any project. And the more complex the project, the more beneficial the method. Your project interests me very much, because it's another acid test, a great proving ground. I believe I can help you, just as I believe that using the methods I'm going to describe to you, can help all project managers."

He chomped down the last of the papaya, snuck a glance at the buffet as if considering going back for thirds, but then looked back at me. "More specifically, your project is well into something that looks like failure. I'm assuming you haven't used the tools I'll introduce you to. In such projects, the tools I'll describe can be very effective and turn the situation around."

Done with the fruit, Michael now wiped his hands on his napkin and said: "Besides, the look on your face when you walked into that bar yesterday would have turned the most wicked sinner into Mother Theresa."

I smiled uncertainly. In a voice that brooked no disagreement, he said: "Let's move to the lobby. It's too noisy here."

Through the large plate-glass windows, Silicon Valley, fully awake now, looked like something out of a sci-fi movie on the verge of an apocalypse: the office towers with their giant logos, the excessively lavish hotels, the heavy, yet orderly traffic, the dull gray sky. The view no longer excited me as it had in the past, I realized; now it felt almost like a screen-saver.

I finished my second cup of coffee and looked at Michael expectantly. Time was indeed passing.

"Your trip yesterday – I'll get to that in a minute. But first tell me, what did you think about the navigation app while you were driving?"

"What did I think?" I didn't quite get the question.

"Yeah. What did you think about the app and how it steered you?"

I took a deep breath. This was not a question I was expecting.

"The truth is that I didn't think anything," I started. "So, forgive me if my answer is off the cuff. As you said, the app identified Eric's Place easily enough, so I didn't think I'd have any trouble getting there. At first, the app showed a twenty-five-mile ride over an hour and a half, so I assumed I'd run into traffic jams.

"I expected the app to figure out a shortcut. I thought the initial calculation was an overestimate. There were no unusual events when I started driving, and the first twenty kilometers were smooth sailing.

"At that point, the app had me exit the highway. I ended up in a maze of crisscrossing streets. I saw that the app was constantly recalculating and changing the directions, but some of them came too late, after I'd already entered the intersection.

"After some turns, I saw I was still stuck in traffic. I asked passersby if they knew a shorter way to Eric's Place, but nobody seemed to know. So, having failed to get there on my own or with other people's help, I went back and followed the app's directions."

"It finally took me out of the football stadium area, but this added some extra minutes to the drive. But it's just an app, you know."

Michael's smile froze. He leaned towards me; his eyes suddenly looked enormous. "Yes, but what did you think of the app's navigation ability?"

I sighed loudly. I assumed this conversation was going someplace, but we were really short on time and the foot traffic in and out of the hotel was making me lose my train of thought. My eyes were following a young porter pulling a heaped luggage cart; suddenly he bumped into someone and the entire cart tipped over. Michael, too, was watching the scene intently.

"His problem wasn't an app, was it?" I said.

"I think you're right."

A harried manager, wearing a too-snug tie started ranting at the porter in near silence. No one was offering any help.

"Look, the app was fine," I continued while watching the porter rearrange the luggage on the cart exactly as it had been before. "At some point, I lost faith in the directions, but in the end the app did a reasonable job. I saw there were lots of options for reaching the destination, so I don't really know if I got there by the shortest route possible."

"Excellent!" Michael exclaimed. He seemed to have heard what he wanted to hear. "I gave you two assignments that were supposed to teach you something about communication as it relates to the management of your project. This communication consists of two parts; communication with the people involved in the project and communication with the people who report on progress.

"These people are usually your own managers, but there are others. Your team also wants to know about progress. The navigation assignment is connected to the way you report on progress. Just to demonstrate, let's take your generous donor. What did you say his name was again?"

"I didn't, but I'll tell you now if you're prepared to keep it confidential. His name is George Madison. Do you know him?"

"Maybe. It doesn't really matter. What matters is that you're not only a project manager; for him, you're the navigation app. This analogy generates some important insights, or, should I say, some important biases you have to avoid when reporting on a project."

"Wait up! I've lost you. Are you saying that the success of a project depends on how you report on it?"

"Hang on! Have some patience! It's important to report correctly on both a successful and a failing project. When I met you, you had just submitted a report incorrectly, regardless of the project's success or failure. But your most immediate problem right now is not the project's success or failure, it's the threat that Madison will withdraw his support," he answered with an edge. "So, to learn to report correctly, follow me closely. Got it?"

I nodded, and he went on: "The first bias you have to avoid is the one I call the 'optimism bias,' and it is linked to the universal tendency of people to be optimistic. Philosophers attribute it to religious ideas and a belief in the unlimited goodness of God. But it makes no difference if you're religious or not."

"A universal tendency to optimism?" I asked bitterly. "Are you sure? I would think the tendency would go the other way."

He didn't answer, simply forged ahead. "When the app displayed the distance, forty kilometers, your tendency was to relate to this as the key factor, even though you knew it was only the nominal distance and that its effect on the drive time was less than that of other factors, such as the traffic, the time of day, or even the weather.

"At the same time, the app also provided a time estimate. The app's time estimate is smart because it takes into account traffic in practice based on the time of day, drivers' reports, and the calculation of specific routes. This datum was much more relevant to you, but you *chose* to think it was less important or at least only as important as the nominal distance, right?"

I shrugged. While his analysis was interesting, I didn't know where it was going, and, in truth, I was sick of talking about the app. I started wondering if this meeting was really that important. Still, I was curious to hear his theory and how it could benefit me.

"In general, you expected the drive time to change for the better," he answered for me, "even though you had no good reason to think so. Is that a fair description of your attitude to your navigation app?"

Again, I shrugged, admitting my guilt.

"So where am I going with this, you're asking?"

"You're absolutely right." I had to smile.

"You see, the way you related to the app's data, is similar to the way Madison relates to your project data. Without looking at your presentation, I can guess they cover two factors. You are used to presenting the nominal distance remaining to the project's conclusion as well as the real distance, which is more relevant. But because of the optimism bias, the real distance fades into the background in Mr. Madison's head. I bet you present the nominal distance as the amount of time for certain activities, and using chains of actions performed in sequence, you arrive at a certain destination. Am I right?"

He didn't wait for an answer: "Anyone with a brain knows it's impossible to perform assignments in that kind of a sequence, yet, we still present them as if it were. You probably also present estimates you get from suppliers about the amount of time needed for a certain assignment or task using their nominal value. This is also a common mistake. To demonstrate, I want you to tell me how long it takes your dishwasher to clean your dishes?"

I took his question seriously, and tried to think about the dishwashing dynamic. I usually used it only on weekends.

"Don't quote me on this, but I think an hour and twenty minutes."

He smiled. He seemed to have taken a shine to me, but he was also impatient. I suddenly remembered a guided tour I took of Beijing, and the Chinese tour guide who knew exactly where he was taking me, but had no patience for explaining the stops on the way and kept looking at his watch the whole time.

"An hour and twenty minutes? You mean that dishwasher works for about an hour and twenty minutes. But how long does it take *you* to wash your dishes in the dishwasher? Obviously, a lot longer! You have to load your dishes and then unload them; first, you have to look for the dishwasher soap, and then you have to wait for the dishes to cool off before you can unload the machine. And all of this assumes that you're standing next to the dishwasher and waiting for the cycle to finish, because unless you open the dishwasher door the cooling off time is very long.

"Not to mention that there may be heavily soiled dishes that have to be rinsed before being loaded. And what happens if you discover that the rinse aid indicator is flashing? All of these seem like trivial events, but we, as project managers, tend to mislead everybody and his brother when we present nominal timeframes that do not provide enough information about the duration of the project."

For a moment, I felt dizzy with fatigue. The navigation app, the dishwasher, the anticipated conversation with Anna, and Madison, holding a stopwatch like a ticking time bomb, hovering over everything; the acrid espresso taste still in my mouth, the hotel porter still heaping too much luggage on the cart, his stressed-out manager, the ugly chandelier suspended from the ceiling.

My feet were starting to feel leaden. The heaviness, I was sure, was about to climb up my legs. I tried to remember what else I had planned for the day, who I had to phone other than Anna, who I had to meet, and how to get out of this conversation without feeling like pureed papaya.

"Look," I started, trying to marshal my thoughts, "there's something to that, but it's clear that the analysis of any assignment requires a starting point. Just like the navigation app. It relates to the datum of distance as a starting point and then makes an informed calculation about the rest of the way."

"Nice! But you, unlike your navigation app, are not obligated to present this datum. You can focus your report on an informed estimate of the duration of a specific assignment and of the project in general."

"Even if that's true, I can't mislead my managers and only present an estimate that serves my own interests as project manager!"

Michael leaned back in his seat. He seemed pleased with himself and the reaction he'd wrested out of me. "That's exactly the point, Gary. Making a presentation while ignoring the bias is exactly what misleads your managers. In fact, you're digging them a hole with your optimism bias. And like every human being optimistic by nature, they're going to fall into it."

"So, you're saying that my problem is that I'm optimistic?" I shot at him bitterly. But, being short on time, he was in no mood for banter.

"Of course, you can continue to use nominal data for task and assignment lengths when you're analyzing the situation, but when you prepare to make a presentation to your managers and employees, you're better off focusing most of the attention on expected performance times rather than theoretical performance times. They're not realistic. They're not even possible."

Michael stopped for a second, glanced at his watch, and then turned to examine me as I was trying to digest what I'd heard.

"I need another coffee," I said and got up. Michael stood up too.

"Not a bad idea. I'll go see if there's any fruit left."

I nodded, and the two of us headed again for the buffet, which was now much emptier than before. We'd been sitting for at least half an hour, and I knew Michael was rushed. But I had to get up and stretch my legs, get some more caffeine into my bloodstream, and continue to mull over Michael's ideas.

I had spoken to several consultants. They were shockingly alike, no matter how professional. They seemed to recite their principles from some secret consultant codex, and they all behaved the same. Michael, though, was different. He didn't try to impress me. He really wanted to share his knowledge with me. And now I felt it strongly; he really wanted my project to succeed. It seemed important to him, somehow. And more than that, something in him believed I would succeed, and this filled me with strength.

In the meantime, Michael had gathered all the papaya remaining on the fruit platter and was looking pleased. We went back to our seats in the lobby. He glanced at his watch again, but seemed less rushed than before.

Suddenly, a group of men, all wearing blue suits, walked into the lobby, carrying items covered in drop cloths. The five of them looked like a soundless ring of FBI agents. They stopped not far from us, next to a long, bare wall, arranged the items side by side, and then, as if on cue, pulled the cloths away to reveal five blue, shiny aquariums. Michael stared as if hypnotized and started to applaud. The prissy-looking manager was heading for the quintet, he smiled at Michael and said, "Good morning, Mr. Hamilton." Michael nodded in return, turned back to me and said, "Beautiful, huh?" I had to agree.

"All right, the clock is ticking and we've got a long way to go. I'm sure you can review the materials you've presented to Mr. Madison so far and easily identify the parts that led to optimism bias. I'll go further: I bet you can remove that material in its entirety without harming the presentation in the least. All it does is create bias. Got it? Can you check on that for me?"

I nodded. "Sure."

"All right. Hold on just a little longer. The next bias I want you to note is the reality bias. Please tell me again why you asked a passersby for directions, even though you claim that you trusted your navigation app?"

I started to stutter something about the app failing, but Michael raised his hand to stop me. "What did you say? It failed?"

I fell silent and nodded in embarrassment.

"What do you mean, it failed? I can vouch for the fact that, every day, at five in the afternoon, the streets are jammed and virtually impassable. You know it's true in every big city in the world. Not only that, but it's clearly impossible to get anywhere in the neighborhood of a football stadium in a hurry half an hour before kickoff, right? So why are you blaming your poor app? How is it the app's fault?"

Many of the hotel workers had gathered in front of the aquariums. There was something mesmerizing about them. I felt a moment's desire to get up and join them, and I think Michael wanted to as well, but he turned his head resolutely and went on. "Please note that you're attributing your failure and success to your app, based on the navigation results on the ground. I'm not faulting you in any way. After all, you have no other reference point that the success of the navigation at that point. I assume you'll agree that your attitude has no basis in reality. It may be that your device did an excellent job, but it can't do anything about throngs of semi-plastered fans in green and white."

I smiled at the image and finished my coffee.

Michael continued: "Mr. Madison relates to you the way you relate to your navigation system. When you're working hard and really doing all you can, but the project is stuck because of clashing tasks and mishaps, Mr. Madison has a hard time separating the project's status from the quality of your work. In his disappointment, he goes to..."

"...his consultants." The end of the sentence was obvious.

"That right. He goes to his consultants looking for support, exactly the way you turned to the passersby. Now, what datum in the navigation app's display might have convinced you to continue to trust it and not ask random strangers for help?"

"If it could have shown me that I was travelling at a reasonable rate, compared to other drivers in the area at that hour. Or, if it could have shown me that other routes were even longer. In those cases, and theoretically, I would have kept my cool and assumed that I was already doing all that I could. But when I checked for alternate routes in the app, it was already too late. I was already stuck in traffic."

Michael clapped with satisfaction. "Right on!" he exclaimed loudly. Some of the hotel staff who, after having stared at the bits of trapped sea, were now returning to their posts, gave him a startled look, but he didn't seem to mind. "See? You can do it!" he continued, without lowering his voice.

"Get it? Just like the app, you can present the feasibility of alternate methods of operation and the reasons to disqualify them."

I didn't respond right away. Michael looked at me questioningly, as if trying to read my mind. He's right, I thought, I could have presented the project status that way. Michael was wiping his hands on the napkin and patting his belly again. "I had too much to eat. I'm not supposed to. Blood sugar. They say fruit is good for you, but it's a lie. They're full of sugar."

I nodded and tried to recall if we'd told Madison and his assistants about alternatives or explained why there weren't any. Was this insight by itself capable of making Madison lean back and relax in his chair while listening to a presentation on our failing project?

"Good," he said, as if concluding. "For our next meeting, I want you to check if your presentations to date included that information, just so that we can compare them to future ones. But – and this is important – to get the most out of this piece of advice and undo the effects of the reality bias, you'll have to pay very close attention to the alternatives."

My phone started to vibrate and the display read "Anna." I swallowed hard, then texted her: "In meeting. Will call you soon." Michael wiped his hands on his napkin and got ready to rise.

"Wait!" I said. "You still haven't told me why you sent me to a closed strip club."

He smiled. "I see you need something to tell your wife, huh?"

I shrugged. "Listen," he said, already standing, "I had to make sure nobody would help you. Everybody in the financial district knows Eric's Place; it's been around for thirty years or more. But, as I'm sure you can appreciate, nobody would cop to knowing where to find it, especially in the presence of other people."

Suddenly, he sat down again and glanced at his watch. Looking somber, he said: "I almost forgot, probably too much damned blood sugar. Whatever. There's also something called asymmetry bias. Try to remember how you felt when you got off the highway and entered the financial district."

"Well, I realized that I had run out of road where I could drive at a reasonable speed and was heading for heavy traffic, which was the cause of the long-time frame given by the app."

"Yes, but what did you feel?"

"What did I feel? I wasn't surprised. I knew that I'd hit traffic at some point. But I wasn't ready for barely being able to move, and it was extremely annoying."

"What if you had, while driving on the highway, gotten a more exact indication of the traffic ahead? Wouldn't your mood have remained more or less the same throughout the drive?"

"Probably."

"And how did you feel when the app added extra time to get you out of the stadium area?"

"At that point, I was ready to throw in the towel."

"Right, so pay attention to the asymmetry bias. When the navigation app showed the route, it didn't provide any data on where you'd be spending most of the time. You knew you'd hit traffic down the road, but had no idea where or how heavy it would be."

"This is like the start of your presentation to Mr. Madison. I assume you tend to present last month's achievements at the start and then try to soften the less-good news later on, right?"

"Sometimes," I lied. This was, in fact, what we tried to do pretty much every time.

"Exactly like what happened when you got off the highway! Mr. Madison also loses his cool when you take him off the highway and drive him into the many challenges created in the last month. Just like you, he would also be feeling better if he were to get a clear indication about the problems of the last month at the beginning of your report.

"That's it," he sighed. "Speaking of time problems, I really must go. But I'm sure we'll talk about it some more. Here's the thing; every period of time has its successes and challenges. The natural

36

tendency of most project managers is to get the most out of presenting the successes to endear themselves to management and then try to survive reporting the negative.

"It's a big mistake. This sort of presentation places the listener on a mental rollercoaster and actually highlights the bad news. For example, were you to focus on one area of activity, and report early on about a difficulty you're having, while also noting a significant success you had the same month, the listeners' feelings would mirror the changes the navigation app made while you were driving down the highway. Obviously, you wouldn't want to tell Madison about yet another challenge while he's stuck next-door to the stadium, would you?

"The right construction of a report provides a balanced situation assessment from beginning to end. Successes and challenges, solutions and difficulties, and issues still under examination. What the listener gets from the report is a sense of uniformity and that the situation is under control."

Michael stood up a second time and motioned for me to walk with him. We passed the aquarium wall and reached the center of the lobby, but Michael's words were still echoing in my mind. I knew that right after speaking with Anna I would have to summarize them, either in my head or in writing, and try to see how to apply them right away.

"Tell me," I said, trying to extract yet another insight from Michael, "why did you ask me to name the worst employee?"

"Look," he smiled, "as I told you yesterday, a project is a social event long before it's an engineering challenge. Which is why I'm trying to find out how you're reporting on it and who's working with you before getting down to the nitty-gritty, the actual project activities and operations. The worst employee can serve as an indicator of your main problem in assembling the project team. Instead of asking you complex questions about each area and what you consider the most problematic, I asked this instead.

"Without really knowing anything about the project, I know, because of my question, that you're having integration problems and that the interface with the group in charge of the hospital's existing systems, specifically with the manager responsible for them, is problematic. Besides, later on, I want to use this employee as a barometer."

"Barometer?"

"That's right. Because there's really no such thing as a terrible employee in a vacuum. There are bad managers or insufficient instructions. There is problematic coordination or there are unrealistic demands. If you change the project's work environment, you can test how your worst employee and interactions with him are affected. If working with him improves, you'll know you're on the right track towards putting together a committed, effective project team."

"Or maybe he should just be fired!" I answered, annoyed.

"Sure," Michael answered confidently, "but in reality, he's not been fired. Maybe he's not really terrible, or maybe he is, but his manager has decided to keep him on. For you as project manager, it makes no difference. He's there. He's a fact of the project's life. And it's an excellent reference point, because it can serve you as a barometer of change. Compare him with your best employee. You can't learn anything about the project from that person, because you're satisfied with that person's work and your opinion will probably not change."

"All right," he said and held out his hand, "now I really have to move. So call me, OK?"

After shaking his hand, I watched him walk out of the hotel. I pulled out my cell phone to call Anna. The empty fruit plates and coffee cups were still cluttering the table.

"Hi sweetie! What's up?" Anna's voice was like a boost of energy from a parallel universe.

I told her all was well, maybe better, because I'd just had a really important meeting. Well, yes, it was with a consultant, but not your run-of-the-mill consultant. We'd met for only just over an hour, but I thought I wanted to see him again. In any case, he opened my mind. I mean, he made me see things differently. Yeah, just like that stupid cliché – outside the box. What about you?

She said the kids missed me, (though she didn't say she missed me) they were asking about me yesterday, and Sean even started to get mad that I wasn't home. My heart skipped a beat and I suddenly felt drenched with longing. In any case, they were at school and preschool now, so I couldn't talk with them.

The minute the project ends – if and when it ends – I'll take some time off, and let her decide what she wants to do. I'm going to make sure that happens.

But when will it end? Despite the tiny flare of optimism I was feeling, I still couldn't see a specific endpoint on the horizon. Meanwhile, Madison's threat continued to hover over every thought. That was really the most urgent challenge.

I wound up my conversation with Anna. The waiter cleared the table and suggested I move to a sofa at the edge of the lobby. I thanked him, but said that I was finishing up shortly. He pulled a face but left me in peace. I took out a writing pad and a pen and started jotting down bullet points.

The optimism bias causes managers to give too much weight to nominal estimates and ignore other information presented. To avoid this, it is best not to present nominal estimates, because it is essentially useless. Concentrate instead on informed estimates of the duration of the tasks.

The reality bias causes managers to blame the reporting party for the problematic reality, even if that party has done a fine job. To avoid this, it is necessary to present alternative methods of action and explain why they are not better.

The asymmetry bias requires uniform reporting on successes and challenges in the right context, so that no undue weight is given to problems just because of where and in what context they are presented.

There really is no such thing as "the worst employee in the project." The employee seen as most difficult can serve as an excellent reference point for forging teamwork.

I finished writing and looked up. For a second, it seemed as if the hotel was enveloped in a purplish haze. My head was pounding with tumbling ideas I had to get in order. I considered going back to the buffet for another espresso, but I'd already lost track of how many I'd downed.

I put my pad back in my briefcase, got up, and meant to head to the elevator bank. But instead, I found myself walking towards the aquariums. Something in the movement of the goldfish and the other species I couldn't name was spellbinding.

Suddenly, one goldfish broke off from its school and started swimming towards the aquarium wall. It bumped into the glass but kept hurling itself at it, over and over again. For a second, I thought to call over one of the hotel staff to alert them to what was happening, but quickly realized how ridiculous I was being, and I started to laugh. It too, just like me, was incapable of seeing the wall ahead. The fish's excuse was that the wall was transparent. What was mine?

At the front desk, Michelle was again on duty, and I asked her for Michael's phone number. Normally, hotels do not share this type of information, but she was willing to make an exception because she had seen us together. I saved the number in my cell phone and, while walking to the elevators, I texted him: "I've decided to stay in town another day. When can we meet next?"

2

The next day, Michael had the same breakfast and again loaded his plate with fruit. We took our coffees and headed for the same spot we'd occupied the day before, not far from the aquariums. The scent of some unknown perfume was in the air, and elevator music tinkled in the background.

Michael took a deep breath, looked at me like a guru meeting a studious acolyte and asked: "Did you have a chance to look at the link I sent you? What did you think?"

I put my coffee down. "Honestly, I was worried you'd directed me to some stripper's YouTube video." I laughed, and Michael smiled back.

The link, had in fact taken me to the text of a speech Winston Churchill gave to the British House of Commons. According to Wikipedia, it was the second of three speeches Churchill delivered in a five-week period in 1940, when the Battle of France was being fought and dramatic changes were occurring in the international arena. The speech was long; it is remembered mostly thanks to a paragraph whose climactic sentence – "We shall fight on the beaches" – became the phrase by which the full speech is known.

Despite the fatigue and despair that filled me yesterday, I read the speech and was moved. Written with much pathos, at a time when Nazi Germany seemed unstoppable, it provided inspiration to leaders everywhere. There was something refreshing and unusual about it, and it suddenly occurred to me how long it had been since I had read anything at all, except for contracts, Gantt charts, and technical documents.

But what relevance did it have to my project? I was really hoping that Michael wouldn't talk to me about leadership. It was precisely what I disliked so much about consultants. It reminded me a little bit of a leadership course I'd done a long time ago. For three weeks, I'd sat in a classroom with wonky air conditioning, listening to a bunch of self-styled leaders who all sounded alike, barking clichéd mantras at a group of dazed wannabe executives.

"What did I think of the speech?" I said, once again sipping coffee. "It was interesting. Very inspirational. And the historic context – the low point in the campaign Great Britain was fighting – is extraordinarily dramatic. I imagine Churchill as a project manager with the British people as his client."

"Look," said Michael, "I'm really not asking you to become Churchill. Only few have the rhetorical skills. But the speech does have meaning in terms of creating a common language when it comes to your job as project leader, and the meaning of communication with all the people involved in a project."

He wiped his damp hands on a napkin. I noticed that he was eating less fruit today, but drinking more coffee, and it seemed that he was stealing looks at the cakes table like one who is perpetually conflicted over taking a slice or sticking to his diet.

"There are many aspects to leadership," he continued. "Leadership may shape and reward, leadership may correct and enforce. These aspects are all relevant to the project manager's job, but if you don't mind we're not going to concentrate on that; leadership is not my main focus. I assume that project managers got to their positions, based at the very least on a reasonable capacity for leadership, and it is this capacity that I want to develop."

He sighed briefly, "I'm trying to decide whether or not to take that piece of poppy seed cake. What do you think Churchill would have done?" His brown eyes crinkled in amusement.

"Churchill would have opted for a scotch and a cigar."

He laughed, "I suspect you're right. I really have to watch myself; it's no joke. Later, when I get home, my wife can tell if I cheated or not. It's as if she has sensors embedded in my stomach. But she's right. I have high blood pressure, high triglycerides, the whole shebang. I can't help myself – I just love sweets and those cakes are calling my name."

His eyes shone with longing, but he collected himself at once, thumped his knees, and said: "All right, let's get back to the text you read, and I'll ask you something else. Churchill had to drive a group of people into a certain mindset at a time of crisis and improve the chances that this group of people would manage to get out of the crisis and function optimally. Is that a fair statement?"

I nodded, and for a second recollected my high school AP European History exam.

"We can spend lots of time talking about the tasks facing the group, the way to accomplish them, and the group's goals. But Churchill chose not to address any of those. Instead, he decided to focus on constructing the ethos surrounding his project. Can you suggest a rationale for this decision?"

"I'll try," I said, "though it seems pretty obvious, actually. The details of how to accomplish the tasks and the goals are usually too numerous, certainly in the case of Churchill and the British parliament. Therefore, leaders try to speak more generally, hoping that it will affect future activity and the people who will turn these goals into activity on the ground."

Michael was about to ask another question, but I interrupted him. "Look, I see what you're getting at, so allow me to refer to the three elements you mentioned yesterday. Did Churchill praise the job done to date? Referring to similar situations in the past counts. He very clearly stressed the importance of the project, and in simple words explained the meaning of the British people's steadfastness and uncompromising will to fight, but didn't balk at noting the situation could grow worse before it got better."

He looked at me with satisfaction and motioned for me to go on: "What impressed me most was his rhetorical ability to set goals and make them attainable, while instilling confidence in his listeners. But victory against the enemy was an existential need more than a goal to be fulfilled. I think that the last words of the speech are what made it so famous, beyond its decisive historical significance."

Michael was beaming at me. After another sip of coffee, he said: "Well done! You're one of the most serious students I've ever had. I'm joking, of course. I'm not a teacher, and you're not a student."

"The truth is that you reminded me of my AP exam in European History."

He laughed and said: "Did you know that I majored in history? I did. Don't ask me how I went from there to here, but truth be told, I think history taught me many important lessons for my job and life in general." He drained the last of his coffee and sneaked another peek at the cakes table. But the waiters were already clearing the breakfast buffet.

With notable distress, he watched his beloved poppy seed cake being carted off. I felt a bit sorry for him and decided that, before our next meeting, I'd pop into George Milner's Bakery, which sells sugar-free poppy seed cakes. I'd buy one and have it gift-wrapped.

"In any case," he looked back at me, "you understand that leaders construct an ethos. That is, they pour the foundation for all the beliefs and ideas that, later on, will reflect the conduct of a certain society in a war, in a factory, or in a project."

I nodded.

"So now that we've seen how leadership speeches are constructed and produced, let's take a step back. Did you consider what exactly they're trying to create? What is that thing you spoke of that can affect people's future actions?"

I leaned back into the sofa. I tried to understand where Michael was going. People would act in the future based on instructions they got in the present. There are specific instructions and there are general instructions designed to define the general direction of a task or series of actions, in a way that allows people to define their own assignments and make independent decisions. But, do they do that in relation to any ethos?

"Gary, stay with me for a sec. I sense that you're in the neighborhood, I really feel that, but you're still finding it hard to apply the right label to our discussion."

I felt like a student who's been rebuked, but the smile on Michael's face was reassuring.

"I'll try to help you using a concept from my management method called the Project Essence. One challenge facing all project managers, especially if the project is large, is the inability to encompass the whole project. Right?

"In any case, to deal with this problem, project managers – consciously or subconsciously – try to delegate authority and give general instruction that will help good decision-making and definition of sub-tasks and goals beyond their reach. I'm sure you've done it yourself."

I nodded again. My mouth was getting dry.

"But, in addition to the tasks and goals, an experienced project manager will try to communicate the project's background and the motivation for its success, even beyond his direct communication.

Above all, he'll try to create attainable meta-objectives that everyone in the project is supposed to know by heart.

"The sum total of these details result in an entity that stands on its own and works on your behalf even without you realizing it. That's the **project essence**. My assertion is that every project also generates a social entity that to a large extent, dictates the project's success."

"When a project essence is minor-key, boring and awkward, it will be tough to enlist resources. The project will suffer from inattention and repeated postponements, and will be unable to make the most out of the resources invested in it.

"Other projects have an intriguing, attractive, responsive, and confident essence. When that happens, the projects will maximize their resources, and even commandeer resources allocated to other projects. Sounds odd, doesn't it..."

I mouthed the words, "project essence" to myself. It sounded like something from chaos theory or quantum physics. Michael was talking about it in so concrete a manner that I was expecting him to invite my project essence to sit down and have a cup of coffee with us, while Michael made the official introductions. I imagined it as an androgynous being in a white dress and a crown on its head, a beard and a mustache. I realized I was grinning like an idiot at the image. I leaned forward and sent Michael a questioning look.

"Now, without over-thinking it, how would you describe your project essence?"

The androgynous figure in the white dress disappeared. I tried to harness my thoughts. How *would* I describe it? I didn't feel like answering. I tried to say something, but my mind's eye saw only dull lines and waves of technical concepts shattering on the shore of our conversation.

"Look," I started speaking without knowing what I really wanted to say, "I'd say that my project essence has lacked confidence for some time. It had lots of buddies in the past; some were even willing to help with a lot of money, but it's losing its appeal.

"It seemed energetic and capable of performing well, but after some key suppliers finished up and left the picture, my essence is naked. My entity is an annoying androgynous nude."

Michael burst into loud laughter that reminded me of galloping horses and that jiggled his potbelly up and down. "That's great! Never heard that one yet!" he chuckled. Turning serious, he asked: "Well, how would you rate its attractiveness?"

I scratched my head and answered hesitantly: "OK, it's been on a downward trend lately. There are far more attractive essences, and it has cut into the attention it had been getting."

Michael was satisfied, but immediately added: "Let there be no mistake. I'm not talking about personification. I'm talking about essence. It's not an abstract or theoretical construct; it's very real. The essence can be constructed according to the parameters I introduced to you today and others I'll get to later. Please, go on."

I tried to understand where I was supposed to continue from. I wasn't sure.

"All right. I see you're stuck, so let me ask you another question. What do you consider to be the ideal project essence?"

"I think it's attractive, rewarding, efficient, self-confident, and resilient, at least at the beginning." I wanted to add that it has no mustache or beard or white dress, but kept silent. I was no longer in the mood for joking.

"Nice," said Michael. "I would add rational, no?"

"Sure, that too."

Suddenly, I saw I had a call. Anna's name appeared on screen. I asked to be excused, and Michael shrugged. She asked how I was doing, where I was, and what I was doing. I told her I was in a meeting with Michael. It took her a second to respond, but then said: "It's nice of you to answer the phone. I was starting to get used to your texts. But I can hear you're pressed for time."

As if trying to turn Anna's last sentence into the beginning of our next fight, I said: "I'll talk to you later, OK?" I shot an embarrassed smile at Michael as if he could hear the other side of the conversation too. I couldn't decide whether she was always calling at the wrong time or whether I was stuck someplace where no time was the right time.

I ended the call and looked straight at Michael, apologizing for the interruption, but he waved it off and went on: "Rationality or consistency is important for the structure of the project essence, because the more uniform, organized and rational the message of the essence is, the greater the distance it can go without you and the greater its effect on many different tasks that are out of your hands."

I nodded, but I felt I was losing him. I was facing a long day of meetings and errands. When I'd answered Anna, I noticed I had missed seven calls, including two from Lisa and one from Fabian, and even though it was still morning I felt time running out like sand between my fingers.

Nonetheless, I was fascinated. I still sensed that what I was doing was meaningful, that it could really turn the project – and my life – around, though I wasn't tempted to think of Michael as a guardian angel who had suddenly descended on me from heaven. That wasn't his style, and who believed in angels anyway?

"Fine," he went on, oblivious to my swirl of thoughts. "Let's assume the speech you give when you get back is the cornerstone for building a project essence that will serve you well in the future. It won't be the last step in that direction, but it can be a very significant first move. To do this, I want us to connect the components of the speech with the essence you want to construct."

Finally! A real assignment, rather than a theory of essences. At once I became focused, as if the vitamins in my body had started a synchronized dance. All the background noises faded into the distance as I started jotting down what he said:

Part one: Praise the work done in the past. This strengthens the project's attractiveness. The rationale is simple: everyone wants to be part of a success and nobody wants to be part of a failure! If you praise the work done to date in the right way, you'll make this project attractive by definition.

In part two, you provide background on the project, and through it you continue constructing its self-confidence and resilience. As the saying goes, "A people without a past has no future." So too the project essence: it needs a past to build its resilience, so it can handle the future.

I continued taking notes, while using my other hand to signal Michael to continue.

Finally, articulating clear, attainable goals serves the rationale and creates continuity, like a beacon towards which all activities are directed and whose light may be used to illuminate situation assessments, complex calculations, decision-making, and the definition of sub-goals and other tasks.

I completed my notes, put the pen down, and stretched out in the sofa. But the look Michael gave me told me he wasn't done. I leaned forward again and urged him to keep talking.

"In any case," he said, "it's important to stress two points. The first is that I could have added other characteristics, but I made do with the ones that emerged from our brief discussion. You can add characteristics that are important to the success of your project and think about how to construct them among those involved in the project. With time, you'll notice changes in the project essence, identify gaps, and close them."

Michael cleared his throat and again wiped his hands on the napkin. He went on: "The other thing is that your speech is, as I said, only the first step. Moreover, it is possible to construct another layer of the project essence in a single sentence, but by the same token a single sentence can also damage it. It can also be done with a few sentences at the beginning of a discussion or in answer to a random question asked in the hallway.

"If you adopt this way of thinking, it will affect not only the project essence but also the way you see the project."

I saw Michael looking at his watch, but I wanted to understand this better. "What do you mean?"

He took a deep breath, and wiped his hands yet again. This seemed to be an involuntary habit, and I tried not to stare so as not to embarrass him, but he didn't seem to care.

"Do you have time?" he asked.

"A bit."

"Another coffee would be nice," he said, wistfully adding, "and a piece of cake."

I walked over to the buffet. Most items had been cleared away, but the coffee machine was still on. I poured two espressos and apologized to a waitress who had no idea why I was saying "Sorry."

After taking a sip, Michael began: "Let's pretend an engineer who's been installing a certain system comes to you and reports that there's a problem. What do you tell him? 'This is terrible news. And it's not the first time it's happened. I suggest you schedule a meeting with your manager to figure out a solution.' Is that something you're likely to say?"

I nodded. He went on. "Or, you could say something like: 'You know how much I value the work you've done to date. It is really important to the core of this project and the achievements we've had. We're coming close to achieving the goal all of us are working to attain, and that is a functional system by year's end. It would therefore be wonderful to schedule a discussion in the right forum to learn more about the issue and arrive at the optimal solution.' I assume you see the difference, right?"

"Sure."

"Great," he said inconclusively, looking at his watch again. "Look, I don't have to hear your speech, but I would like to meet with you at the hospital next week after you've had a meeting with your employees to help you move on to the next stage, and start talking about the operational aspects of the project. I'm going to have to meet with your team to see how you manage schedules, tasks and risks. Is that all right?"

49

"Of course!" I answered, feeling at last that something was happening. I was truly grateful. I watched him get up, wipe his hands one last time, and start to put his things away.

"Listen," I said, "like I said, I'm not a huge fan of consultants. But what I've experienced since yesterday is very different from working with any other consultant. I really appreciate your offer to come out to us next week, but I can't have you come unless you agree to be paid. I insist. We have a budget for consultancy we haven't used up yet. And of course, we'd cover your expenses."

Michael thought for a bit, then said: "I won't argue with you. I would certainly expect you to cover my expenses and I can let you know my minimum consulting fee. But I want you to understand – and I did tell you this yesterday up front – that I have consulted for companies in the past, but it hasn't been my chief interest for a long time. In recent years, I've concentrated on developing innovative project management tools and my real profit will come from the feedback you give me after you've used these tools for a few months in a field in which I've never worked."

"OK. That's not a problem."

"Fine, but you need to know that these tools require a very high degree of self-discipline. I still don't know the project managers who report to you, but I can assure you that some of them are going to find this a very difficult process. It's important that you know that I'm very limited in terms of time. I can't offer you a long-term consulting process. I won't be available to you on a daily basis. I hope you can live with that."

"I'm absolutely fine with it. Thank you."

We shook on it and he left the hotel. I glanced at my watch. I still had half an hour before leaving for the airport. I tried to summarize the key points. I opened my notebook and realized that what I'd jotted down was all illegible. Just like my grade school teacher said, all I saw was chicken scratches. Good Lord! How right she was. The words ran into one another and some of the letters were only partially formed. I felt like taking the page and tossing it in the trash. But the ideas were still fresh enough in my mind: **A project is,**

above all, a social entity before it becomes an operational challenge. The project essence can be created, and it is possible to fashion it out of a range of characteristics.

A project that is well-constructed in the consciousness of all those involved will function well, enjoy a wealth of resources, and have high chances of success. Many characteristics may go into a project's essence, but most importantly it needs to be attractive, rewarding, resilient and rational.

Sounds elementary. So simple, yet so true.

I placed a call to Anna.

"So, how did it go?"

"Great!"

"I'm so happy to hear that."

"No, you're not."

Anna laughed. "Why not?"

"Because now we start implementing the project essence."

"The what?"

"Doesn't matter. We'll talk later."

Chapter Three

To Speak for the Project

1

Before I took the job at the hospital – in fact, before it occurred to me to manage a project of this scale, though I sometimes dreamed about it – I worked for a well-known high-tech company for six years. I was very successful in the position, but I failed utterly in my attempt to climb the rungs in the organization.

After suggesting myself for more senior positions three times, I left, slamming the door behind me. The hospital was looking for "a senior project manager" and I fitted the criteria. This was not a promotion or professional advancement, but I had no choice. Sean had just been born, I hadn't found a better position, and I had to work.

After a grace period lasting several weeks, in which I had time to study the hospital and its organizational structure, I was appointed project manager to replace equipment in the cardiology department. It was a complex project, which was supposed to last a year, and it involved several interfaces. A real challenge, no doubt about it.

I was eager to get to work in a completely new field, but was bothered by the fact that my career arc was again moving laterally rather than vertically. I only hoped my disappointment wouldn't be too obvious so as not to damage my team's motivation.

But I couldn't hide it from Anna.

At first, she tried to cheer me up by hosting a small family dinner in honor of my new responsibility. Later on, she bought me one of those small audio systems as powerful as an old-time hi-fi setup, so that I'd always be able to play music in my office. Those small boxes have always fascinated me. Even though I grasped the technology, the transition from three-foot tall speakers to something as big as a paperback in phosphorus colours seemed absurd. Nonetheless, despite the gift, my face was as glum as ever and the distress started eating away at my insides.

That's when Anna suggested that I consult "the forum." The forum was a small group of long-time friends I used to meet over a beer every once in a while.

"C'mon, men don't talk about stuff like that at a bar," I protested.

"There's always a first time," she shot back. "What works for half the human race may just work for the other half too."

At the bar the following week, the forum members asked me about my new job right away. My first instinct was to say that everything was fine and shift the talk to sports, but then I remembered what Anna said and decided to pick up the gauntlet she'd tossed.

"I don't know. I feel stuck. I don't see anything new, and it's wearing me down. I know how it starts and how it's going to end. I have to do things differently, but I don't know in what way. I have to do something that will advance my career, not just the project I'm managing."

Nobody said a word. This diverse group of men seemed willing to help, but didn't really know how. What was I expecting? I asked myself. There were four of us who'd grown up together and remained friends from elementary through high school. One of them was a fading soccer player, the second a transport pilot, the third a psychologist, and me, the fourth, a project manager who was going nowhere fast.

"Can't the two go together?" the soccer player asked. Maybe in your world, I thought. Score a goal and get promoted. Or not, like you.

"Not necessarily."

"Sorry," he said, "I don't really understand your field."

"Neither do I," said the pilot.

The psychologist on the other hand, looked at me with frank curiosity. He always does this, thinking he's got some sort of telepathic power to will you to speak. He scratched at his little goatee (we'd given up trying to convince him to shave it off – "Who do you think you are? Freud or something?" the soccer player had asked), brought his chair closer to mine, and waved the waitress away.

Maybe he did possess a bit of telepathy, because I started telling my buddies how, after only three months and one meeting at my job, I'd already saved the organization ninety thousand dollars by simply changing the way one of the projects was being managed, thereby making one of the suppliers redundant.

The soccer player quickly grew bored and stared outright at one of the giant television screens showing a baseball game. He always complained that nobody in this country understood sports, that soccer was the real game – not baseball, not football, certainly not basketball.

In any case, I continued explaining that not only hadn't that helped, but only earned me the enmity of the purchasing department, which refused to cooperate with me for months. How can you be promoted in a company where an entire department sees you as public enemy number one?

"Great Will Smith flick, no?" said the soccer player, who continued to stare at the screen on his left.

"All right, but that's an extreme example," said the pilot.

The psychologist remained quiet. His silence was starting to get on my nerves. He continued to look at me inquisitively, only this time asked the waitress for another round of beers. "Three please. You're not drinking," he said to the soccer player, "you have practice tomorrow."

The soccer player scowled at him. "It's at night," he grumbled.

"It may be an extreme example, but it's not the only one," I said, frustrated, and continued telling the table how, for two years, I'd been in charge of the company's biggest project for one of the company's biggest clients. Thanks to my work, income from that client, who was thrilled with our progress in development, was steadily rising. During those two years, there was an opening at the next level, "But what did they do? Picked that insufferable Steve Fletcher. I still can't believe he got that job," I added, feeling the rage building in me.

"Maybe he was better than you?" the pilot suggested.

"Are you kidding? No way!"

I added that he had less experience and was significantly less involved in the company's major projects. He spent most of his time on unimportant projects that didn't interest anyone. And still, one day I found myself reporting to him rather than him reporting to me. "It was humiliating. I mean he had this smug look on his face. And he was constantly telling me what to do, even though he knew perfectly well that I knew what I was doing."

"Ego is a problematic thing," said the psychologist and sipped some beer.

I'd already drained my second pint. The soccer player's gaze was still glued to the screen and seemed a little glazed.

"Remember when we were kids and used to play Jenga?" the psychologist suddenly asked.

A soft wave of nostalgia washed over me; Jenga was a fun game of fifty-four rectangular wooden blocks that are at first arranged crisscross in threes to create an eighteen-story tower. The goal of the game is for each participant in turn to pull out a block without toppling the structure and place the pulled block on the top. As the game progresses, the tower becomes increasingly unstable, and the loser is the one who extracts the wrong block and causes the whole structure to come tumbling down.

"Of course! What made you think of it now?"

He finished his beer, fixed me with his stare, and said: "I'm sure you remember that you can't move a block that will cause the tower to collapse. What you do is look for a block that feels loose, one you know the structure doesn't rely on. The blocks holding up the structure won't be touched until the end. And the more important a block is in its current location, the chances that someone will risk moving it drop. Right?" The psychologist smiled and continued: "Simply make yourself dispensable. This will make them promote you."

I guffawed. "Great idea!"

"I'm totally serious," he insisted.

I sucked the last drops of beer from my glass, put it down, and said: "Are you quoting Freud now?"

Now it was his turn to laugh. "No, Freud was much too needed."

"I feel I've become dispensable," said the soccer player.

The pilot got up. "Needed or not, I gotta hit the head and settle the tab. I have to get an early start tomorrow."

* * *

"So how was the forum?" Anna wanted to know in the morning. We were eating breakfast, the aroma of good coffee filling the kitchen nook, the bold colour of autumn crowding the handsome bay window.

"They said I should make myself dispensable to climb to the top of the structure. Like in Jenga. So perhaps I have to try to do less to succeed more."

Anna either didn't hear the sarcasm in my voice or chose to ignore it. She got up and busied herself with our mugs of coffee and the kids' sandwiches, closing up her own briefcase as soon as she was done with Sean's and Marianna's lunchboxes. In the meantime, I was stuck in yesterday's forum discussion, still not understanding the advice I'd been given.

"If you think about it," she said, bustling around me, "it's not that stupid. It's actually fairly sophisticated. You've been hard at work for a very long time and are burning out. Maybe you're not operating right. Making yourself dispensable doesn't mean doing less; it means allowing your work to go on without you.

"Now, don't jump down my throat. I didn't say you're not working hard. It's damned hard work; don't put it down. The truth is that one day you really won't be needed in the project. But if you succeed, why wouldn't you be promoted so that you can do the same thing elsewhere? Try to look at it from your supervisor's perspective."

I looked at Anna, wondering for a moment if the entire universe had tilted, but she seemed totally serious.

56

"OK, we're off," she said, kissing the top of my head. I got up to give the kids a hug. Sean was stuffed into a parka, so thick it was hard feeling his little body inside. And Marianna in her where's-Waldo cap, looking both goofy and pensive.

I finally had the kitchen to myself. I put my mug in the dishwasher, and wiped down the counter with a cloth. If I'm critically needed in my present position, the manager can't pull me out. Because, if he does, there'll be a hole where I used to be. It's much easier to promote someone who is less critically needed in his current job. Somebody dispensable. I had to admit that the whole thesis was perfectly logical.

If I become dispensable by not working, no one will appreciate me for it and I certainly won't be promoted. Is there, then, a positive way to become dispensable? I asked myself. Well, I answered my own question, you have to try. What's the worst that could happen?

* * *

It didn't happen all at once. In my first few months at the hospital, I tried to become dispensable in a positive way. Gradually, I saw it was possible. I had to work in a way that felt counterintuitive, and concede being in key positions. When I identified situations in which the system became dependent on me, I made sure to change the process, train others, invest more in mentoring and explanations. Slowly but surely, I saw that my day-to-day work was becoming smoother.

It worked like a charm.

Changing my patterns reinforced what I'd always known: what was leading me to succeed in one job was only the foundation for the success of the next, and would not necessarily continue bringing me success automatically. Sometimes it stood in the way and had to be ditched.

At the beginning of my career, I was known for my attention to detail and thoroughness, but pretty quickly I understood that I could never get all the details if I wanted to encompass many issues. There were simply too many details. There are always too many. Contrary to the cliché, God isn't always in the details. Sometimes he's to be found in the bird's eye view. I had to learn to tell the wheat from the chaff. Now, I also had to concede my own need to be needed, and I worked hard to make myself replaceable.

After a year, I was called to the manager's office where I heard about the plan to expand the maternity wing. I was told that management was pleased with my work on the current project, but it seemed that everything was proceeding well and that I could go on to something else. I smiled inwardly. My plan was working! Kudos to my psychologist friend. I would have to take him out for a beer soon. And Anna – well, I owed her my gratitude as well.

I was told about the professional team being put together and the idea to place me at its head. I already knew Lisa and Fabian, but not Laura; the rest of the talk floated past me. When it stopped, I thanked everyone and said all the right things. But I hadn't yet taken it all in. It was only when I was in the stairwell that I suddenly felt my pulse accelerate. I did it! I told myself. I landed an amazing project! I got my promotion! I got everything I wanted, everything I'd dreamed of. It was really happening.

I stood on the twelfth floor and looked out at the city past the hospital, the traffic arteries, the roofs. I saw a great flock of birds and the pale autumn sun that, through the cloud cover, was heart-shaped. I opened the window to let the fresh air into my lungs. My chest expanded. For a second, I felt like lifting my arms and giving a victory cry. I was gliding on air, like the swallows above. Maybe I was now at the top of the Jenga tower. It was stable at this moment. From its top, the whole city, the whole world, was visible, the whole expanse of the human ego. At that second, I wasn't thinking about the next stage and what happens when one falls off the top. How much does it hurt? And what do you hit down below?

2

Now, back at the hospital, we were about to start the meeting of the expanded project staff. I cleared my throat and saw Lisa going back to her seat. The stage was all mine, in every sense. As project manager, I had very little occasion to address so many people at once; I generally only had small staff meetings and reported to my supervisors. I was reminded of an episode of *Sponge Bob* I'd seen with the kids, which recommended that if you have stage fright you should imagine everyone in their underwear.

For a split second, I tried to do just that, but realized how ridiculous it was. I didn't have stage fright; I had no fear at all. I was at once filled with resolve and thought of Winston Churchill and what he'd had to face. The ethos, I reminded myself.

"As you know," I began, "a few years ago the hospital decided to expand its maternity wing and embarked on a process to identify the appropriate donor, or donors, who would help finance the project. A group of visionaries had the idea to upgrade the department much beyond merely expanding the building, but do it in a way that has never been done in other hospitals."

I could feel everyone's attention and the unspoken question of what I wanted to say and why I was so far stating only the obvious. I continued: "The vision was to improve the experience of the user, in this case the mother and her companion, by an integrated visual communications system that accompanies the mother from the time she enters the hospital grounds until she leaves after a short postpartum stay.

"The vision involved many components in the process of care and hospitalization. A great deal of thought went into the smallest details. For example, the mother's prior registration through the hospital's new computer portal is supposed to allow her into the hospital without checking in at the front desk. I assume that at least some of you have had the dubious pleasure of being stuck in a line of visitors' vehicles while a woman in labor is panting in the passenger's seat."

A few scattered snorts and murmurs of assent rippled through the crowd, and for a second I remembered Marianna's birth – the insane pressure, the wasted time in the car – and suddenly I was struck by the realization that this vision was real. I could actually see the project take shape in my mind. I understood this wasn't just another technical assignment, involving equipment and computer codes: it was a fundamental change that would in some way improve the human experience. A tiny bit of pride along my spine made me stand a little straighter and the neon lights suddenly seemed soft and blue.

When I'd parted from Michael a few days earlier, he'd urged me to call him at any time if I had any questions or requests, and warned me, with a smile, that "if you don't wake me up in the middle of the night, I'll wake you!" Then, when I entered the airport terminal, it occurred to me that Michael had said something about gathering the staff, but he hadn't elaborated. So, only an hour later, I found myself calling him to ask for an explanation. He answered with a snort: "I really didn't think you'd call so soon. What can I do for you?"

A little taken aback, I asked him my question, and he answered: "Curiosity killed the cat."

"Excuse me?"

He laughed some more.

"I know the group," I said, "but they're really not my cup of tea. And I doubt you mean a British pop band from the eighties."

"A band? Never heard of them. Any good?"

"Not really."

"But that's beside the point. What I wanted to say is that you bring them to the gathering and pique their interest."

"Pique their interest?"

"Yes. Look, the hundreds of people involved in a project are a human fabric with characteristics that are important to the project's success. You can leverage these characteristics to have a successful gathering. I assume that you use some sort of meeting scheduling system."

"Sure."

"Fine. Send everyone a message saying that at such-and-such a time next week you're not going to be available because you're participating in an urgent gathering about the project's status. In the message, be sure to note that anyone who is interested is welcome to join and listen, but that participation is not mandatory."

"Is that it?"

"Well, yes and no. You're going to have to generate buzz around the gathering. Curiosity is a tremendously powerful human characteristic. It makes people travel, open themselves to new cultures, go shopping, you name it. It can also help them connect to your project on condition they choose to do so."

He paused, took a deep breath, and went on: "Curiosity is a project characteristic that generates much attractiveness. If you build it right, it will be part of your project essence. I know it sounds vague and conceptual, but it is one of the most practical recommendations I can give you. And you can quote me on it, graffiti it all over the walls, and repeat it to yourself around the clock, but no matter how you look at it, you'll realize it is both very simple and very true."

"I agree," I said, "I just wonder how to do it in the best way possible."

"Look," he continued, "I suggest you talk to a few people who have nothing in common with one another and persuade them to sign up. Make sure you have a good mix: both managers and team members, old timers and recent hires. After you do that, allow nature to run its course. I promise you that if the project involves a hundred people, as you told me, a hundred and fifty will show up to the meeting."

"Great," I said, "no problem." My own curiosity was certainly piqued.

"And call me whenever you want," he added.

"Yeah, well, I've already done that, in case you hadn't noticed."

"Oh, I had, I had," he laughed.

3

I sent the message to the expanded team while the plane was still on the tarmac. A series of brief phone conversations told me how many team members and managers I could expect at the gathering. I said I had had a series of meetings with George Madison and that I wanted to keep everyone informed of some important developments. We did have weekly project meetings, so I stressed that this was not a routine gathering. The responses I got were matter-of-fact; no one suspected the plan that was roiling my mind. At takeoff, I had to turn my phone off. I stared out at the clouds, then closed my eyes, and within seconds fell into a deep sleep.

I awoke five hours later, just as the plane was descending. Leaving the terminal, I switched my phone back on and saw I'd missed fifteen calls. Fifteen? God help me, I thought. I also had several text messages, almost all with questions about the coming meeting and its purpose.

What had occurred while I was on the plane I learned from Lisa two days later. It seems that my message had captured the attention (or curiosity) of many, and quickly a sense was created that whoever didn't attend would remain outside some imaginary circle of those in the know.

The number of registrants crept steadily upwards. Lisa had to reserve larger rooms twice, until finally she had no choice but to book the training hall that, on a good day, held eighty but was now supposed to contain a hundred. Michael was right. Curiosity killed the cat. While it was theoretically possible to gather all involved in the project in other ways, this approach clearly showed the internal forces at work in a project group, simply by virtue of the fact that the group was made up of people. In other words, I felt the project essence crystallizing before my eyes.

The direction looked promising. Standing in front of so attentive an audience, I felt the need to call Michael and share, but he would not have been surprised. Somehow, I had the sense he was sitting right behind me, a Cheshire Cat-like grin on his face.

I took a breath and continued: "In addition to improving the user experience, the vision also wanted to incorporate an information system for the caretakers – the doctors, nurses, midwives, and so on – so that information would be provided just one time but be available on many occasions. Not like today; we know that a birthing mother has to recite all her information each time a new staff member walks through the door.

"Furthermore, the steering committee came up with a locator system based on entrance controls to various parts of the hospital, so that the information system could follow the mother's physical location in the various departments. This would help retrieve relevant information and prevent errors by means of a series of rules and conditions.

"At the outset, the steering committee created several presentations designed to explain the vision to potential donors, and the hospital started a search for the right one. Without boring you with details about meetings that produced no results, I will just say that about a year into the process the steering committee was asked to present its vision to a philanthropist named George Madison. You know the rest."

Everyone more or less already knew this background, but the people in the room seemed to enjoy hearing a full overarching narrative. While speaking, I understood what Michael – and even Churchill – had meant by an ethos, also a critical part of the narrative. I was speaking about them, and patting them on the shoulder.

"George really liked what he saw," I went on. "He connected to the modern vision and the unique user experience it would provide. He also understood that such a project would be a flagship project for other departments and hospitals, and felt it was a worthy cause to support. I want you to know that George Madison is an unusually ethical donor; most of his philanthropy is dedicated to social projects designed to make life better for everyone.

"As you probably know, it took almost another year until we actually received the funds. The project got under way immediately thereafter, the project because of which we are now gathered here. You all know how difficult the process of initiating the project was. All of you put in – and are still putting in – a tremendous amount of work to make this vision a reality."

All eyes were on me. I saw something else in them now. Attentive, sure, but also resolute. Perhaps even a spark.

"Myself and the hospital's management know that the distance between the vision as described in the presentations and implementation in practice was great, perhaps too great. Many of you have had to work day and night to deal with issues the steering committee did not anticipate or did not sufficiently develop.

"I want to take a moment to note in particular the integration team. You are the ones who, at the end of the day, are in charge of linking all the systems to a single functional entity. I know that in recent weeks the integration team had been the target of a great deal of criticism despite the fact that it has had to deal with limits imposed by the hospital's systems and could therefore not make progress. I think that, here too, excellent work was done."

I had decided to begin with the integration team because it was the most unexpected thing I could have done. The team manager, whom I had described to Michael as being the worst employee in the project, was a tough nut and caused the team innumerable delays. But there was no doubt that his people worked hard, maybe the hardest of all.

I continued to highlight other departments and their great efforts, but then I noticed a slight murmur in the group and realized I was starting to lose people's focus. I decided I'd made my point. Lisa was looking at me and I tried to read her expression, but it was tough. I filled my lungs before starting the second part of my speech.

"Look, it's no secret the project is in trouble. For about a year, we've been caught in a gradual process of losing our grip on the timetables and commitments. Despite all the hard work I just described, we've been finding it tough to coordinate our operations in relation to the goals and objectives we defined.

"Over the past years, we have recalculated our schedules almost every month. I know that many of you are uncomfortable with this; my team and I are also unhappy about it. But, to an extent, we've all gotten used to it, maybe even made peace with the notion that this is how the project will proceed until it's complete."

If I'd heard murmurs before, now the room was utterly silent. It was the right moment to drop the bomb.

"You're undoubtedly asking what I want to say. Well, it is one very clear thing: This state of affairs might have continued indefinitely were it not for the fact that, last week, something happened that could upset the whole applecart. Throughout this period, George Madison and his consultants have shown a great deal of patience and understanding and have taken the delays in stride. But last week, his patience ran out. Only a few of you know that Mr. Madison has a clause in his contract, according to which he can withdraw his funding unless the project is completed within four years. We are already three years into the project. And because we can't present an orderly plan for the future, he is seriously considering that option."

The bomb was now in freefall.

The murmurs quickly grew in volume until people were talking out loud. I knew I had to give them a minute or so before continuing. Lisa gave me a worried look. It seemed as if she wanted to come to the podium and help me quiet everyone down, but I smiled at her serenely and my hand motion told her everything was fine. She looked back at me, bewildered.

I waited for the hubbub to subside, making sure everyone was calmer and looking at me. I waited for the last murmur to die out; a brittle silence descended. With a slight smile on my face, I went on smoothly: "Just to clarify, you all know that the new wing is completely constructed and at least half of the investment is already executed.

"But the implementation of the vision as presented to the donor is far from done, and without that component, the project as a whole is in danger. It's not only a threat to further financing of the project; such a move would create a budgetary hole that would require the hospital to find funding for the work already done. I have no idea how the hospital would manage that.

"So, we have no choice. The situation is critical. It requires each and every one of us to rethink, from management to team members. The method we've used to date can only lead to disaster. We urgently need to find new tools and creative ideas to ensure the completion of the project."

I waited through several long beats of silence. I saw their concentration, saw them waiting for my next words, curious like cats.

"Look," I continued, "with a great deal of effort, I succeeded in convincing Mr. Madison and his team to give us another opportunity, another three months, to show them that the project is going in the right direction. But what can we do to prove it? That's a good question.

"My team and I intend to turn over every rock and think outside every box to give you the tools to provide you with better control of the work. To succeed, we need your cooperation and commitment to the process.

"You should know that we are in contact with a consultant who specializes in crises. Next week, we will hold several meetings with him to study new tools to help us confront the situation. But it is important that I clarify that there is no chance of completing the project in the next six months."

More audience murmurs. Some people were leaning towards one another, exchanging information and impressions, while others just looked stunned, unsure whether to sink into despair or lift their heads high and carry on with more grit than ever.

"Listen!" I said authoritatively. "There are no magic bullets to the situation we're in. It is best not to commit ourselves to targets we're not sure we can attain. But still, it is important to me – actually, to all of us – that we set some doable goals for the short- and mid-term. These are attainable, and, with their help, we can create the necessary change in the project that will convince George Madison we're on the right track."

I motioned to Lisa to turn on the projector and show the only slide I'd prepared. The slide on the screen consisted of only three lines; I'd tried to make it simple and catchy.

"As you can see," I went on, "the **first goal is to change the project management method this coming month**. This goal will be achieved by working with the consultant I mentioned, and it will be led by my team. I don't promise that the process will be easy, but I promise to do the utmost so that only effective, valuable steps are taken. **I am going to be personally responsible for reaching this goal**."

"The **second goal is to articulate the real achievements that are attainable** in every area in April, May, and June. Please note that I am not saying what those achievements will be, but they have to be significant enough to indicate movement in the right direction, things we can present to Mr. Madison in order to regain his trust. Next month, I will present those attainable aims to Mr. Madison. In three months, I want to be able to show him the aims were in fact attained. **Fabian will lead the work to reach this goal**."

"The **third goal is examining the current plan and rethinking it to redefine the plan to complete the project**. The current plan is expressed in a Gantt chart, but we've been unable to execute it. We need a different plan, one we can stand behind and use to rebuild trust with our donor. I intend to have this goal completed by May. **Lisa will be in charge of reaching it**."

I was done with the slide, but sensed some discomfort in the room. I had piqued the people's curiosity, but I felt I – and they – were capable of more, and I didn't want the moment to slip out of my grasp. I cleared my throat in an exaggerated manner, tapped my fingers on the mike, and again had the group's full attention.

"Look, maybe these steps seem a little anemic compared to the threat to the project's very existence. But they are crucial. They will change the way we manage the project from the ground up. I could have spent an hour up here exerting pressure on each of you to make a more aggressive effort to make things happen faster. But to accelerate so complex an activity, we simply have to generate new tools with which to advance the projects. The steps I just outlined are **the steps needed to make these new tools**. Is this clear?"

Most heads nodded in agreement.

"I hope that this day will be remembered as the project's turning point. This hope is not just a possibility; it is a necessity without which the project cannot go on. The situation might deteriorate even further before we have a chance to improve it, so I'm going to ask you all to be patient and allow us to carry out this critical move for the good of the hospital and the good of us all. I am sure that, next year, we will be proud of our achievements."

Other things needed to be said, but I decided to stop there. All in all, I thought I'd achieved what I wanted: praise the work done to date, provide a full background to the project's status and stress its importance, and, of course, define clear, attainable goals for the future.

"All right, folks. I don't want to take any more of your time. You're all busy. I just wanted to thank you for your hard work, keep you in the loop about the situation, make sure you understood the risks we're facing, and knew the new goals as well as I do. I'll be happy to explain more in the next few days. Please do not hesitate to talk to me or my team. We're happy to answer all questions. Thank you."

I stepped off the stage under the watchful gaze of the assembled. I thought some were on the verge of clapping, but it would have been out of place. I headed for the hallway while Lisa stayed to talk. I grabbed some orange juice off the drinks table, and guzzled down half a bottle before coming up for air. In all that talking, I hadn't noticed how dry my mouth had become.

Within moments, more and more people gathered around me. I knew they had many questions and I was ready to explain myself, but, on the other hand, I wondered if it was better to keep them in suspense.

Chapter Four

The Team

1

In the second week of April, I picked Michael up from the airport. He was wrapped in a black raincoat and wore a woolen hat, so at first, I didn't spot him and his gleaming bald head. When he approached me, and stretched out his hand, I was filled with joy. I was truly happy to see him.

The sand in the hourglass counting down the three months George Madison had given us was already trickling. Every day, I imagine the sand pile at the bottom growing a little taller. There was no room for error, and I had many expectations from the meeting with Michael. Maybe too many.

I helped him with his small suitcase, asked him about the flight – because that's what one does – and he mumbled that it was fine, adding he hoped the day would come when flying would be like taking the bus, without all the waiting and the lines and the fatigue. Get on, fly, get off. End of story.

"I hear you. That's a project I'd love to manage."

He smiled. "One thing at a time."

"Sure! Let's finish this first and then – a real vacation."

On the way into town, I told Michael about last week's meeting and the strong sense I'd had since then that we started well, but that it was necessary to seize the momentum. Michael nodded, yawned hugely, and apologized. He was tired from the flight but was sure a cup of coffee would perk him up.

"I'll have a whole carafe waiting for you," I answered.

"I'm glad to hear it."

"And poppy seed cake. Sugar-free."

He laughed. "Good man, Gary!"

After talking a bit about Churchill's speech, the circumstances under which it was delivered, and how I understood it and used it in my own speech, he started asking me about the hospital project.

"It's time for me to get a bit involved in the details," he said, swallowing another yawn. "Pay no attention to my yawns. It's oxygen for the brain. I'm wide awake, and curious like a cat."

I smiled forgivingly, and said: "All right, as you know, we're talking about an expansion of the maternity wing spread over four floors. The construction used an existing space that was previously used for parking. Parking is now underground, on two levels, and above, we added about eight hundred square meters on every floor.

"The first floor consists of the entrance and all non-medical services, such as the cafeteria, visitor seating, the information desk, the elevator lobby, and so on. The second floor houses the ER with reception rooms, labor rooms, birthing rooms, operating rooms, and recovery rooms. And the third and fourth floors are for postpartum hospitalizations.

"Now, the construction was done about six months ago, and that's where our story begins. When the expansion of the maternity wing was approved, we had a vision of the whole building being computerized and synchronized by means of advanced telecommunications systems. Am I going too fast?"

"No, no. It's all clear. I'm yawning to stay alert."

"OK. Anyway, unlike other hospital departments, the maternity wing deals with women who are generally healthy. This means that women can register long before their due date through the hospital's internet system via a dedicated interface. The vision was to do a computerized intake of the mother the minute she enters the building, and her progress from that point onwards would be monitored through advanced information systems. The system would track her location in the building, show wait times at every stage, and retrieve the relevant data for all staff members, including personal information gathered long before the birth. The aim was to give the mother the sense that the hospital knows her and personally accompanies her every step of the way. This feeling is supposed to add to her sense of security and calm, and therefore also has medical implications.

"All of this required the development of a unique information system and relevant applications. But beyond this we had to distribute a network of information screens for the patients and their families, provide the medical staff with terminals connected to the information system, connect the medical equipment to integrated information systems, and define whole sections of the vision and its implementation that the steering committee failed to articulate."

Michael seemed focused, processing the information while I was steering my way through traffic, wondering if I should have used my navigation app. A quick phone call to Lisa ensured that we'd have hot coffee waiting for us. I had ordered the poppy seed cake ahead of time. I had also arranged for a huge fruit platter with lots and lots of papaya.

It wasn't a matter of placating our guest. I believe that when you pay attention to the small things, you affect the atmosphere and the setting of any discussion. I was trying to communicate to Michael the sense that we were excited to see him but also had high expectations.

"Anyhow," I continued, "the department managers and steering committee together created marketing materials long before any application existed, in which an expecting mother is undergoing a semi-automatic computerized check-in while entering the building and moving through the hospital.

"This was supported by a very fancy presentation that stressed the uniqueness of this approach. It wasn't a technological challenge that had never before been applied elsewhere, but what we wanted was a fusion of existing technologies and capabilities to create a completely new and unconventional service to the woman: building a preliminary information base, distributing wireless ID card to registered women (like cards used in hotels), using entrance control linked to a computerized center, gathering computerized information, while progressing through a pre-defined process, and more."

A traffic jam greeted us just blocks from the office. This time I really wanted to turn the navigation app on, and again I remembered Michael's first assignment. A rueful smile tugged at my lips.

"What do you say – turn on the navigation app?" he asked, as if reading my mind, an impish smile creasing his face.

"There's no point," I answered, "we're almost there and I know the area well."

He nodded.

"We're making good use of the time, and that's what matters. The other thing I wanted to say is that, for a whole year, the hospital tried to find a donor who would help finance this vision with no success, until the steering committee was invited to take a meeting with George Madison, whom I've already mentioned.

"George and his team were introduced to the vision and the marketing materials, and this played an important part in his decision to finance the project and implement the hospital's vision. Not only that, but at the outset, the department managers wanted to involve several donors, but George insisted on donating the entire sum."

Michael looked surprised. He motioned for me to go on.

"He thought it would speed things up," I said with a measure of bitterness, "and this is how we got to the point where, although the building is up, we have a great deal of work left before we can declare the project done. And George's threat to withdraw his investment is not only the death knell to the project and the vision, but is a budgetary and legal nightmare for the hospital, whose ramifications I can't even begin to consider."

Traffic was suddenly flowing again. Michael hunched his shoulders and straightened up again. I imagined he needed to stretch after the flight. My plan was to take him to a nice seafood restaurant near the hospital, but first there was the meeting with the team.

But, as I entered the hospital's parking structure, I was suddenly beset by niggling doubts. What if none of this mattered? What if the consultancy only postponed the inevitable? To what extent could Michael really be a part of the project? How much responsibility could he assume, if any? Did he really understand the reality the hospital – we – were facing?

"Michael," I said after a short silence, "are you sure your method is relevant to our project? You yourself said you had no experience in the field." As I spoke, I hoped I wasn't being too forward. Besides, wasn't it a little late to be asking?

"That's for you to say," Michael answered confidently and laughed briefly. "Projects can differ widely in terms of contents, complexity, duration, goals, and field of business, but are really quite similar. The key to project management lies in understanding its structure, which is a direct derivative of the participating groups or its areas of activity – we'll get to that later. Multiple groups and multiple areas of activity require coordination, a need that is common to different projects and makes it possible to adapt a similar management method to all. Clearly, very simple projects and very monotonous projects will benefit less from using my methods. But they are relevant to most cases, certainly for a complex one like yours that encompasses construction, technology, high demands, and strict medical standards – you have it all."

I allowed Michael to persuade me, at least for now. Parking the car, I dismissed all my other bothersome concerns. The momentum was positive, no doubt about it, and, maybe, as Michael was saying, that was the important thing. There was momentum and it would allow us to soar.

2

We went straight to the conference room, and Michael, in the straightforward style I had come to recognize, was eager and ready to begin without further ado. Obviously, he poured himself a generous cup of coffee to begin with, and nibbled at a couple of slices of poppy seed cake. "Are you sure it's sugar-free? It's tastes too good to be..." For some reason, the fruit platter hadn't shown up yet, but the coffee and cake seemed enough for now. I asked that my team come up, which they did just a few minutes later.

We sat down at the polished table. After some brief pleasantries, we began the round of introductions I had planned. The project managers were to give their names, list their realms of responsibility, and then bullet-point their future plans. Lisa was supposed to go last, and I had asked her to segue right into a review of our Gantt chart.

I motioned to Fabian to begin. He wore a shiny black button-down shirt, and his long hair was gathered in a ponytail. Fabian had grown up on a farm, and as a child he had risen early to take care of the animal pens whenever his father was away. He has many wonderful qualities, but he's not especially detail oriented. And sometimes he looks as if he wants to leap through the window straight back to the farm where he can talk with goats instead of people.

Once, after work, over beers, I mentioned this to him. He denied it strenuously. "I've had it with goats. I can't stand their smell. Can't look at them, can't milk them. Seriously, dude. That whole thing is so over."

As was his wont, Fabian stood to give himself space to gesticulate as he spoke. He likes attention and enlivens his presentations with jokes and stories. "Hi. I'm Fabian. I've worked with Gary for eight years, three of which have been devoted to this project."

Michael nodded. There was a knock at the door, but I shouted: "Not now, please," and wondered if I'd been too loud.

Fabian continued. "I'm a machine engineer by training, but I worked only a little in that exciting field. I quickly realized that I'm a much more sophisticated machine than any I worked with, so we parted ways. On amicable terms, I should add. Most of my career has been spent on construction and technology- and integration-intense projects. The more operational challenges, the merrier."

Michael gave a Mona Lisa smile. I already knew all of Fabian's lines.

"In this project, I'm in charge of all technological aspects of the new wing, from installing robotic arms to setting up and integrating the computer network and all the tools needed to begin operations. I work with various providers, some good ones, some so-so, responsible for the communications equipment, testing, and applications."

Fabian was giving Michael an appraising look. For a moment, he seemed to be considering how to continue. Did he have to make a good impression at all costs? Either way, he spoke the way he always does, which I appreciated. He cleared his throat and continued: "A snapshot of the present shows that we've started activity in every area; there isn't a single technological aspect that still hasn't been addressed at all. Everything is in process. In fact, I'm managing fifteen projects simultaneously, and every project involves development, installation, testing, and putting into service of some system or another."

He paused for a moment and looked at me as if asking whether he should continue. I honestly didn't know. I suppose he could have gone on, but at the same time I felt he had summarized the situation well. There was another knock at the door and, again, I yelled "Not now, please." Just then I saw that Michael wanted to ask something.

"Can you estimate the amount of time you need?" Michael looked at Fabian, who didn't seem to have expected the question.

"I don't really know. When I was a kid and hadn't finished milking all the goats on our farm, my father would say, 'You should have gotten up an hour earlier.' Here, even if I get up an hour earlier, I'm dependent on many factors without which I often can't proceed.

"I'll put it this way: If I wasn't dependent on anyone else, I'd milk the entire herd of projects in three months. But we've had delays that lasted that long in and themselves."

Fabian looked at me as if to read my face; I wasn't sure what he was seeing. He sighed briefly, and resumed: "For example, on one occasion we waited two months for the hospital's general communications department to give us lines we could connect to, which caused pretty much all of our activity to grind to a halt. Despite the fact that Gary is friends with the manager."

Fabian winked at me, thinking of the worst employee. Michael didn't get it, but attributed no importance to it.

"OK," I said, "you laid it out like it is. Laura – your turn."

Fabian shot me a dissatisfied look, which I ignored.

Laura took a deep breath, sipped some water, and began: "All right, I'm Laura. I'm a doctor by training and worked as an OB-GYN for about a decade. I joined the project after construction started, so I've worked with Gary for only about two years."

There is something a little mysterious about Laura. She's seems to be from nicer side of the tracks, a kid who always wanted to be a doctor because it was expected. And she'd done it, with flying colours. She'd come to project management with a bit of an attitude, and it blew up in her face. At the beginning, she'd talk to me about her problems, but after a while, I told her, gently: "Laura, don't take this the wrong way, but I don't want to hear about the problems. I want you to solve them. I want you to come to me only when you can't do that on your own."

She was probably insulted, but I'd had no choice. Since that conversation, she stopped bothering me with small and medium-sized issues, but, one time, walking past her open office door, I heard her screaming at someone over the phone. The secretary at the end of the corridor seemed amused, and when I asked her about it said: "It's OK, it's just her husband. She yells at him every day. It's her escape valve, and it helps her solve problems at work. Or so she says."

"Nice to meet you," Michael said, and rose to pour himself a second cup. I was wondering what happened to the fruit platter. If we're incapable of having a fruit platter delivered, how can we build a new wing? Bad thinking, I decided. Sometimes you just have to let go of the little things.

"So, as I said, I'm an MD. When the construction of the new wing was complete, I was involved in acquiring the necessary medical equipment. After most of the acquisitions were decided on, I moved to Gary's team to complete the mission and take receipt of the equipment as it arrives."

Michael nodded again, and looked more curious than usual. Fabian scrunched his eyebrows, managing to look bored. I knew that he was sometimes a bit hyperactive, but I didn't want it to tip into disrespect. I gave a look that communicated, Shape up. I nodded to Laura to continue.

"I have to say that project management is a new field for me. In the last two years, I've learned a lot from Gary, Fabian, and Lisa, and I really like the work. But I feel that while we're really making tremendous efforts, we're having a hard time controlling the project."

She went on and on, as was often her tendency. It was necessary to cut her off without being rude. I was on the verge of doing so, but Michael preempted me by asking: "How much time do you think you still need?"

Suddenly, Laura blushed, as if he'd asked an inappropriate personal question. She sipped some more water, looked at him seriously, and said: "I estimate I need three months to complete the project. But I can't tell you the starting date."

"You can't tell me the starting date?" Michael echoed. "What do you mean?"

"Several systems in Fabian's field aren't ready yet, and some are needed before it's possible to start working. Connecting medical systems to other communications systems can be very problematic and requires a very high degree of precision.

"We're having trouble reaching that degree and testing it before the systems are actually in place. Also, we don't have all the delivery dates. Some providers demand that I commit myself to a date for taking delivery of devices. As long as I can't commit to the infrastructure being ready, they keep postponing the delivery date. It's really frustrating. A chicken and egg situation."

"What kind of medical devices are you talking about?" Michael wanted to know.

"Good question," Laura said uneasily. "The most complicated issue would seem to be the operating room, but this is one place where we haven't actually bought anything new; we simply copied an existing OR and equipment for the new wing. Most of the new devices we bought consists of advanced imaging equipment, and most of those are mobile.

"We're also talking about all the medical equipment installed in examination rooms and the hospitalization wards. From unique lighting pieces to disposable items and dispensers."

Laura walked over to the sideboard to pour herself some coffee, and I assumed she was done. Michael seemed to have heard what he needed to learn. Now it was Lisa's turn. She was not only the most professional of the team; she was also the toughest. Telling her that she had to work differently wasn't going to be the easiest thing in the world. Mentally, I was wishing Michael a lot of luck.

Lisa quickly introduced herself. She spoke without smiling, and was at times quite forceful. Her penetrating gaze was focused on Michael, as if weighing up their balance of power. She mentioned her background to make an impression and to ensure our guest didn't doubt her professionalism, but Michael's blank face revealed nothing.

At a certain point she sighed, and slumped back in her chair. "In this project, I divide my time pretty much into two equal portions. One portion I devote to the Gantt chart. Other project managers submit their parts to me or I help them construct it. I have a weekly schedule in which I update the Gantt for my own benefit but don't share it. Once a month we do a more thorough job to prepare the materials for the monthly meetings with George and his team, which I sometimes attend.

"With the other portion of my time, I'm in charge of developing an information system and applications together with a provider. This includes planning the development, receiving the parts whose development is complete, testing, feedback, and more testing, until the system is stable."

"Lisa is in the Critical Chain," I said, immediately second-guessing my statement.

"I don't think I'm in the Critical Chain," she said, looking at me. "Most of the time, our development provider sits and waits for us. The biggest problem, which is getting worse, by the way, is that his attention is waning. He signed a two-year contract, not a four-year one, and it is clear that his ability to complete the work is in doubt. I'm sure we'll get another demand for payment soon."

The room fell silent. I thought I heard another knock at the door but wasn't sure. In any case, I didn't bother to say anything. Michael, on the other hand, seemed eager to speak. Just then, the door opened to reveal Chantal, the secretary, holding an enormous fruit platter. Everyone called out in excitement.

"I'm so sorry to barge in," she apologized. "I knocked a few times and you told me not to come in, but I was starting to feel sorry for the poor fruit."

Michael stared at the platter with glittering eyes, then looked at me and nodded in appreciation. I merely shrugged. Fabian used the opportunity to go to the bathroom. We said we'd wait for him before continuing the discussion. Laura, who seemed somewhat down, tugged at a small cluster of grapes, but didn't eat any. Lisa still seemed to be in fighting mode, while Michael attacked the papaya with glee.

"Excuse me a second," I said, "I'm just stepping out to call my wife. I'll be right back."

Michael was fine with it, but Lisa sent me a warning look as if saying, don't you dare leave us alone with him.

When I called Anna to ask about things on the home front, because I'd promised I'd check in with her more often, Fabian was already coming back from the washroom. I saw he wanted to talk to me and probably also say something to Michael. I signaled that I was busy but that he should go back inside. Anna wasn't answering. I left her a voicemail telling her I missed her and the kids. I moved towards the doorway to re-enter the conference room and collided with Laura and Lisa. "We'll be right back," they said in unison. Frustrated, I looked at my watch. We still had plenty of time, but I felt we were being rude.

3

When we had all finally reassembled, the expression on Michael's face told me that, from his perspective, the meet-and-greet part was over. He wiped his hand on a napkin, sipped some water, looked at Lisa, and, as if no time had passed, asked her: "On what basis do you say you're not on the project's Critical Chain?"

I suddenly sensed tension and saw Lisa trying, unsuccessfully, to swallow. But she pulled herself together and her body language became more aggressive than ever. Too aggressive. She leaned forward and said: "Based on the Gantt. And I see the project's general structure and its constraints. In the past year, we never hit the point where someone was waiting for a development to be completed. It is always development that waits for installation and testing to be complete to get feedback and make corrections."

"And who was on the Critical Chain at the beginning of the process?" Michael asked.

"At the outset, the project structure was completely different, and I was on the Critical Chain," Lisa replied. "The situation changed the moment we took possession of the building. While I was able to do much of the work with my provider in tandem with the construction, Fabian and Laura's work was only starting. Very quickly the Critical Chain was elsewhere."

"Where?" Michael wanted to know.

"To be honest, I don't know." Lisa's answer stunned me. "As Laura pointed out, the last update shows that it starts with the communications infrastructures on Fabian's side and only then goes to Laura and the installation of the medical equipment. But given the scope of changes every week, our analysis is incapable of following up on what's happening on the ground. At best, the Gantt reflects current reality, not any kind of forecast."

"So, what you're really saying...," Michael was also leaning forward, speaking loudly, "is that the Critical Chain analysis did not predict the current crisis and isn't particularly helpful in managing it."

"If you put it that way."

"In which case, the Gantt is pretty useless, wouldn't you say?"

For a second, everyone's expression froze. The silence was so profound we could each hear our heartbeats. I followed Lisa's eyes, wondering what she was thinking.

"It's useless if there's something to replace it," she said. She looked impatient. "It's what project managers do, isn't it? Their job is to maintain the project plan."

Michael saw her distress but didn't seem to care. "You see," he said, "there are many project managers who think that if they track and update the Gantt they are managing their projects. But that's just not true. Swimming doesn't make you a fish. Standing in a parking space doesn't make you a car. And operating a Gantt doesn't make you a project manager. If you want to be a project manager – or a fish – you have to do things very differently. You also have to relate to coordination among teams, risk prevention, problem solving, plan presentation, and level of team involvement. Without those, your Gantt diagram might as well be a scribble. I will try to show you that, even as a diagram, the Gantt is far from adequate."

Lisa didn't know what to say, and shot me a helpless look, as if I had the answer. Michael perceived the discomfort in the room, but seemed ready for it. Fabian's face alternated between smug and tense, as if trying to decide what to say. Laura's mouth was open, as if she were watching a play on a stage. Maybe that was the remove she craved.

Michael shifted his bulk in his seat to the extent he could, and then said: "Please believe me, it is not my intention to insult anyone, certainly not Lisa, who is, according to Gary, the most professional project manager in the organization.

"But I'm here to move you out of your comfort zone and, come hell or high water, I intend on doing just that! The project is in crisis.

Nothing's moving. And you're busy with a plan that you say isn't helping anyone. So, what is really going on here?"

Michael stopped to look at each of us in turn, trying to assess the impact of the stunt he'd just pulled. It was one of those moments when the silence was too much. But, I told myself, it wasn't just a stunt; it was part of his methodology. And, above all, it was the price we had to pay. It was painful, yes, but necessary.

"Look," said Michael, and stared hard at me for a while, then shifting his eyes to Lisa, "I'm going to try to convince you that there are inherent problems with using Gantts and managing projects on the basis of the Critical Chain. But even without my methodological analysis, you know as well as I that nobody like Gantts, right?"

Fabian guffawed awkwardly. Michael went on: "As Lisa said, it is presented monthly. You work so hard at it, giving it time and effort. And what do you get in return? What value is created at the project's operational level? Who even looks at it? These are the questions we have to ask to figure out if there is any point in using the method at all."

Michael got up. For a moment it seemed he was lingering next to the drinks and fruit, but resolutely turned to face us and said: "All right, before we start: Would any of you buy a car with two gears and a top speed of forty-five miles per hour?"

We were all mystified. How was that relevant? The skeptical team was attentive, but no one answered. Not even I, who was by now fairly familiar with Michael's stock of metaphors (though I'd never told anyone about my trip to Eric's Place and never would), knew what to say.

"It's like this. I'm going to introduce you to a nice guy. The name is Henry Gantt. Unfortunately, he's no longer with us. In 1910, our dear Mr. Gantt invented the chart bearing his name, in use even now. At the same time, there was another, much more famous Henry around. Henry Ford. I know you know him.

"In 1910, Ford sold no fewer than ten thousand Model Ts. It had two gears and its top speed was forty-five miles per hour. The starter was manual, mind you. The same decade that Gantt invented his chart, Ford increased the manufacturing capacity at his factory from ten thousand a year to one million!"

Michael scanned our faces to see the effect his last statement had. Today, one million doesn't sound like much, and only Fabian seemed impressed. Laura and Lisa both looked bored or maybe impatient, but they continued meeting his gaze and waited for him to continue.

"Clearly, back in the day, it was the biggest thing to hit industry. And that was the business environment where Gantt got the idea for his chart. Everything was aimed at production and, specifically, at making it more efficient and increasing its volume. So, Gantt's idea was meant for factories and production lines, and everything related to the chart comes out of that world."

Michael tried to assess if we were following his example. Satisfied, he went on: "So, you refused to purchase that classic car. Too bad. In the antiques market, the car is now worth twenty-five thousand dollars, even though it originally sold for just eight hundred and twenty-five.

"OK, let's move forward from 1910, because several developments were added to the Gantt chart over the years. In the 1950s, the concept of the Critical Path, and afterwards Critical Chain, came into vogue. The critical path was then calculated on PERT – project evaluation review technique – or Gantt charts. Its effect on the optimal length of activity fascinated its inventors.

"Now, I don't want to bore you with too much history, but I ask you to stick with me just a little while longer. This whole field of theory got an enormous push when the first computers came into wider use in the 1970s. Suddenly, it became possible, even easy, to calculate the critical path, and generally be able to control long lists of tasks.

"And that's how, in 1984, we got to the development of the Theory of Constraints and the Critical Chain. The innovation in the way of thinking and how these concepts was transmitted to managers at the time made the terminology ageless.

"In fact, we use it to this day. Bottleneck, Critical Chain, smart management of surplus time, what we call the buffer – these are not only the foundations of project management, they are the basis for talking about project management even now.

"So, given all of this, I'd like to offer you a much better car. A much more modern Ford, the Ford Escort Erika. It has a top speed of one hundred and ten miles per hour, but has no modern safety features. Would you buy it?

"Of course not! Who buys a car without antilock brakes these days? Who buys a car without airbags? Or distance sensors? Obviously, as consumers, we understand that what was fine in 1984, no longer meets the standards thirty plus years later. We understand that the Erika drove, drove well in fact, but today we need so much more than that."

Michael was speaking very lucidly, and I thought everyone was following and agreeing. There was another knock at the door and Chantal popped in to hand Lisa a note. She glanced at it, seeming not to take it in, and stuck it in her pocket, but then, for some reason, took it back out and crumpled it in her fist.

"When I failed to be enthused by your Gantt, I didn't mean to criticize any of you," Michael said and turned to Lisa who was still mashing the note with quiet fury. "Using the Critical Chain and the Theory of Constraints to analyze and manage a project is important, but unfortunately it is not enough anymore.

"It doesn't matter how many expansions or adaptations we apply to the Theory of Constraints, which was inspired by theories related to manufacturing, as if we were still stuck in a world of interconnected machines. The capacity of the method to help us manage a project is limited. You understand why, right? Today, no project is an assembly line. It's something much more dynamic."

We were all nodding. And I wondered how, indeed, it had happened that, even though projects had grown increasingly complex, the tools had remained the same. Maybe they'd worked for a little while...

"Look," Michael continued, "when I first started out, I used these methods too. In fact, I went further and managed the allowable buffer and use of surplus time as a function of a project's progress.

When I saw it wasn't enough, I also started to manage less Critical Chains, and I attached maximal buffers to them too so that they wouldn't become critical. But despite all these steps, I saw the method has many limitations, and I know that you know most, if not all, of them."

Michael was gauging the team's response, and watched us all thinking and digesting. His eyes sparkled. He started walking towards the whiteboard, but the secretary once again entered, this time carrying a tray with take-out boxes. Turning to Michael, she said: "I hope you like Chinese."

He looked surprised but charmed. I, too, was pleased. I didn't remember us asking her to place an order. I scanned the faces around, and realized by her look that Lisa had made the arrangements. It was only then that I noticed it was already one o'clock.

Fabian, not unexpectedly, volunteered to open all the containers. My mind's eye could already see the MSG fumes filling the room. "It smells great," Fabian noted, while Michael watched me intently. I had eaten great Chinese food in China, but I couldn't stand the Western take-out version. I'm pretty sure no Chinese person would recognize any of that stuff as something from back home. I hoped they had at least ordered eggrolls so I wouldn't starve.

"Thank you so much," Michael said and smiled at Chantal.

"Just remember to get rid of the cartons."

He nodded as if to say, I'll make sure it's done. Fabian had already opened everything and spread the contents over the conference table. Lisa handed everyone chopsticks and napkins.

"How long will you be needing the room?" the secretary wanted to know.

I shrugged and looked at Michael. He'd already started to root around in the pickles, but he looked up, and with a warm smile answered: "Oh, I should think several hours still."

She nodded and left.

"Several hours?" Laura gasped. "In that case, I have to call my husband."

She got right up, left the room, and probably headed for her office to vent for a while.

"The walls will soon be shaking," said Fabian, chewing a piece of sesame chicken.

I snorted silently. Searching the offerings on the table, I finally spied two crisp and greasy eggrolls and a container of sweet-and-sour sauce.

"Leave some for Laura," Lisa told me, "I ordered those mostly for her."

"Fine," I said and made do by scoffing down just one of them.

4

After collecting all the left-overs, we tossed everything in the garbage can, and even cleaned the table with some wet wipes. Michael went up to the whiteboard where he wrote "Gantt: Major Limitations." He kept writing:

The chart is half-empty!

He turned to his laptop to show us a typical Gantt chart on his screen.

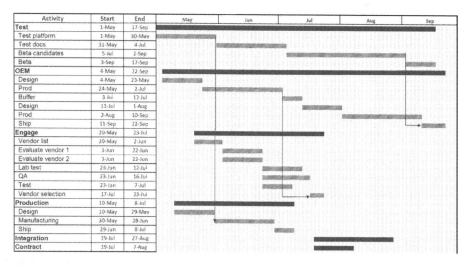

Activity	Start	End	May	Jun	Jul	Aug	Sep
Test	1-May	17-Sep					
Test platform	1-May	30-May					
Test docs	31-May	4-Jul					
Beta candidates	5-Jul	2-Sep					
Beta	3-Sep	17-Sep					
OEM	4-May	22-Sep					
Design	4-May	23-May					
Prod	24-May	2-Jul					
Buffer	3-Jul	12-Jul					
Design	13-Jul	1-Aug					
Prod	2-Aug	10-Sep					
Ship	11-Sep	22-Sep					
Engage	20-May	23-Jul					
Vendor list	20-May	2-Jun					
Evaluate vendor 1	3-Jun	22-Jun					
Evaluate vendor 2	3-Jun	22-Jun					
Lab test	23-Jun	12-Jul					
QA	23-Jun	16-Jul					
Test	23-Jun	7-Jul					
Vendor selection	17-Jul	23-Jul					
Production	10-May	8-Jul					
Design	10-May	29-May					
Manufacturing	30-May	28-Jun					
Ship	29-Jun	8-Jul					
Integration	19-Jul	27-Aug					
Contract	19-Jul	7-Aug					

"Look," he said, "even if you've never noticed it before, a Gantt chart is inherently hierarchic, and is therefore full of holes. Today, when most information is viewed on smartphone screens, who can afford blank spaces? This manner of presentation has become irrelevant."

He continued writing:

It's too big; it can't be presented like this!

Michael went back to his computer where his screen was showing a whiteboard and said:

"I want to relate for a second to the work process. Let's assume we're now talking about a new project. We've sat in the room and jotted some ideas down on a whiteboard, just like in this example."

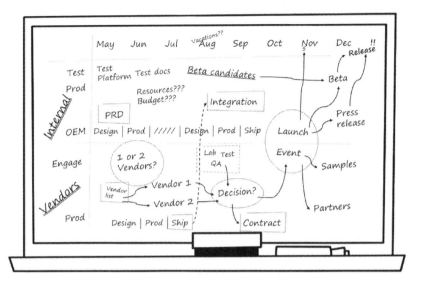

By now, we were staring as if hypnotized. The so-called Chinese food had infused us with renewed energy, though heartburn was sure to follow.

"Lisa," said Michael, indicating he wanted her to answer, "the meeting that produced that board is over. What happens next?"

Lisa, full of Szechuan chicken, sipped some water and answered: "A discussion about that disorganized board. Maybe we'd change and erase some things, add tasks or question marks. Afterwards, I assume that somebody," Lisa frowned and pointed at herself, "would be asked to summarize the discussion and add this information to a Gantt."

"Sounds like fun times," Michael said with a grin. "Turning this into a Gantt must be a real doozy. Tell me, Lisa, how do you turn this chicken-stuffed eggroll into a Gantt?"

Lisa's face finally relaxed into a smile. It seemed that she and Michael were now on the same wavelength. Moreover, it was the first time she'd smiled since the beginning of the meeting, and it made me feel we were finally getting somewhere.

"OK," she said, still smiling, "when I transfer a plan to a Gantt, I have to consider a particular starting point from which I can begin building the Gantt's task tree. I assume I would choose to start at the most significant sequence of activity and then add other tasks until I'd covered everything.

"To maintain a dynamic plan and logical sequences of activity, my experience has taught me that it is necessary to add tasks in great detail and also add them in other links to keep tasks from moving automatically to the wrong place on the time axis. It's not a simple task, and it requires experience and time, otherwise the results are useless."

Michael's face was expectant and shiny. I concluded that he felt we were on the right track. Then I realized it had been a long time since I spoke. It felt weird. Usually in these meetings I had to talk and talk and talk, organize and organize, manage and manage. And just as suddenly, I experienced this supposed passivity as pleasant. I felt like a spectator, but I knew I was really a learner. We were all learners, something we hadn't been in a long time. For too long, we'd been responding like mechanized robots, stuck in our operating command. And the sense that different operating orders were being installed at this very moment was wonderful. Cleansing.

"So, what you've described hints at a high level of changes the plan must undergo to make it fit the Gantt's structure!" Michael exclaimed in surprise, although I'm sure it was just for effect.

"That's right," Lisa replied.

"It's a way of massaging the data. It's not exactly what was on the board."

"True."

"So, what would you do after the Gantt's done?"

"What would I do? I'd try to understand the implications and find a way to present them on the next occasion we met."

"I don't follow you," Michael was in full-blown actor mode now. "Why not just present the Gantt?"

"Seriously?" List wanted to know, losing both her patience and smile. "You know as well as I that you can't bring a Gantt to a meeting. At most, I'd copy a piece of the chart and apologize that it wasn't legible. Afterwards, I'd go on to a more general presentation or speech that would summarize the main points, through which I'd steer the discussion to the points that seem right to me?"

"Seem right to you?"

"Yes."

"Another manipulation of the project data?"

No one said a thing. The truth was that none of us had thought about the process in quite this way before. In Michael's description, the process suddenly seemed absurd. And, who knew? Maybe all of us seemed absurd. Nobody likes that feeling.

"Fine," Michael pushed on, saving us from the tense silence, "let's say you had the meeting, and you talked about the points Lisa considered right. At the end of the meeting, you're asked for a copy of the information. How do you provide it?"

"I attach the presentation to the meeting summary," Lisa said.

"Thank you, Lisa," said Michael. "You can't imagine how much you've helped me to present the solution I'm offering you. Please pay attention everyone!" Michael's body language indicated that the back-and-forth with Lisa was over. "Please note the very problematic nature of the process you've just described, even though it is prevalent and is normally done just the way Lisa said in virtually every project."

Fabian looked frozen, as if someone were trying to pull the rug out from under his feet. Laura, too, hardly opened her mouth, only shook her head occasionally. She seemed hunched, as if wanting not to be seen, wanting her presence, her very existence to be forgotten. Still stooped, she got up to pour herself some coffee and started to slowly nibble at the last piece of poppy seed cake from this morning. Suddenly I noticed that all of us, except for Michael, were sighing, or yawning, or stretching our legs. Laura, remembering herself, asked: "Who wants some coffee?" Fabian barked a short laugh, as if Laura had actually asked, "who wants to jump out the window?"

Michael studied us. "All right, let's stop and think. We turned the whiteboard into a Gantt, and the Gantt into something that can be presented. After two steps of processing, what resemblance

90

between what we put on the board and what we presented remains? How much information from that intuitive process that happened on the board and that encompasses so much of the project's intelligence is actually left?

"I would argue; not much. And once you have to add, the little that's left is not to be shared! To share it, Lisa against mentioned a process in which she decides what's important. Now, stay with me for just a bit: we have a five-stage process going on!"

He got up and, with great enthusiasm, wrote on the board:

Create a general overview of the project on a whiteboard using words, symbols, etc.

Information processing stage 1: Somebody sits down and turns it into a Gantt.

Information processing stage 2: Somebody sits down and turns the Gantt into something "presentable."

There's a discussion about the previous point – after much of the original information is already lost.

Information processing stage 3: To summarize the discussion, somebody sits down and indicates the important points.

We all looked at what Michael had written.

"You have very legible writing," Fabian noted. Michael smiled, but turned back to the task at hand. "The process is tiresome, inefficient, and, worst of all, one that fails to preserve the information generated in the first step. Right?"

Like an obedient student, Fabian echoed: "Right!" Lisa and Laura, on the other hand, said nothing, just continued to stare at the board.

"So, what are you suggesting?" Lisa finally said. She seemed to be on the verge of tears. I've often thought she's made of steel, that she has a strength I can't begin to fathom. But now she was looking very different, though I didn't really believe she'd break down. If anyone was going to, it would be Laura, but why would she?

"Hold on," Michael smiled, "I'm happy you already want to know what I'm suggesting, but I'm still explaining the drawbacks of the current method. This will only take another couple of minutes, all right? Fabian?"

Fabian shrugged and said: "I'm following."

Laura laughed artificially. Michael gave her a curious gaze. She motioned to say everything was fine and that he could go on. I glanced at my watch. Four in the afternoon. The meeting was taking the entire day. Precisely as I was trying to think of the most urgent tasks I had to accomplish, because there were always emergencies, Chantal walked in again, this time with a note for me. It said, "your wife asked that you call her." Right. We never did touch base.

"A five-minute break?" I suggested.

"Sure, but in a minute."

"All right."

Michael poured himself another coffee, went back to the board, and wrote: **3. We can't see the forest for the trees,** as a preview for the rest of the meeting. Fabian chuckled: "We used to say: 'We don't see the field for the goats.'" Laura laughed again and Michael smiled broadly.

"A Gantt for a year-long project may contain six hundred or more lines. This means at least six hundred dependencies, in other words, tasks that can start only once the previous ones are done. Sometimes there are as many as one thousand. How are these links – all of them – supposed to catch our attention as project managers? They obviously can't. On the other hand, the links describe the anticipated flow of the project so they are, by definition, critical to its success. What links are we supposed to discuss in the first project meeting?"

"The Critical Chain," Lisa shot back.

"Traditionally, the industry tends to relate in particular to the links that form part of the Critical Chain. It may be the right thing to do, but it comes with the embedded assumption that the important links are found in the Critical Chain.

"Look, Lisa, the Critical Chain contains the longest path to the end of the project, but is it also the most important one? I want to try to demonstrate that it is not! That sometimes the Critical Chain is not the part we must focus on."

He turned to Fabian.

"Fabian, let's see how critical the Critical Chain really is. You interact with a vast range of providers, what I call 'the good, the bad, and the ugly.' How would you describe a good provider?"

"One that gives good delivery estimates, isn't too expensive, reports on changes... Is that the sort of thing you mean?"

"Exactly. And a bad provider?"

"The opposite. Makes scheduling mistakes, asks for too much money, and doesn't keep us informed if something goes wrong."

All of us burst out in involuntary bitter laughter. We knew exactly what Fabian meant, or more precisely *who* he meant.

"And the ugly?" Fabian was ahead of Michael. "The one that puts me to sleep."

"I disagree," Lisa interjected. "The bad lacks all capability. Even cheaters are good at something. But those who can't assess the duration of the work are the worst."

"And where is the Critical Chain?"

The Critical Chain? The wheels in my brain were turning rapidly. The Critical Chain represents the longest path. A good provider gives a good assessment of the duration of the work and can therefore be expected to be longest, and is therefore on the Critical Chain. Oops. It would seem that this type of thinking really is liable to make us focus on the wrong things, because chances are that problems are not going to arise with the good provider.

"Nice," I said, suddenly noting that, as all heads turned my way, I was speaking out loud. "We walked right into your trap."

"Think about it the next time you discuss the Critical Chain. The bad and the ugly are off to the side, screaming with laughter, while you drive the good provider crazy just because he's on the Critical Chain."

Lisa sent him a meaningful look; it seemed to hold a smidgen of admiration. Her body language changed, and she seemed more at ease, more open. Her smiled returned; it was minimal but consistent. Michael noticed, though it was as if everything that had happened that day in the conference room was following a script he knew by heart.

"The dependencies system – the Holy Grail of Gantt – creates more than a forest of interdependent tasks, and its entire function is to maintain the calculation of the Critical Chain, which isn't even critical to begin with! And this is how we're forced into a situation in which we're looking for our keys under the streetlight when they're actually hiding somewhere else."

"I'm sorry to interrupt, but I really have to excuse myself to call home," I said.

"Yes, me too," said Michael.

"And me," Laura added. "I was horrid to my husband before. I have to apologize."

Fabian snorted, and Laura gave him a dirty look.

Lisa remained seated.

"Don't you have a call to make?" Michael asked her softly.

She smiled. "Always, but I need to sit and process for a bit."

Michael looked at her appreciatively. The gleam came back to his eye and, looking at me, made a face as if to say, she really is something else.

"OK, ten minutes? Will that do it?" he asked.

"Let's reconvene at five. I have to check my email, or I'll get antsy later," Fabian said.

Michael looked at his laptop. "Excellent. Five it is."

"Hang on," I said to Michael before we scattered, "what are your plans for tonight?"

"The truth is I haven't made any special plans. I figure I'll head back to the hotel and watch some TV."

I looked at my three team members. "What do you say? Shall we take our guest to that new seafood restaurant?"

I could see them thinking.

"I'm sorry, I can't. Family obligation," Laura said.

I gave her a disappointed though understanding look.

"I'd love to," said Fabian. "I'm in favor. At the hospital's expense, right?"

I nodded. "That's your first question?"

"Of course!"

Michael smiled and answered: "It's really nice of you but don't feel you have to. You'll be tired after today."

"No, it's fine. I'm stoked," Lisa said and smiled both at Michael and me.

"Great. It's a date."

"But I'll want to pop back to the hotel to shower and change."

"Of course," I said. "I suggest we end the five o'clock session at six thirty or seven. I'll make reservations for eight thirty. That should give you plenty of time, right?"

"Oh yes. Excellent."

5

Fatigue was evident on all our faces, especially Laura's. It always happens at some point during the day. The afternoon hours are always less efficient and can only be used for certain things. Sometimes it feels that time slows down, and the fall weather, with its earlier sunset, contributes.

Suddenly, everything looked and felt like night, though it was still day. It was as if our emotional state was dictating the time rather the other way around. But despite being tired, everyone still seemed interested. Michael looked as if he'd washed his face and seemed fresher than ever.

"OK, we don't have a lot of time left today, and I hope you don't make me keep talking at dinner. Well, maybe just a little," he joked. "In any case, I am now going to address another problem with the Critical Chain." Michael faced the whiteboard and wrote: "**Fixed thinking.**"

"Whose?" Fabian shouted even before Michael had finished writing.

Michael didn't answer, but he smiled, and for the first time I saw that fatigue was taking its toll on him too. He looked longingly at the coffee pot, wondering about a last cup, then rejecting the idea.

"When you concentrate on the shortest path to completing the project, there is, in the background, an assumption that all the other factors are fixed. Even if you never thought of it this way, the Critical Chain is presented to you as a puzzle with many fixed data items and one Critical Chain you have to identify. Correct?"

Everybody nodded, though Laura was also trying to vanquish a yawn that threatened to topple her out of her chair.

"As curious human beings, it is only natural that you'll want to solve the puzzle. The more complex the situation, the greater the intellectual challenge, and finding and updating the Critical Chain well represent accomplishments in and of themselves. In such a situation, the chances that someone will say that the basic operating assumption of the puzzle are wrong are low."

Michael sighed and went on: "Let's talk a moment about the travelling salesman problem. In that classic puzzle, you are given several destinations the travelling salesman must reach and the time it takes to go from one to another. Your job is to find the shortest route. To enhance the effect, you're also told that there is a path that is shorter than all the others and that entices you to make sure you get the right solution."

Once again, I remembered Eric's Place, but I didn't laugh. I was too tired. Suddenly, taking everyone out to dinner seemed like a terrible idea, but it was too late to back out. Michael had seemed genuinely touched by the invitation and Fabian was keen to go.

"All right," Michael went on, "the assumptions underlying the problem are that the travelling salesman must reach each destination, that it's impossible to shorten travel times, the routes can't be moved, and so on. The problem is that the moment you begin considering the problem, it's highly unlikely that you'll suggest moving the travelling salesman around by helicopter. And you won't question why he has to reach every destination.

"But it's possible to think in other ways. Maybe we need two salesmen? Maybe we should get a subcontractor with ten salesmen to do it? And what does the salesman do at every destination to begin with? Why can't it be done online? Why shouldn't the clients go to him? And so on and so forth.

"The fixed way of thinking is created very naturally the moment the first analysis of the project is generated. Even if we assume that on the day the first project plan is made it is possible to maximize resources and accurately define the project's contents, so that the optimization process of the Critical Chain is perfect, there isn't a snowball's chance in hell that everything will remain static over time.

"For example, we're three months into the project. The Critical Chain is at a certain place. But what happens if we double or even triple the resources of an activity that is currently defined as critical?

"What happens if we call a meeting and announce that we can save a month if the department managers agree to forego this activity? What happens if we pay a provider more money to speed up the work? What happens if we take more risks and shorten the testing process? It may very well be that we manage to shift the Critical Chain elsewhere and significantly shorten the project time."

Fabian looked exhausted, as if all the air had gone out of him. His eyes were swollen and red. Laura, too, looked lifeless. Only Lisa was alert and fresh.

Michael looked at each of us in turn and then glanced at his watch. "Look, I can see you're tired. So am I, even though it's only six twenty. Let's stop here, OK?"

He looked and me, and I nodded.

He leaned back and stretched, and I saw the relief on my team members' faces. Still, despite the exhaustion and long hours, nobody looked bored. Everyone seemed to want to hear more, and soon. They were curious. Curiosity, I recalled, killed the cat, or at least exhausted it.

"I'll be picking you up at the hotel at eight fifteen," I said.

"Yes, see you there," said Fabian, and got up.

Laura got up and, before heading for the door, said: "I'm sorry I can't join you tonight. How long are you in town?"

Michael shrugged. "Tomorrow morning for sure. I intend to pick up exactly where we left off now. I've booked a flight tomorrow night, but we'll see; it's all up in the air." He stopped to consider. "On second thought, maybe we'll continue talking over dinner, at least until we're served. You think we can manage?"

Fabian answered for the rest: "I think so, but Laura will miss out."

"Can't you fill her in?"

Laura's hand was on the doorknob. "I may be able to make it... We'll see. No promises," she said, and left.

Once I was alone in the conference room, I told Chantal I needed another couple of minutes. She looked at me frustrated, but didn't say anything. I photographed every part of the whiteboard, the four points Michael has spoken about when trying to convince us of the drawbacks of current methods:

A Gantt, by its nature as a hierarchic chart, is mostly empty, and doesn't use the presentation space.

Because of its size, it's impossible to present and it's hard to explain its essence.

A Gantt contains many details but doesn't present the general picture: we can't see the forest for the trees.

Focusing on the Critical Chain creates fixed thinking and prevents innovation in project management.

I tried to think of the most effective way of preserving the information, but I was tired. I told myself that, at this stage, it was important simply to retain it. Afterwards, maybe on its own – wishful thinking – it would get arranged in the best way possible.

I made sure nothing was remained outside my smartphone camera's frame, and called Anna. She didn't answer. Just then, Chantal entered and said: "The room smells. Why didn't you air it out when you finished eating?"

Embarrassed, I shrugged and left.

6

Atlantis, the restaurant (which, in my head, I thought of as Bikini Bottom, for the town in *SpongeBob SquarePants*), with its blue and white walls, looked like an ocean. I thought Michael would appreciate the enormous aquarium at the entrance. It wasn't an ordinary restaurant; every night, its small stage hosted a different band playing covers of soft rock hits from the eighties. The enticing aromas of grilled seafood and cocktails, wafting all the way to the sidewalk, were impossible to ignore.

Michael seemed more relaxed than earlier. Oddly, he failed to remark on the aquarium, but again expressed his gratitude for the invitation. Fabian and Lisa looked refreshed. They, too, had had time to shower and change, Fabian into a Star Wars T-shirt.

Once seated, a waiter hurried over to bring us menus. Fabian, who had arrived before us, used the opportunity to order a second beer.

"Michael, the way you were talking this afternoon, I think you could start a whole anti-Gantt movement," Fabian remarked.

"That's funny. Never thought of it that way, but, yes, I seem to have some sort of emotional issue with the damned chart. By the way, do you know how porcupines make love?"

"No," said an amused Fabian.

"Very, very carefully," Michael answered. "Look, today, projects consist of many partners, clients, and providers. Even if you somehow managed to construct your Gantt and you're happy with the result, how do you relate your plan to the plan someone else has constructed? In that case, even the care that porcupines have to take won't help. It's simply impossible."

Fabian started to laugh, while Lisa smiled and looked around the room. She was wearing a sleeveless, knee-length sheath in red, and looked positively glamorous.

"That's a great image," said Fabian, "pretty unforgettable."

"I'm glad to hear it. Look, a joint program, which is complicated to begin with, becomes operationally impossible. Linking two differently constructed Gantt charts is a whopper of a challenge. And for what? When several partners are involved, a joint Gantt – if it can be made in the first place – is not only illegible, but outdated before it's ever presented."

Several forty-something year old guys got up on stage. I didn't catch the band's name. Luckily, the stage was on the other side of the room, and the muted music didn't interfere with our conversation.

"We'll be playing your favorites from the eighties, and we'll start with..." the soloist with the bushy sideburns and leather pants clearly enjoyed keeping the audience in suspense, "well, you'll figure it out for yourselves." The guitarist immediately banging his instrument, but I remained mystified. I didn't seem to be the only one unable to tell what he was playing.

"I love eighties music," Fabian commented.

"Maybe they'll play something by Curiosity Killed the Cat," said Michael, looking at me with mischief. The joke flew past Fabian and Lisa, but I smiled and answered: "I doubt it, but who knows?"

The waiter was back, dotting the table with many appetizers I didn't remember ordering. It seems Fabian had seen to it all, planning a meal that would consist of dishes to share, exactly the kind of meal we loved. You couldn't go wrong.

Suddenly, I felt ravenous, and remembered that all I'd had to eat all day was a breakfast croissant and a single eggroll at lunch. I pounced on the plate of shrimp, as did Michael, though somewhat more delicately. He turned to Lisa and, abruptly, instead of holding forth on Gantt and linked tasks, started to sway to the music, which by now was recognizable as Bruce Springsteen's "Born in the USA."

"That brings back some memories," he said.

"Same here," said Fabian.

"It a really good cover."

"I'm more of a Nirvana kind of guy," I said.

"You're a depressing kind of guy," Fabian added.

Lisa smiled. "I can't remember what kind I am. I only listen to music in the car."

As the music played on, we heard a voice behind us: "I hope you didn't wait with the food." We looked up as one to see Laura in a wine-red, furry-looking top, looking at us with an edgy smile.

"Laura!" we said, as if we hadn't seen her barely two hours ago.

"I'm so glad you made it," Michael said, pulling an empty chair towards the table.

"Yes, well, it wasn't easy," she said, a faint blush covering her face. "What did I miss?"

We looked at one another, and realizing we had no idea what to say, we burst out laughing.

"Hmm. I see," she said, while the diners clapped for the band.

Then, from the stage, came the unmistakable opening chords of "Smells Like Teen Spirit" from Nirvana's *Nevermind* album. Michael looked at me with satisfaction. "Just for you, eh?" he said with a wink. A shiver of joy went through my back, even if the performance was too upbeat for my taste.

* * *

"So, Michael?" The band had finished its set and the restaurant, now filled to capacity, was playing soft instrumental music. Fabian seemed a little drunk. Two beers and most of a bottle of wine can do that to you. "What happened to make you wake up one day and decide all this?"

I, too, wanted to know, but I'd been waiting for the right time to ask.

Lisa chimed in: "Yeah, I'm dying to know the answer."

Michael put his cutlery down. He seemed full. He sipped at some wine, gauged our level of interest, and said: "All right. It's a long story but a good one."

"We have time, right?" Fabian asked the table. "Having a personal life is a rare privilege," he added. Lisa sniggered. Laura seemed serious, as if he'd touched a raw nerve, which he probably had.

Michael ignored the aside, wiped his mouth, leaned back in the chair, and began. "About ten years ago, I was stuck in a project that was going nowhere. At the height of the crisis, my daughter dragged me to some parent-child to-do at her school. I showed up with a killer headache, the kind only project managers get. This event at school was the last thing I needed, but, you know, sometimes you just have to."

"Parent-child? Sounds disastrous," Fabian said. "I once took my niece to one of these indoor play spaces. I needed the whole weekend to recover. The sensory overload…"

Michael chuckled. "I hear you. Anyway, this was different. Parents were invited to give short presentations to the kids on any topic of their choice. But when I got there, I saw all six hundred kids accompanied by one or both parents crammed onto the playground, the only space big enough to hold everyone.

"Anyhow, a single teacher was in charge of the whole thing, and she didn't seem stressed at all. In fact, she seemed to be enjoying the energy. People were milling about in twosomes and groups, assembling and reassembling like amoeba. At some point, she tried to call for everyone's attention so that the official program could start, but nobody was paying her much attention."

Michael stifled a yawn, and took another sip of wine. Fascinated, we waited for him to resume the story.

"In any case, when she saw it wasn't working, she tried at different tactic, and simply put the day's program on the central screen. It worked. The people who were scattered all over the playground slowly quietened down and all eyes focused on the screen. Here, in my briefcase, I have an example of that chart from one of my lectures."

Michael bent down to retrieve a piece of paper, which he placed at the center of the table. The table looked like this:

Location	9:00	9:30	10:00	10:30	11:00	11:30	12:00	12:30
Gym	Jewelry making	Carpentry	Architecture		Bridges	Cranes	Building a Seesaw	
Classroom		Abseiling		Jogging	Pigs are not what you think			Horseback riding
Library	Baking		Reality TV	Dolls	Being an Olympic Athlete		The Lowest Place on Earth	
Lab	Yoga	Brain Physiotherapy		Drafting		Materials	Exploders	Treading Water
Art room	Climbing		Going to Lapland		Nordic Walking		My Bike and I	Thailand
Playground	Raising Fish	Fruit Trees	Anemones		Butterflies			Raising a Dog

"The teacher running the activity was pleased that everyone's attention was now on the schedule. 'We want to start,' she said, 'and we have a busy four hours ahead of us, so I need your attention for the day to run smoothly.'

"She continued to explain. 'Every child has the chart you see here on the screen, and I invite you to use it throughout the program. You can see the topics being presented, decide which lecture to attend, and accordingly build your own schedule. As you can see, off to the side is a list of school locations. The lectures will be given one after another in these locations. After a twenty-minute lecture, there will be a ten-minute break to allow you to move to the next lecture.'

"'All in all, that comes to half an hour. If the lecture is forty minutes long, you'll have twenty minutes to get to the next lecture and maybe pick up a cup of coffee on the way.'

"'Please note that we didn't ask you to pre-register. This means that some lecture spaces may fill up and you'll have to choose a different one during the ten-minute break. We have six locations with six to eight lectures in each. Every half hour, the school's PA system will sound a bell, your sign that we're moving on to the next set of lectures.'

"I would ask parents to stay with their children, and lecturers to end their presentations on time. The first lecture begins in fifteen minutes. This is the time to look at the chart and decide on your personal schedule for our parent-child day.' I remember pretty much every word she said, because I repeated her speech to myself on the spot and later wrote it down."

Fabian gave him a questioning look, not really getting where Michael was going and how, from a day that sounded like an utter nightmare, he'd managed to extract and refine an entire theory of project management, while disproving past axioms and laying down a better path for the future of our project and the field as a whole.

Laura, who'd finished eating, was surprised to see the waiter putting down more plates, and said: "What's this?" Fabian said: "I should have warned you, but you looked so happy inhaling the appetizers I didn't want to interfere. These are the main dishes." She was caught off guard, but still looked lighter and more open, as if sitting with us outside the confines of the hospital had filled her with a different energy. And maybe the rest of us too.

"So," Michael went on, "when she completed her briefing, hundreds of parents made sure their kids were next to them and they all looked at the print version of the chart. My daughter was ready with ours, and had even marked her top choices, but, to please me, she let me pick one lecture and promised to take my preferences into account if I behaved nicely.

"To be honest, I doubted the ability of a relatively large crowd to scatter and follow the teacher's directions. As a project manager, I knew that moving a large group that has only had a five-minute explanation is no small feat.

"The chart my daughter was holding was identical to the one on the central screen. With her help and that of a friend who joined us, we quickly decided our schedule. And, so, I found myself starting the day with a lecture on jewellery making instead of mountain climbing. We marked our transitions with a pen. When we were done, the program looked like this."

At this point, Michael took a pen out of his pocket and marked up the paper still placed at the center of the table.

"When we were done, I looked up to see hundreds of parents going off in different directions, exactly as they'd been told. The lecture started at nine o'clock sharp, and dealt with silversmithing. At some point, we heard the bell, so we looked back at the chart to see where we were heading next. I looked around and saw that everything was working almost perfectly. At that moment, I decided I had to find the teacher and ask her how she made this happen."

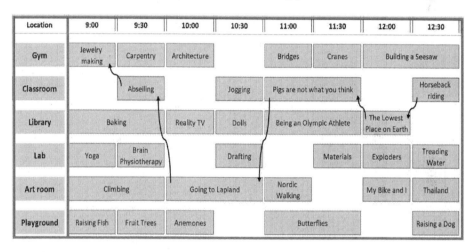

Location	9:00	9:30	10:00	10:30	11:00	11:30	12:00	12:30
Gym	Jewelry making	Carpentry	Architecture		Bridges	Cranes	Building a Seesaw	
Classroom		Abseiling		Jogging	Pigs are not what you think			Horseback riding
Library	Baking		Reality TV	Dolls	Being an Olympic Athlete		The Lowest Place on Earth	
Lab	Yoga	Brain Physiotherapy		Drafting		Materials	Exploders	Treading Water
Art room	Climbing		Going to Lapland		Nordic Walking		My Bike and I	Thailand
Playground	Raising Fish	Fruit Trees	Anemones		Butterflies			Raising a Dog

Michael stopped talking to take a few bites of the gnocchi with crab meat. The rest of us used the pause to dig into the food again – a banquet that seemed to go on and on. Knowing Fabian, I was sure he'd gone the whole hog, and pre-ordered desserts and after-dinner drinks.

"This is superb. Everything is great," Michael mumbled.

Lisa, still chewing, nodded. "You're right. It's my first time here. I think I'm walking home with three new pounds."

Laura snorted in derision. "Ha! You can use another three pound. I, on the other hand..."

Fabian shushed the two women. "Enough. I don't want to hear about diets, nutrition, or calories. It'll do you good to remember to enjoy food every once in a while."

The women said nothing, and Michael smiled in their direction.

"Hear, hear! That's what I tell my wife all the time."

"I can say it all I want, but it won't eliminate the calories," Laura sighed.

Michael leaned forward: "Tonight we're going to eat without feeling bad about it, OK? We go back on the diet tomorrow." Everyone nodded enthusiastically, and he continued: "Anyhow, at the end of the school day, I introduced myself to the teacher and asked her how, with so many people around, she'd made it run so smoothly. 'How did you do it?' I asked."

"'How did I do it?' she repeated, and looked at me all innocent. I explained what I meant, and she said: 'I'm not running anything except for the transitions. What happens in the mini-lectures doesn't concern me. All I care about is that they start and end on time and that people know where they're going. The most problematic transitions are those where people want to go from one activity area to another.'

"I started asking her what happens if there is a problem she can't see because it's too far away. She gave a little laugh and said: 'That's easy. I have someone in every location who makes sure the talks start on time and end on time, which means that I don't have to worry. And, if there is something truly wrong, they'll call me and let me know. Otherwise, I don't interfere.'

"And then she added that the activity cycles simplified the program. The minute all talks are the same length, it's much easier to do crowd control. That's why she decided on twenty-minute breaks after the long lectures. It was so that everyone would be synchronized."

The waiter was now clearing the empty plates and the band was back on stage. With no introduction, they launched into Supertramp's "Breakfast in America," and many of the delighted diners started to clap and some got up to dance. I thought Michael wanted to join the dancers but felt obligated to finish his story first.

"In any case, I stood there and felt as if I'd been struck by lightning. Well, not really, but I sensed there was something in this system that had to be applicable to my world as well. I mean, right in front of me, I'd seen hundreds of people being managed after a five-minute explanation. It still seemed miraculous."

He stopped when the waiter, back now, started to put down red, white, and blue desserts.

"Oh my God! Fabian – what are you doing to me?" Laura moaned. Fabian looked pleased. Creamy mousses, molten chocolate, berry toppings, and other dishes I didn't recognize dotted the table.

"You know Fabian. He heard there was a free meal to be had and went to town!" I shrugged.

"Ah, but it's not for me; it's all in honor of our guest," Fabian laughed.

"Sure, sure," I laughed back.

"But, seriously, what am I supposed to do now?" Laura was not amused.

"Ignore," said Lisa, "that's what I do."

"Not me," said Fabian, and reached for a cheesecake with blueberries.

"I must ignore too, if you don't mind. I'll make do with fruit. These are just too much. Not so good for my health," Michael said.

Fabian shook his head. "I respect your health, but you're missing out."

"I know what I'm missing, but I also know what I'm gaining."

By now, all the plates were scraped clean. At some point, Lisa too had offered her "help" in finishing what the rest of us couldn't. We were leaning back in our comfortably padded chairs, staring at Michael like fattened fish. The band was playing its last song, something I didn't recognize, but at that stage I doubt I'd have recognized anything.

"You want me to go on?" Michael asked, seeing our looks.

"Yes, please," said Lisa. "Our brains are awash in sugar. We're as awake and focused as can be."

Michael smiled, sipped his espresso, and said: "So, what elements made the control of the parent-child day so simple? Division into activity areas, somebody in charge of each one, focus on transitions, and the clock. Right?"

We nodded as one.

"And the diagram we all saw made the program clear at a glance. It was constructed on the basis of activity areas, and the teacher encouraged us to plan our transitions from one to the next, basically in exactly the same way she planned to oversee the day.

"So, I asked myself: In my project, were there 'activity areas' and did I have people in charge of them? Mostly yes. Was that visible in the plan? Mostly no. Our plan consisted of a long line of tasks and was not designed to reflect activity areas. Another question: Did I know how to handle transitions between the different areas?

"In any case, that's the story. It all started with that parent-child day, and later continued in many different locations. And now – here we are. Tomorrow, I'll show you the method that came out of that story."

"It's a great story," said Fabian, his eyes thoroughly bloodshot.

"And, now, with your permission," Michael said, "I prefer not to talk about projects any longer."

"Yeah, me too," said Fabian. "If you want me in the office in the morning, I'm going to have to get to bed soon."

"Me too," said Lisa, stretching.

I signaled the waiter for the bill and, to Fabian's great amusement, paid with the company's credit card. Sated and a wee bit tipsy, we headed for the door. The minute we stepped outside, a cloudburst beat down on us. We started running with no destination in mind.

A minute or so later, we found shelter under the overhang of a grey building to wait for the rain to taper off. Fabian dug a hand into his inside coat pocket and lit up a cigar. Gleefully, he blew the smoke at us, despite Laura's cries of protest. It was then that Lisa noticed that Michael wasn't there.

"How odd! Where did he go?"

I shrugged. I was clueless.

"It makes no sense," said Fabian, "I saw him running with us. Wasn't he?"

I didn't know.

"I think he's been kidnapped by aliens," Fabian concluded, making Laura laugh out loud. "They kidnapped him and took him back to their planet so that he could advise them on their next intergalactic project. That's it. From now on in, we're on our own."

"He didn't even say goodbye," Lisa said.

Fabian lifted his face to the drizzling sky: "Come back to visit planet Earth sometime soon," he yelled.

Clearly, Michael had headed to the hotel, but it was, without a doubt, an odd way to end the evening. But I was also sure he remembered that we were meeting in the office in the morning to continue from precisely where we'd left off.

The rain had slowed considerably. I announced: "That's our cue. See you all tomorrow."

Chapter Five

The Project Map

1

"Good morning!" Michael exclaimed and entered the conference room, where we waited with some confusion. "I'm so sorry about yesterday," he continued, breathing heavily. He stripped off his jacket and hung it on the back of his chair.

"We weren't sure we'd be seeing you again," said Lisa. "Fabian was saying you'd been kidnapped by aliens."

Michael laughed and poured himself some coffee. "Well, if they did, they wiped any memory I might have had of the event."

"Fabian thought they wanted you to consult them on some intergalactic project," Laura added.

Fabian seemed embarrassed, and shrugged in apology. He was badly hung over. Two cups of coffee had failed to wake him up. Michael took it all in stride, and clapped him on the shoulder to show no hard feelings.

"Shall we?" he asked, sitting down. He was bursting with energy.

"Of course," I said. "We can't wait to hear what you did after that parent-child day."

"What I did? I slept really badly. I was in my office before dawn. I went straight to the Gantt we'd been using in that project I told you about. As I already knew, the chart wasn't arranged by activity area. It only showed chains of tasks hierarchically distributed, based on the structural rationale that guided us back then.

"I imagine it might have been possible to arrange the tasks in several different configurations, but we opted for a particular one in some sort of intuitive way. In certain places, the hierarchic structure of the tasks was fairly detailed, involving five or six levels.

"In other places, we'd made do with headings and a single line underneath, in other words a two-level hierarchy. I wanted to turn all of that into something resembling the parent-child day chart, but I didn't have a tool to do so. Instead, I used an electronic form and tried to copy the tasks from the Gantt into lines like that teacher had done."

Just then, Fabian groaned loudly. "I'm sorry. It takes me a while to wake up, but I'm getting there," he promised. Michael used the interruption to thank him again for last night's dinner, and then picked up his narrative. "So, what seemed like a simple task turned out to be quite complicated. I had a hard time organizing the tasks in a sequence similar to the sequence of the lectures of the day before.

"It was a challenge to insert the more complex tasks chains we'd created in certain parts of the Gantt into the two-dimensional structure of a simple block chart. I soon realized that this direction wasn't taking me in a fruitful direction. I knew I needed a different approach.

"I decided to put the list of tasks aside for the moment and instead tried to think about the project's main areas of activity, parallel to the activity areas where the lectures were given the previous day. The simplest division I could think of was too basic, so I subdivided each activity area and tried to express the decentralization that characterized the project. By the end, I had a chart that was designed to document activity in the first two months. It looked like this."

Now Michael turned his laptop around to show us a chart on his computer. I assumed it was saved as his go-to example to demonstrate his new method. It resembled the one he'd shown us last night at dinner, but this time, instead of lectures, it contained project activities. Michael continued: "Some of the chart was very easy to fill out. Block by block, a simple sequence of actions planned until we had an application we could present to the client. But a different part of the project was happening on the client's side. What was going on there? I had no idea."

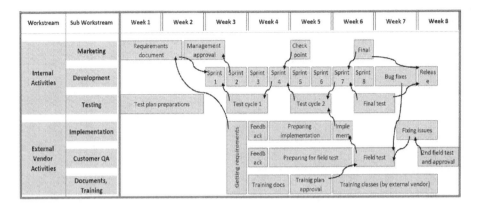

Workstream	Sub Workstream	Week 1	Week 2	Week 3	Week 4	Week 5	Week 6	Week 7	Week 8
Internal Activities	Marketing	Requirements document	Management approval			Check point		Final	
	Development			Sprint 1 / Sprint 2	Sprint 3 / Sprint 4	Sprint 5 / Sprint 6	Sprint 7 / Sprint 8	Bug fixes	Release
	Testing	Test plan preparations		Test cycle 1		Test cycle 2		Final test	
External Vendor Activities	Implementation		Getting requirements	Feedback	Preparing implementation	Implement		Fixing issues	
	Customer QA			Feedback	Preparing for field test		Field test	2nd field test and approval	
	Documents, Training			Training docs	Training plan approval	Training classes (by external vendor)			

Michael didn't answer right away.

"Something secret? Having to do with aliens?"

Michael laughed. "No, not at all. The project was a failed attempt on our part to develop a coupon application for one of the largest malls in California."

We laughed, but Michael was serious. "You can't imagine what a project that was. Today, there are thousands like it, but back then we had no idea where to start. And neither did the mall's subcontractor..."

"Hey, sometimes this hospital also looks like a mall," Fabian said.

"For sure," Laura chimed in. "We're the shops and the patients are the shoppers. Or is it the other way around?"

Michael smiled. "In any case, what you see here is the full chart. But to get there, I cut out all the empty lines and sent them to the project managers on the client's side, to help me understand the activity on that end.

"Unintentionally, the process of constructing this chart forced me to define a person in charge of each activity area, just like that teacher did at the parent-child program. Moreover, the way in which I sent the empty chart to the people in charge of those areas, informed them that I had appointed them to be in charge, and that in turn motivated them to define plans within their areas. What happened, in fact, was that I generated involvement on the part of the team members in constructing the project plan and raised their level of commitment to it.

"Reactions started coming in right away, and the activity area managers submitted plans in the new format. I collected all the responses and created the chart I showed you, which presents all planned activity, though without links between the actions. And, as you can see, it looks a lot like the chart from my daughter's school, before we decided which lectures to attend.

"It's true that a decision on what lecture to attend next, is nothing like creating a conditional connection between activities. But the manner of representation is identical and very clear in both cases. I again sent the chart to the managers, this time in its full format, and asked them to mark the connections as they saw them. Although the managers were located in different places and didn't even work in the same organization, none of them had any difficulty understanding the picture that emerged from the chart."

Michael now went back to the more detailed chart. "At that point, I had a chart representing the project, and this was before holding a single meeting based on the new method. Or perhaps we *had* met, in a new way – a virtual and involving way," he said.

"I noticed that nobody bothered marking links within their own activity area. It was clear from the chart that whatever appeared within a sequence was exactly that: a piece of a connected sequence. This, to a great extent, reduced the number of links on the diagram, and consequently simplified its visual complexity.

"So, what did I do? I went back to the list of principles the teacher had formulated: division into activity areas – check; somebody in charge of each one – check; a chart based on the activity areas – check. What was left was to focus the discussion on transitions between activity areas, marked by arrows, and create the timing the teacher dictated by making sure all the lectures were the same length.

"Concentrating on the transitions really appealed to me. In my mind's eye, I could see that smug teacher in the middle of the playground, commanding hundreds of people only minutes after meeting her. Could this method provide project managers a space for controlling, leading, and focusing on building a coordinated plan for the really important things?

"I thought I had great potential for creating a coordination program, with an internal hierarchy stressing important links rather than trivial ones. As it was, the people in charge of activity areas had never been too keen on talking about internal problems connected to coordination within their own groups.

"My plan was to have the first meeting focus on the links between the activity areas, and I hoped that such a discussion would lead to a different and clearer discourse about the things that would make the project progress as planned.

"I had a hard time determining the time frames. The activities in the project were not twenty minutes long, and I couldn't plan breaks in order to get everyone back on the same schedule. To create some kind of rhythmic element, I divided the horizontal axis of activity into segments and weeks and gave them names.

"I hoped this would create a shared language for the different groups engaged in activities taking place in different locations and times. Which is exactly what the teacher tried to do at the parent-child day: create a shared timing language for many activity areas."

"I'm wondering how all of this connects to coupons," Fabian interjected.

"Me too," Laura added.

"I get it," Lisa said. "The topic of the project doesn't matter. I mean, it matters, but it must always be seen as a project."

"As the project essence," I added. Michael looked pleased.

"In any case," Michael went on, "I won't talk too much about that first meeting. In hindsight, I realized that I didn't have enough time to prepare for it, and the few days I had were not enough for me to develop the new method to my satisfaction.

"But, in a way I didn't fully grasp at that time, the chart made the team come to the meeting better prepared, and the entire discussion was conducted from the perspective of the activity areas and coordination between them. The topics we covered were all the most important ones, touching on the challenges we'd always failed to meet – passing the baton from one activity area to another.

"Although the new method wasn't fully developed, it was clear to me that, at the next meeting, I wouldn't be going back to the Gantt. A different shared language had already been created, one that was much more effective in terms of the project.

"During the year after the parent-child day, I tweaked this method in many ways. With time, I started to understand what makes it so clear. Unlike the tools we had used till then, the parent-child day chart, which I had in the meantime renamed 'The Project Map,' shows projects the same way that people think about projects and doesn't force them to engineer a project into a non-intuitive structure.

"I don't have that much more to say, so stick with me just a little longer. There were two elements that made The Project Map clearer.

"**The first was the fact that, when people think about projects, they think in terms of activity areas**. When they are asked to describe a project, they don't begin by talking about a series of tasks. They start by describing the parties involved.

"In many cases, they'll also mention, in the very same breath, the people in charge of those parties, exactly the way The Project Map sets out. Without any division into activity areas, it is tough for a project manager – and for any observer – to capture the project's general outline. This void turns into a real lack of understanding.

"**The second element is the fact that people tend to think of activities in sequence**. That's how they'll describe the process of changing a tyre, baking a cake, or their morning routine. Even if they opt to present parallel activities, they'll do it by presenting a parallel sequence, and describe the links between that sequence and another. This way of thinking also lines up with The Project Map's presentation, and allows for an intuitive grasp of the sequence of activities at different levels of detail.

"But these insights were only the beginning. Later on, I understood the operational value of working in activity areas. The discussion about transitions between them again and again touched on the problems at the core of the project.

"Looking back, this isn't particularly surprising, because we all know that projects hit snags, precisely when the baton is being passed between groups or where there is a dependency between activity in one group and activity in another.

"After a year or so, the project was over. And I knew that the next thing I had to do was document this method and construct a generic project map. Which is more or less what I ended up doing and was still doing when I happened to run into Gary at a bar in San Francisco. The truth is that I thought I'd told you everything I had to say yesterday, but I guess I was wrong. I had planned to talk about something else today, but it's all good."

"Impressive," Laura commented.

"Thank you," Michael answered, blushing slightly.

"So, what now?" Fabian wanted to know.

"Now – to work," I said.

"Sure, boss!"

"Whoa, wait a minute," Michael interjected, "not so fast. I have to tell you something important. I am convinced beyond a shadow of a doubt that you will succeed."

"Thank you," said Laura, "that's really good to know."

I suddenly realized that this was the first time Michael had expressed his complete faith in us, and I also understood how important it was to me to hear that short, simple, and oh-so reassuring sentence. It filled me with confidence.

"And I also think your project is interesting, not to mention groundbreaking," he added. "And now, my friends, I have to leave for a couple of hours. We'll resume this afternoon."

"Another parent-child day? Off to the mall? Thank God my niece hasn't tried to drag me there yet," Fabian quipped.

Michael only smiled enigmatically.

2

In the afternoon, we again gathered in the conference room. It turned out that the VP of finance claimed to have booked the room. I sent Lisa to duke it out with him. She left the room like a hungry lioness and came back a few minutes later with a satisfied smirk.

"It's a good thing you didn't send me," said Fabian, "I can't stand the guy."

"You can't stand a whole lot of people," Laura reminded him.

He nodded at her as if to say "touché" and rocked back and forth in his chair.

"Try not to fall on your ass," Laura added caustically.

Michael bustled in. "So how are we all? Did you have a chance to get some work done? I trust all is well."

The atmosphere was great and we were ready to get back to work, but suddenly the VP of finance appeared in the doorway. He was a mousy-looking fellow in his fifties. Everyone said he was a financial genius and it was all thanks to him that the hospital was in the black and functioning. But he had a way of making everyone around him feel uncomfortable, and it wasn't helped by his intrusive glare. It was as if he'd come to see if we really needed the room, but Michael's presence made it impossible for him to argue.

Once he was gone, Michael began by saying he would try to present the tool he had developed in recent years to prepare the project map. "The Project Map is an alternative to the Gantt chart you know and hate. It offers a different and intuitive approach, while utilizing the whole diagram space to plan activities across a timeline and to follow up on execution. I wouldn't declare the Gantt dead, but, for many projects, The Project Map will replace it. Its simplicity makes it possible to grasp the state of the project at a glance, and preparing the map requires a minimal investment of time."

Fabian gave Lisa a pitying look, as if offering his condolences on the loss of the Gantt. She saw his look and smiled back completely unruffled. Fabian was still rocking in his chair like the hyperactive kid he'd once been.

"Let's do a small exercise, shall we?" Michael suggested.

"Let's!" I answered for everyone.

Michael strode to the whiteboard. Across the top, as befitting a project that was supposed to be completed within a few months, Michael wrote May, June, July, and August, and each of these he divided into weeks. He left the rest of the board blank.

Now he turned to my team members and said: "Each of you – please take a marker and come to the board. Try to document the activity you anticipate by the completion date in the most intuitive manner you can. The only limit is time; you have ten minutes to set the project map down on this whiteboard. Go!"

It took Fabian, Lisa, and Laura half a minute to recover from the shock, but then they rushed at the board to jot down whatever had been on their minds for the past few months. Without an orderly planning process, it seemed that the project's problems were fighting for space in different coloured markers.

Michael and I went to the other end of the room to try and not to make them feel we were breathing down their necks. It wasn't the first time I'd seen projects thrown at a whiteboard at the initial planning stage, but never this far into an existing project. I was curious to see what Michael would do with the result.

At the end of the allotted time, Michael and I strode over to take a look. The team members looked very pleased, as if putting the information on the board had eased a burden that had been weighing them down. I stared at the result and was lost. I had no idea what to do with the illegible mess I was seeing. It looked more like a piece of abstract art than like anything practical. Now what, I wondered.

I took a deep breath and looked more carefully. I saw they had created some horizontal lines where Michael had left the board empty. Each was given a different label, such as "installations," "software," and "construction." In each activity area, several different activities had been sketched intuitively.

Fabian's green marker dominated the "installations" line, while Lisa's blue one was prominent in "software." Laura's red marker had left arrows connecting the tasks; she had tried, unsuccessfully, not to smudge the squares, circles, and other symbols covering almost every square inch of the board. The time limit had also resulted in several questions marks being scribbled where an activity's link or placement seemed to be in doubt.

Inwardly, I groaned. Question marks were an accurate description of my state of mind.

We sat down in a hastily-arranged semi-circle in front of the board, staring at the colourful doodles. The team members were undoubtedly asking themselves if this mess was the best they could do.

After about a minute of silence, Michael asked: "What's the matter with you? In shock?"

Fabian chuckled. "Not at all," and leaned back in his chair, ignoring Laura's warning glance.

"Look," Michael continued, "what if I gave you a tool that made it possible for you to create an intuitive plan, just like you did on the whiteboard? After you're done, it'll be possible to discuss the project map that emerges and finally share the original image with everyone, even people looking at the plan on a six-inch smartphone screen."

"We're in favor of that," said Lisa.

Michael went on: "Not only that, but the tool I'm going to give you doesn't leave the decision on what's important and what isn't, or what's discussed and what isn't, to any one person. It turns important links into an action plan and critical problems into a risk-prevention program. Those two pieces are presented in the background and require the project team to provide solutions. This information, too, is sent to everyone and can be freely shared."

"Well, if you're telling me I can be tall, ripped, handsome, and rich all at once, who am I to say no?" Fabian laughed derisively. "Seriously, you can't tell me you have something that really works like that!"

"See for yourself," Michael retorted and hooked his laptop to the room's projector. As usual, the projector refused to work. Lisa groaned. "It's got to be the worst projector in the northern hemisphere."

"I'll get someone to help," said Laura, and left the room to find a technician.

"Can't we buy a new projector with our budget?" Lisa asked me.

I shrugged. "Maybe. Somebody's got to look into it. But I think projectors are inherently a bad idea. They don't connect to just any old computer. Sociopaths."

"My dream is to build a company that makes no-fail projectors," she said, rolling her eyes dramatically.

"I think you need a more realistic dream," Michael responded. Lisa snorted.

Laura was now back with a grim-faced technician in an ill-fitting jumpsuit. He pushed one button, and – lo and behold! – the project lit up as if by magic. We looked at him, embarrassed, but he must have been used to it because he just turned on his heel, probably cursing our incompetence under his breath.

Michael opened the application so that we would all be able to follow the process. The tool Michael was using had a graphic interface with which he started to sketch a general example of a project map on the screen, based on what the team had put up on the whiteboard.

With great speed, he dragged graphic shapes into place, matched labels to them, and arranged them in accordance with the activity areas the team had defined on the board. Like the board, Michael opted for a weekly division along the timeline, and every dividing line was dated with the last day of the week.

We were all staring at the screen, trying to understand what we were seeing. It looked simple, yes, though I still didn't grasp the full picture. I was impatient to hear his explanation.

"Before I say anything about what I did here, you must have noticed that, in a very short period of time, I can copy everything you did into this tool. In fact, we could have used this tool to do what you did on the board. But do note some of its other features."

Michael cleared his throat, sipped some water, and then continued. "When you were asked to plan intuitively, you opted to present tasks from the perspective of activity areas. As we said yesterday and this morning, this is not coincidental. It's the way most people would choose to present project information, and it's the way most people would want to see the project plans at a later stage.

"The project areas you defined intuitively turn the project map into horizontal lines representing these areas. The project map not only allows you to present data this way, but it actually forces this kind of presentation. You'll see why in a second.

"Had Lisa tried to turn all this into a Gantt, she would, at best, have used tasks to follow that structure or ignored this division altogether. As Lisa has noted, Gantt's preference is for thinking about hierarchies of activities rather than sequences. **Systems prefer hierarchies, but people prefer sequences**. They're simply clearer."

The VP of finance was back, staring at us through a crack in the door. Fabian sniggered. "What's up with him? Is he still waiting for the room?"

Lisa shrugged. "I told him we were here for the long haul and suggested he use the other conference room, but he won't let go."

"I think he has the hots for you."

Lisa guffawed. "I have to say that I don't always get how your mind works, Fabian. Or perhaps I do, but don't know what I think of it."

Laura smiled. "I get it, and know exactly what I think of it."

Michael laughed. "Hey, you, stick with me. Let's try to be efficient before the financial genius breaks in with CPA commandoes, armed with Parkers to throw us out of here, OK?"

Like obedient soldiers, we fell silent and turned our attention back to the tool.

"As you saw," he continued, "even though you were instructed to do so, you decided to make a limited number of connections between

121

tasks. The connections you did make are clearly linking different activity areas, right? Yes?

"It's not very surprising. When I asked you to describe your jobs, you all displayed confidence in your ability to control coordination and oversight of your own part, and you attributed anything problematic to the link with other parties. A direct byproduct of this logic is that we have to pay particular attention to connections between activity areas, assuming these connections are more critical to the project's success than internal links within a specific activity area and demand the attention of the project manager and the team.

"The project map easily locates these connections because it already sorts activities by area. The project map has at least three levels of connections. Following?"

Everyone nodded. The VP of finance was gone as if the ground had swallowed him, though I almost suspected he'd be back with an angry battalion of accountants.

"The first level consists of the connections within the activity sequences, important in analyzing the project but not requiring particular attention on the part of the project manager or the team. The second level involves the connections between the different sequences within the same activity area. This level is important for follow up, and may require a coordination plan."

He took a deep breath before going on. "The third level consists of links between activity areas, and these are the most problematic. Projects rise or fall based on project managers' ability to coordinate them. The Project Map forces the team to handle these links by means of a detailed coordination plan.

"As I said, the Gantt doesn't make a single move towards a coordination plan. Each of the hundreds of links in Lisa's plan is of equal value."

Lisa let out a loud sigh that sounded like "Wow."

"Are you OK?" I asked.

"Yeah, it's just that it's the first time in the last two days that I'm saying, 'Wow.' It's the type of information that simply doesn't exist in any other system. Do you have any idea how many hours I spent on the Gantt – all of us – without getting anything like this in return?"

Fabian's eyes lit up. He stopped wiggling in the chair and said: "With that time, we could have built an entire hospital, not just a maternity ward."

"Hey, no need to overstate things," I said, "and, besides, everything in its time, like they say."

"Who's they?" Fabian demanded.

"I don't know, but somebody has undoubtedly said it."

Fabian was back to his rocking, and now leaned the chair all the way back against the wall.

"All right," Michael resumed, more determined and focused than ever, "you drew several question marks on the board. I assume you were alluding to anticipated problems, or unclear areas, or risks. The Project Map does not calculate risk, but only relates to what I call the perceived risk. The Project Map translates the risk you marked into a risk prevention plan you have to construct, so that you don't lose the information you put down."

"Another important thing I want you to notice," he said, giving me a hard stare as if addressing me in particular, "is the use of the presentation space. You made a point of using every available space on the board and filling it with as much information as possible. The ability to preserve information requires excellent utilization of the planning area and preservation of the structure you created on the board: the activity areas on the vertical axis, the timeline on the horizontal axis, and the placement of tasks within the chart.

"But that's not all. In a second you'll see that The Project Map functions like a Google map, and has several layers at different levels of resolution that can be observed while zooming in and zooming out, and this is a huge advantage for small screen. The top layer is the general picture; the bottom layer is the breakdown of activities; and the middle layer is the one we just created. Is this clear? Any questions? Don't be shy. Ask questions even if you think they're dumb."

"Hear that, Fabian? Feel free," said Laura.

But just then Fabian, instead of answering, was busy falling out of his chair. He ended up sprawled over the floor. Laura broke into frantic laughter, while Lisa leapt up to see if Fabian was all right. I, too, stood up. "Are you OK?"

Fabian was on his back, like a stranded junebug, though smiling. When I helped him to his feet, he said: "No dumb questions today."

Laura failed to tame her fit of giggles. "Excuse me," she apologized, and slipped out of the room.

"Maybe a break is a good idea," a confused-looking Michael ventured.

"I'm fine," answered Fabian, back in his righted chair.

"Maybe so, but the others..." Michael answered.

"Five minutes," I declared. The VP of finance might see us wandering around and decide to seize control of the premises."

"Yeah, fortify himself with calculators," Lisa chuckled. "Let's not abandon the room altogether. I need the bathroom, but when I get back, you can go out."

3

"Do you think you're beginning to understand how to adopt The Project Map for your project?" Michael asked. It was ten minutes later, and we had all reassembled in the conference room. Laura had clearly washed her face and was trying to look especially serious, though stealing occasional glances at Fabian, who, for his part, was rigid in his chair, like a frightened first-grader.

"Let's try to understand how to take what I created and fill it with your project's contents. Let's start from the milestones on the timeline.

"We've added two milestones, the more important one, of course, being the submission deadline. Now we'll try to better define the project's main activity areas and their leaders. So far, we have whatever construction is left, under Fabian's responsibility; communications – also Fabian." Fabian nodded, and for the first time in a long while he looked absolutely serious. He was attentive to every sound coming from Michael. I was astounded by his transformation.

"In addition, we've defined medical equipment and its installation in the system – Laura's baby; system development – that's Lisa; certification and regulation by labs and professional bodies – back to Laura; and alpha testing – that's all of you.

"So far so good, right? Can I continue?"

And, so we did, and very quickly went on to filling every activity area with the expected activity contents. We started with the major tasks and described them by means of long-term activities of a month or even more. Despite the relatively general description, the map contained about fifty activities that, in a Gantt, would have covered several pages. Here, they coexisted on the same page without being particularly crowded. And, most importantly, the project's structure was very clear. Michael noted that it would have been possible to add greater detail on this layer and the general picture would still have been clear. Alternately, we could use another layer of the map to spell out shorter tasks of weeks or days.

In addition, we worked on creating the links between the activities, which made the plan completely dynamic; the visual presentation allowed unlinked "floating" activities to be seen and prevented them from disappearing and being forgotten.

We created a web of links between integration activities, under Fabian's leadership, and the gradual introduction of medical equipment, under Laura's purview. We linked the end of each integration plan to a cycle of subsequent testing. At the end of every testing plan, we assumed there would be negative feedback and that it would be necessary to fix the flaws discovered. We therefore linked the end of testing to the next, somewhat shorter, integration process.

We similarly added links in the certification area. We marked the earliest point it would be possible to get to a standards lab or professional certifications body, and at the end of the certification stage (similar to the end of the testing), we assumed we would have to deal with feedback. This area remained critical, because medical equipment must undergo testing and calibration before being used. Failure of the certification process meant we would not be able to proceed to field testing.

Another thing we did was document activities we considered risks, which we entered directly into the risk prevention program of the project map where they were marked with a red line. The question marks the team had drawn on the whiteboard became red squares scattered across the project map[1].

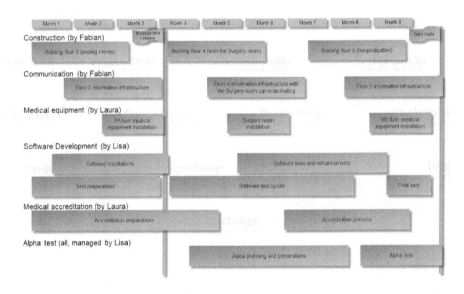

By now, it was late afternoon. I texted Anna, saying I was still in a never-ending session and that I would talk to her later.

Suddenly, I felt a hand on my shoulder. I turned around to see the VP of finance looking at me despondently and asking: "I'm sorry, but when will you be done?"

---

[1] Please check our website projectmap.solutions to review a more detailed plan.

I shrugged, "I have no idea, but we'll try to keep it short."

He glanced at his watch. "You know what? At this point, it doesn't make any sense for me to wait. But you should know that Chantal reserved the room for both of us. She made a mistake, it happens, of course. But you should know that I'm paying for her error."

I didn't know what to say other than: "I'm sorry." I was sorry for his wasted day, but how sorry could I be for someone else's mistake? I watched his back receding down the hallway. I had the feeling it wasn't the last I'd hear of him.

4

"It's impressive, I admit," said Fabian. "I mean, we must have set a speed record in creating this plan. You really think its visual advantage is that significant?"

Michael leaned back, his eyes gleaming. "I would say you can't exaggerate the importance of the right visual method, because it helps resolve the number one problem in every project, namely; the involvement of the organization and the team. An incredibly precise plan that is hard to grasp won't help the project function. On the other hand, a clear plan, even if its level of detailing is pretty basic, will have a decisive effect on creating a common language, the ability to pull together the project team towards common goals, and the way in which the project is executed."

"I hear you," Fabian nodded. "Again, I'm really impressed."

But Michael wasn't done. He stood up, and making sure we were all listening, said: "A clear plan presented right, visually speaking, helps resolve this issue at several points along the project's life. It makes it possible to engage in joint planning, just as we did here today.

"It's not Lisa sitting alone in her office for hours on end, constructing something nobody else can hope to understand. It's something we did, together, all of us. This results in greater commitment on everybody's part."

Lisa looked satisfied, and I wondered when I'd last seen her that way.

Michael went on: "Additionally, when we ask an employee to provide an update on a task, we can show him or her the task visually and in the context of the relevant sequence of activities. This presentation produces an immediate indication for the meaning of checking a task off as done, and alternately the meaning of an overdue task.

"It's very easy to mark a piece of data noting a postponement on a chart without assuming responsibility. Let the project manager deal with that later! But that mark provides a graphic indication that the entire project is now delayed... How easy is *that* to report? Raising the level of responsibility in reporting is very important in getting genuine, timely reports. No one wants to show up at the next meeting as the one responsible for holding the entire project back."

"Very true," Fabian murmured.

The room fell quiet. We all looked at the chart while occasionally peering at Michael. One could almost see the pieces falling into place in their minds. I'm not a particularly spiritual person – I've never been, and probably won't ever be – but in that moment, I thought we'd all had an awakening of sorts, a moment of insight, at least within the confines of this limited world of the physical and the practical.

"It's certainly a very intuitive presentation method," said Lisa, finally breaking the silence. "But what about all the information that's gone now? On the Gantt, we have six or seven hundred lines; no way is The Project Map going to contain seven hundred activities. You're losing tons of information that, as a project manager, you really need. And you're omitting the links among the tasks and an accurate analysis of the Critical Chain. That, too, is important data you're losing."

"I'm losing nothing," Michael answered confidently, as if having anticipated the question. "I'm simply dividing the information up differently and presenting it in a way that encourages thinking and initiative. You'll agree that anyone who's ever constructed a seven hundred-line Gantt chart is terrified that someone will ask for a change. It's a nightmare scenario, right?"

Lisa nodded thoughtfully and then looked pointedly at me. I didn't remember having asked her for changes, but, who knows? Maybe I had.

"Clearly, then, the Gantt manager, and consequently the project group as a whole, will prefer as few changes as possible, especially big ones," Michael continued. "When a Gantt is constructed for a year-long project, sticking to it becomes a significant burden after just a few months, while reconstructing it is an effort everyone tries to avoid.

"So, getting back to your question: I'm not proposing getting rid of any data. The information I left out when I shifted to using The Project Map is less relevant for presentation and follow-up. The information not included in The Project Map will show up in risk management charts, process documentation, sub-plans disseminated to various managers, and so on.

"In total, we won't be losing any information; on the contrary. But we'll use The Project Map as the working tool that contains exactly the right amount of information needed to manage the project, without being weighed down by extraneous data. Don't you agree, Lisa?"

All of us, not only Lisa, nodded in agreement. Then Chantal reappeared. Her hair was pulled back in an intricate do and glossy purple lipstick coated her lips. "Will you be much longer?" she asked, clearly flustered.

"Is it that VP of finance again?" Lisa demanded angrily. "What's wrong with him? Can't he take a hint? Hasn't he found another damned room yet?"

"That's not it," she answered.

"OK, so what is it?" I intervened. "Because we reserved the room until seven tonight."

"There's a surprise party later."

"Surprise party? Here? For whom?" I wanted to know.

"It's a surprise."

"Is it someone's birthday?" I asked around the room. "Because it isn't mine."

The secretary smiled. "It's not for someone here and it's not a birthday party."

"Wait a minute!" Fabian clearly knew what was really important: "Are we invited? Because I didn't get an email."

"Everyone's invited, and the party begins at seven sharp. So, please, if you can, finish up a little earlier so we can set up."

"No problem," I assured her. The secretary, relieved, nodded and left.

"What kind of a surprise?" Fabian asked.

"I have no idea, but I don't think it has anything to do with us. All the surprises we've had have been unpleasant."

Michael smiled reassuringly. "I truly believe that will change soon."

"Soon, maybe," I said, "but not today, and not like this."

Michael, smile still in place, checked his watch, seeming to calculate how much longer he'd have to stay seated. "Any questions? Now's the time, before I go."

"All right, then, I have a question," said Laura with visible discomfort.

"Even if it's a dumb question, it's fine," Fabian added helpfully.

"Look," Laura said, ignoring Fabian, "let's assume we can use everything you taught us to define what we want to do at every stage of the project. But how do we make the project team move in the right direction? A wonderful management method without leadership is not going to bring about the change we need."

"It's fine, don't worry about my feelings," I said, semi-jokingly.

Laura smiled in embarrassment. "That's not what I meant, Gary, and you know it."

Michael nodded at Laura. "I hate to disappoint you, but I don't have a clear-cut answer. First, people differ in their charisma and leadership abilities. Some people are always listened to while others are ignored. Now, quite apart from the issue of personality, leadership is created in many different ways. There isn't a single magic formula that will make a project team follow the piper's lead.

"Nonetheless, there *is* a combination of elements to project management that slowly but surely gives the project manager leadership position: good communication, teamwork focused on achievable goals, presenting rational and easily understandable plans, and expressing appreciation for progress. If you maintain these, you generate a critical mass of high-level management activity that the people involved in the project will recognize and value. I believe it will help you produce the change you want."

Even this failed to satisfy Laura, who still seemed worried. Michael, sensing her distress, decided to take a different tack.

"I'm going to tell you a joke that may clarify my point, OK?"

"I haven't heard a good one in a long time. Certainly not here," Fabian snorted.

Michael leaned forward. The little bit of fatigue he'd shown earlier seemed to have vanished. "It goes like this. The European Union came to the conclusion that too many cab drivers were cheating tourists trying to get to their hotels from the airport by not taking the shortest route. Everyone at the EU agreed that it was unacceptable, so they decided to define this as an issue needing improvement and allocate resources to eradicate the phenomenon.

"For a whole year, many different activities were undertaken to put an end to the practice. At the end of the year, the EU hosted an international conference to present the results.

"The first to speak was the French representative who said: 'I am very proud to present the improvements made in the past year. According to our surveys, a year ago, ten percent of tourists complained that taxi drivers had cheated them, whereas this year the number was only three percent. On behalf of the Republic, I am very proud of this achievement.'

"The second to speak was the German. 'I am very proud to present our improvement. Last year, we had eight percent who complained, and this year it was only two! I am proud that our drivers are behaving better.'

"The third to speak was the Italian delegate, and here is what he said: 'I am very proud to present our achievements. Last year, fifteen percent of tourists complained, and this year we had only three. I am proud that the rest of the tourists weren't paying any attention.'"

"Good one," said Fabian as we all sniggered.

"Now, consider the joke and how it relates to what I was saying," added Michael.

"I was wondering where you were going," Fabian said thoughtfully.

"Excellent," Michael answered. "Let me know when insight strikes."

The conversation ground to a halt. Michael sighed. My team members needed time to digest everything Michael had suggested before attempting to apply the ideas to our project. I thought we'd come a long way and felt a kind of energizing buzz that made me look forward to the future. I was curious to see how all this would start taking shape beginning next morning, and wondered when I'd be able to prove to George Madison that we were on the right path. It was obviously much too soon, but it was no longer a fantasy. At that moment, I felt the change would happen, hopefully soon.

"Michael," I said as he was packing up his things, "what do you have planned for us tomorrow?"

"I don't think there's any point in discussing other topics. I think I'll spend the day observing activity with you and the team. I'm happy to help you keep working on the project map so that you can begin from a better starting point." He got up and moved towards the door. Just before leaving, he turned to us and asked: "Say, have you celebrated the project's progress yet?"

"Celebrated? What do you mean?" Lisa responded.

"I mean having some kind of event to mark the fact that the project is making progress. If I understand correctly, construction was completed a year and a half ago, right? So, was this honored in any way?"

We looked at one another. It hadn't occurred to any of us. And why would it? What was the point?

"Look, one way to express appreciation for work done to date is to highlight it. Successes should be noticed, either impromptu or with a small, planned celebration. There is no doubt in my mind that progress must be marked. It is critical for the project essence."

That last sentence was directed at me. I don't think my team understood what he meant.

"What do you propose? I have to tell you that we don't have the budget for events. At best, we'd be shoved into this room with a couple of poppy-seed cakes and some soft drinks."

"We're talking about negligible costs," Michael retorted. "A few bottles of wine, a few cakes, an hour and a half off from work to say a few words of appreciation. You don't even have to make sure everyone is there; you'll always have someone who can't make it. But, believe me, the money you spend on wine will be the best investment you can make in the project."

"I'm in favor," Fabian said loudly.

With his hand on the doorknob, Michael had one more thing to say: "It will send a very clear message to everyone that something here is changing, that it's a good idea to stick around for this project. All right. Till tomorrow, then."

He left and closed the door. I turned to my team and asked: "Any ideas?"

Before anyone had a chance to answer, the door opened and Chantal bustled in with a bouquet of helium balloons and a cart loaded with refreshments. "Hey people, it's six thirty. Time to go home. C'mon on, get out of here," she said cheerfully.

"All right, all right, we're gone," said Fabian, sneaking a cookie from the tray and making his exit.

Chapter Six

Building Trust

1

The intensive work with Michael and the team jarred something loose, something I could finally wave at the hospital's management to show we were really making progress. I actually had two bosses; not only was I obligated to report to George Madison, I also had to keep the hospital's management abreast of developments.

Every now and then, I would be invited to management meetings and given fifteen to twenty minutes to provide a project update. The discussions weren't deep. Management was mostly concerned with George's level of satisfaction and with what I was doing to improve it.

In the past, I had tried to present the Gantt chart and show some details of the plans and the progress we were anticipating, but the forum would quickly lose focus, and I realized that this form of presentation was irrelevant to the managers. They wanted simple, quick, clear messages. They wanted bullet points and the bottom line.

But now, with the new, visual project map tool, I felt it was time to try to present the plans to the managers, and also demonstrate that we were working with an advanced method and making serious efforts to fundamentally change our manner of work. I had about two weeks until the next management meeting. The project map was already fairly detailed, covering coordination plans and a good level of risk management. I looked at the project map and felt pride. It was indeed a clear, effective, condensed tool, something that management could look at and understand.

I rehearsed a couple of times and realized I'd need about ten minutes for the presentation. Afterwards, I planned on saying that George and his team had also seen the map during our monthly update meeting and were favorably impressed. I wanted to project optimism; somewhere within me, I felt that my own optimism would inspire others.

"Good luck," Lisa said to me as I went off to the conference room.

"Sock it to 'em!" Fabian encouraged me.

"Where's Laura?" I asked them.

"On a fancy vacation with her husband," Fabian informed me.

I entered the conference room. As usual, the meeting appeared somewhat sleepy. My slot had been scheduled deep into the second hour of the discussion. The sad-looking left-over pastries jumbled on a tray and used coffee cups littering the table indicated that the meeting was winding down.

The VP of finance kept sending me patronizing looks. He clearly still held the conference room snafu against me, and it occurred to me that this might be a problem for me. On the other hand, if I managed to be sufficiently persuasive and focused, there was nothing he could do.

I started connecting my laptop to the projector, hoping that, for once, it wouldn't give me any grief. Maybe we ought to buy a projector for our project's exclusive use; it was impossible to rely on other projectors, especially at the hospital where it could take years to replace the ageing equipment with normal HD connections.

But, today, luck was on my side. As the project map came up, I saw that I didn't have to do a lot of explaining. The managers grasped the presentation format almost immediately and related to it as if they were good buddies from way back when. Even the VP of finance nodded with satisfaction; at least, that was my impression.

Just to be safe, I started by talking about the activity areas we had chosen to focus on and I saw that even this basic datum organized the discussion and allowed it to segue easily to the details and the connections between various activities.

As Fabian said, I felt I was really socking it to 'em.

Within ten minutes, I'd covered the new plans in general and had already answered a few questions and noted some gaps I had to close. I added that George had seen the project map at our monthly meeting and had approved its continued use as a tool for charting progress.

Because I had some time left, I mentioned Michael's involvement and that the method originated with him. Everything went by the book. And, yet, I noticed that throughout the discussion, Chris Dumoulin, the hospital director, who was leaning back in his plush reclining chair and looking a million miles away, did not say a word. He was a tall man; six foot four of austere dignity. He was rumored to have been a division chief at the CIA, a rumor he neither admitted nor denied.

Now he cleared his throat, indicating he wanted a moment of silence before summarizing the meeting. The room quietened down, awaiting his pronouncement. I was still standing next to the board. I took a step back and assumed a pose of polite attention, expecting a few concluding remarks and the meeting's adjournment.

"Look, Gary," he said slowly, glaring at me with a troubled expression, "give me a reason to trust you."

I felt my heart thud. I thought everything had gone so well. Where was this coming from?

"A reason to trust me?" I parroted, partly in shock, partly in an attempt to understand how much trouble I was in.

"That's right. It's not that I don't trust you; it's not a question of trustworthiness. But a few months ago you came here and showed us your Gantt, right?"

The hospital director didn't wait for my answer. "We didn't go into much detail; perhaps we didn't want to. But it *was* your presentation and it had dates and goals that you hadn't met. Now you're showing us something else. And I have to admit, I haven't seen so clear a project presentation in a very long time, and in that sense, I'm hooked."

He breathed deeply, then leaned forward, elbows splayed, and fingers interlaced on the table. "But still, I have to ask you again: Give me a reason to trust you."

Suddenly, all eyes were on me. I felt that I was caught in the crossfire, the management's accusatory eyes being the weapons.

Dumoulin continued: "Your presentation, nice as it is, doesn't provide me with any assurance that you'll manage to meet your goals this time. And what is possibly even more troubling is the fact that it doesn't provide you with any such assurance either."

I felt the time had come to respond with a counterpunch, because unless I opened my mouth and started talking I was liable to damage myself even more. And not just myself – the whole project. I felt as if a sword were hovering over my head, inching closer.

"All right," I said, trying to sound confident, "that's a reasonable position. I, however, would claim that what I presented here today does, in fact, represent a higher degree of assurance for several reasons. First of all, the project map is generated intuitively on the basis of a group discussion. It is not an attempt to stuff a project plan into a method for the management of a production line, and that is a huge advantage."

The questioning looks in the room told me that the managers' level of interest in project management methods was not especially high. So, I took a somewhat different direction.

"Second, the project map is constructed by activity areas. Division by activity areas allows a more detailed analysis of problematic nodes between areas, and focuses the project group on the links between the activity areas where most of the problems occur.

"Generally speaking, a better method of presentation is not to be dismissed. Just as all of you here, today, understood the plans better, so every project employee and manager understands the plans, the problem zones, and the risks better, and that of necessity, leads to better cooperation, better coordination, and better performance."

The room fell silent once again. It was clear I hadn't been terribly convincing. The truth is that what I said could have been presented better, had I been prepared for Dumoulin's challenge. It's tough to persuade an audience uninterested in working methods that one method is better than another. The VP of finance smirked at me, as if watching me dig my own grave.

"Look," said Dumoulin, "I accept what you're saying. The presentation does look better, and so the level of coordination is improved and maybe also something at the analytical level, but you'll have to excuse me if I don't understand this completely. I still want you to show me a marker, an index, an indication that you're on the right track. Do you get my meaning?"

I nodded even though my neck felt as stiff as a rock.

"I want to you to tell me that, last week, you were at eight out of ten and that this week you're at seven plus. Do you follow? Something that will spare you the need to persuade me of the appropriateness of your method. That way, both of us will know what the index says and why it's a good one.

"And after you show me that, continue your presentations with the project map, because it's great. And continue following the coordination and risk control plans, because in those areas I really do trust you."

Somehow, I felt that the sword had stopped an inch above my skin. The VP of finance was no longer staring daggers at me; his gaze was wandering the conference room, looking for something else to settle on. But the hospital director's eyes would not leave my face. In that moment, I could easily imagine him in a CIA black-ops site interrogating an unwilling suspect.

"Look," I started, "you can extract such an index from tracking the project's buffer consumption. In that way, I can…"

"No, no, no," Dumoulin interrupted me impatiently. "I know all about that and that's not it. Or, more accurately, I take my own buffer and calculate how you, as project manager, deal with it… I'm not asking you to show me the exact same thing."

Through the glass panel in the door, I caught sight of Lisa and Fabian peering in, trying to make sense of my expression. I hoped I looked better than I felt, but I was determined to fight through this, fight against the sword whose movement had been stopped, though it was still hovering nearby.

The hospital director went on. "Allow me to explain by using an example. Yesterday, I made a hotel reservation in Romania, OK? I know nothing about Romania, but the relevant website rates the hotels, OK?"

It was starting to sound like one of Michael's anecdotes, which oddly made me feel a little better.

"In fact, the breakdown is such that I can see the rating given by businessmen, so that I'm not moved by a rating based on the jungle gym at the pool, OK? So, after doing a little browsing, I reserved a room on the basis of its rating, pretty certain I'd made a good deal. Now I want to be able to look at your map and feel certain that the project is a good deal too. Got it?"

"Got it."

I left the room realizing I was stuck with a task I had no idea how to execute.

Fabian was waiting for me right outside the room. "How did it go?" I held up a hand. "Please, not now," and he looked at me with concern. My cell phone buzzed. Again. I had so many text messages to deal with, including several from Anna. I gave the conference room one last glance. The managers were already on to a different topic, but the eyes of the VP of finance were again boring into me.

2

I went back to my office where Lisa was waiting for me. Perfect timing, I thought. Lisa was just the person to talk to about project management methods. Her extensive experience included enough successes – and failures – to construct a good perspective on a suitable index.

But she had other plans for me. Lisa proceeded to deluge me with the latest developments with the computer systems supplier. A few minutes of chatter all but made me forget about Chris Dumoulin's request. At the last second, after Lisa had already opened my office door to leave, I remembered.

"Hang on a second! I need your help."

Lisa was gripping the doorknob and looking at me with a trace of worry.

"That doesn't sound good."

I ignored her incisive deductive skills and told her, in brief, about the discussion with the hospital director and the challenge he had issued me.

She closed the door, gave a little sigh, and said: "I also don't like using the buffer, but I don't know any other method that will produce a high level of assurance or at least a way to manage the risk level. Do you remember Alex's going-away party?"

Alex had been the previous hospital director.

"Yeah, I remember the party, but why are you bringing it up now?"

"Simply because I wanted to explain to you why I don't like using the buffer. You know how everyone was afraid of Alex? And the last thing anybody wanted was get on his bad side at the party? His personal assistant invited the hospital's management and other people, using a code only she could crack.

"Anyhow, she told the people in logistic there would be fifty guests and asked that the hall be set up accordingly. The logistics manager was afraid there wouldn't be room for everyone, so he asked the purchasing department for supplies for a sixty-person event. The purchasing department issued a tender for seventy people, and the supplier whose bid won decided to prepare eighty places so that there would be room for everyone.

"The day of the party, Alex's assistant got nervous and worried that she'd cut things too close. So, she made an urgent call to the logistic manager and asked to increase the number of spots. And everyone else, in turn, added another five to the original number and the hall was set for one hundred guests. You know how the story ends, right? The hall was prepared for a hundred guests and only fifty showed up. It was mortifying. And that, I think, is the problem with using the buffer."

I looked at her with new eyes. At the time, I hadn't given that going-away party much thought, other than considering it a social obligation I couldn't get out of. I had never particularly liked Alex, and the going-away event was a relief; at least he was on his way elsewhere and I would no longer have to see his arrogant face in the hallway. In fact, I experienced a moment of unwilled schadenfreude at the minor fiasco Lisa just mentioned.

"So, what are you trying to say?" I asked.

"Let me give you the highlights."

I sniggered. "I see that Michael has rubbed off on how you talk."

"I would argue that, but never mind. The buffer has a tendency to grow in direct ratio to the pressure felt in the project's environment. Sometimes, it has nothing to do with informed reasons that require you to store spare time. In the case of the going-away party, not only was there no point in creating a buffer; in the end it was actually detrimental.

"Another important point is that the moment there is legitimacy to save the buffer, it is difficult to control its extent and, perhaps more importantly, control who can save it and manage its consumption."

I was still looking at her with awe, waiting for her to go on. "The outcome of all this is inefficiency. Instead of being managed according to an organized plan, the buffer is managed from the basic assumption that it's possible to cheat. And the truth is that the buffer will almost always be used if it exists."

"Michael would be proud of you," I said, "and I am too."

She blushed faintly and continued. "In an ideal world, I suppose it's possible to define the perfect project and manage it perfectly so that any surplus time is managed as such. But I've never seen it happen in practice because of the reasons I just gave."

She sat down. Fabian knocked and stuck his head through the door, but I signaled him to come back later, and he did an about face. It was still morning, and out the window I saw heavy clouds moving in our direction. I was convinced that one of them was shaped just like a sword.

"Excellent," I said, "but still – what can we do to produce assurance that the project will in fact be managed according to plan?"

"I really don't know," Lisa admitted. "I don't know a method or tool that provides anything like that. At the end of the day, it's down to your manager's ability to trust you or have a discussion and ask enough questions until he trusts you. I don't have a better answer."

"Well, that's an answer Chris Dumoulin is not going to accept. We'll have to think about it some more."

Lisa shrugged, glanced at her watch, and said: "All right, I have to get going. We'll talk later."

She left, and I was sure Fabian would come bursting in, but he seemed to have found something else to keep himself busy. I looked down the hallway. There was little movement, a few telephones ringing, some rustles here and there, distant thuds of heavy equipment, and the constant whoosh of the air conditioning system.

For a moment, I was tempted to get out, find a nice park with a bench, and sit amid greenery and birdsong. That, however, was a privilege I couldn't afford. And I could easily imagine Fabian start demanding we hold all staff meetings in the park! So, I closed my door, took a deep breath, and asked myself: What will make Chris trust me?

* * *

It was midday. The skies were even darker than before, and I couldn't see myself heading out for lunch. I wasn't even hungry, but Anna had told me I had to remember to eat, though I still forgot from time to time.

I remembered Chris using the example of the Romanian hotel. He'd wanted to see a rating to be able to make a reservation with confidence. I had an idea. I took a marker and started writing on the board:

A potential customer surfs travel websites.

He looks at hotel ratings and prices as they appear on a site.

He makes sure the ratings are relevant to his category, i.e. businessmen.

He becomes convinced that a certain hotel is good enough for his needs and reserves a room.

How would I copy this general idea to the field of project management? I asked myself, noticing that I was speaking out loud. I was trying to produce a rating for the project, the way the hotel ratings were generated. Great. But how?

"Hi there!" The door banged opened. Fabian, of course. He looked especially determined, striding into the room. "You look like Rodin's *Thinker*. Soon there'll be smoke coming out your ears. What's up? Hospital on your mind?"

"More or less. I'm trying to figure something out."

"So, share. I'm pretty good at figuring. And I promise not to ask you how the management meeting went."

Feeling worn out, I looked up at him and asked: "Have you ever made an online hotel reservation?"

"Is there any other way?" he answered my question with a question of his own.

"I'll take that as a yes. How do you decide on a hotel?"

Fabian noticed how serious I was and took his natural boisterousness down a notch. "It depends on how much time I have, but generally speaking I decide on my price range, look at the ratings, read some reviews, look at the photograph, and make my choice. Does that answer your question?"

"Yes... Well, no... Maybe I didn't phrase the question right."

I tried to organize my thoughts. "OK. Why do you trust the information you gather about the hotels? For example, how do you know that the hotel hasn't planted hidden ads in the form of vague positive reviews?"

"That's not so complicated. I guess it might happen here and there, but in principle you can look at the timeframe in which the various ratings are submitted and see that the reviewers are relating to relevant aspects and that criticism is balanced and the compliments not too flattering.

"If a certain hotel gets good ratings over several years and the reviews essentially similar or consistent, then the hotel is probably a good one. A sequence of more reserved reviews or low ratings tells me to stay away."

I didn't answer. Fabian caught my eye and asked: "So where are you off to?"

I laughed ruefully. "Nowhere, I'm afraid. But I do want to set up a rating system for projects."

Now it was Fabian's turn to laugh. "Are you kidding?"

"Nope. I'm dead serious. We have to find a way to apply the same mechanism that makes people trust today's method for making hotel reservations to our project."

"In that case, you have to look at the way the rating is created," Fabian said. "Someone stays at the hotel, has either a negative or a positive experience, leaves, and submits a numerical rating plus a few words. Each such process is another brick in the overall impression the hotel makes. A rating generated by many reviewers seems more trustworthy than one generated by just a few, and the words the reviewers use add to that sense of trustworthiness."

"OK, so…?"

"Hey, I'm just thinking out loud. All right, where was I? Ok. So, if a project is like a hotel, we can say that every project activity is like a hotel stay. In other words, if we rate the different activities, we can generate a general project rating."

"Now it's starting to get interesting," I mused, "but on what basis would we rate an activity?"

Fabian scratched his head. His grin was gone, replaced by a serious, professional mien. "We could think about it some more, but here's an off-the-cuff suggestion: We could give every task an initial rating from the gut and then continue to update the rating, just as additional guests update the hotel's rating."

I looked at Fabian, and he looked at me. We didn't know if this brief exchange had generated something of interest or an idea that would seem off-the-wall after a day or two.

"Fine," I said. "Let's stop now and agree to think about it some more. At the team meeting, I'll give a more in-depth explanation for this conundrum. I've already spoken about it with Lisa – really just touched on the topic – but none of this is urgent."

"All right," said Fabian. "I'm going home. Tonight, I have a party I've been anticipating for months. Want to come?"

I smiled but shook my head.

"You won't regret it," he added.

"That I'm not sure about, but thanks for the invitation."

"Rain check?"

"I doubt it."

3

Over the next few days, I was busy with routine project tasks. Chris Dumoulin hadn't said when I had to get back to him with an answer, and therefore I didn't make time to think about the matter. It was actually Fabian who brought it up at the end of a team meeting. He acted like a very industrious hen who had sat on her eggs all week and was eager to stretch her legs.

"What are you guys talking about?" Laura inquired. She was the only one not yet in the loop.

"It's like this," Fabian started. "I've been thinking about the hotel rating system. Not only does it produce a rating that potential customers can refer to when making an online reservation, but it also creates an interest on the hotel's part to improve its score.

"What do I mean? Hotels know that guests will be asked to rate the level of several aspects, say cleanliness, the food, and staff courteousness, so they make a point of being good in those categories while also checking in with guests during their stay to see if there are any problems. This leads an overall better hotel experience. So, the rating system is not some kind of heaven-sent punishment, but something the hotel can use to make positive changes."

"I don't get it. Are you trying to put together a hotel vacation for all of us?" Laura wanted to know.

"You just got back from a vacation," Lisa said, with a certain amount of grievance in her voice.

Fabian, sighing, stopped to explain why we were on the topic.

"And now," he finally continued, "getting back to the project: If we succeed in creating a similar project index, it would not only serve Gary as a means for updating the hospital's management, but would also motivate the project group to engage in a constant process of improvement in order to raise its rating. And you know what? I think this is a really promising avenue to explore. And I'm not aware of such a mechanism in existing systems."

"Other than hotels," said Laura. "And thanks for asking, by the way. We had a great time."

We took her sarcasm in stride. None of us really wanted to hear about her great time.

"So, what do you think?" Fabian wanted to know.

"About what?" Laura said frostily.

"Laura, there's no reason to get bent out of shape, but I don't really feel like hearing about your massages and aromatic oils and health foods, all right?" said Fabian.

Laura had the decency to blush. "I'm not offended." And to prove it, she asked: "So how exactly would you determine the rating of a project? I don't understand; it seems to me like artificial intelligence. The question of the project getting done or not getting done depends on so many factors. It's not like a hotel that you rate on the basis of its rooms."

Fabian looked readier than ever. "I've given this a lot of thought, my dear. I knew the question would be asked; I even knew that *you* would be doing the asking."

Laura was still rolling her eyes when Fabian flipped the whiteboard over to reveal the four lines from two weeks ago I'd jotted down for myself about hotel reservations. I was a little taken aback. "What have you been doing for the past two weeks?" Laura was now looking at me. "Are you working between team meetings? Writing a book about project management?"

It was my turn to blush now, but I brushed her off. In the nick of time, I saw Fabian erasing the evidence and putting down the following:

Every activity in the project map will be given an initial rating representing the level of assurance that the activity will be carried out as planned.

The rating may go up or down during the time the activity is executed.

The initial rating will be fairly high, because we assume that the initial projected timing is based on solid information.

The rating may go up or down based on three parameters:

The nature of its prior/preliminary activities. If it is linked to many other activities, the rating goes down. If the coordination plans cover these links, the rating may be raised.

The risk attributed to an activity will lower its rating. But, as with 4.a, if the risk prevention plans cover it, the activity's rating may be raised.

Sign-off from the activity owner: If the activity owner states that s/he accepts responsibility and anticipates it will be executed on time, the rating may be raised. If no such assurance is given, the rating will drop.

The rating of the project as a whole is, the weighted ratings of all activities at a given point in time.

Lisa, Laura, and I were all gaping at Fabian with amazement. I couldn't believe he'd run the idea and done it so well. For a cynical second, I wondered if it had been his way of avoiding the boring daily routine for the past two weeks, but then dismissed this unworthy thought. This, too, was part of our day-to-day working life. In fact, it may have been the most important part of it at this stage of the game. He had clearly given this a great deal of deep consideration.

Having written all of that down, Fabian now spoke about two more points he felt were significant: the first was sticking to comprehensible indexes rather than advanced algorithms. Precisely to avoid falling into the AI trap Laura had noted, Fabian had made the decision to stick with a transparent rating whose rise and fall – the hows and the whys – could be explained simply. For example, changing the duration of an activity wouldn't affect the rating either way, because such a change could be explained in two ways: either extending the duration could indicate an increase in certainty, as the activity was reassessed and had now been given the right amount of time to stay on schedule, or, alternately, extending the duration could indicate a decrease in certainty, as the extension was a result of problems in execution.

Fabian's second point had to do with the rating's overall positive effect on the project. The moment the method used to calculate the rating was shown to be easy to grasp, the project group would make an effort to raise the rating. And raising the rating, too, was easy: getting the activity owner to sign off, improving the coordination plans, and improving the risk prevention plans. These steps would result in raising the rating and raising the sense of assurance that the project would come to fruition as planned.

"I'm floored," said Laura. "Really, I'm thoroughly impressed. And you know that you don't impress me that often."

Lisa nodded in agreement. I examined Fabian's proposal as it appeared on the board, trying to gauge if it had enough depth to calculate the project's assurance level. I suspected that another round of discussion would bring the indexes he'd considered into greater relief, and that, over time, we'd have to test the indexes in practice and perhaps add or change some things. But here, without a doubt, was an interesting approach worth testing.

"What do you think?" I asked Lisa.

"I'm not sure," she answered.

"I guess I failed to impress you," Fabian said half-jokingly.

"That's not it," Lisa corrected. "It's a very interesting approach, but I would want to construct a simple spreadsheet that would calculate the rating and then see what we get over time. I also think that we can – maybe should – calculate a rating not only for activities and the project as a whole, but also by activity areas. That would tell us who was contributing to raising the rating and who was responsible for it falling."

"Brilliant!" Fabian was enthusiastic. "We could generate a kind of covert – or maybe even overt – competition among managers of the activity areas just as there is between hotels!"

"Yeah, but the question is if this wouldn't push them into hiding risks or dropping links just to raise the rating..." Laura, as always, was thinking practically.

"Good point," granted Fabian, "but blank coordination or risk prevention plans would be a red flag that not enough thought and in-depth analysis had been given... This rating wouldn't be the only one a manager would consider. I think it's possible to find a balance."

"I propose again that we prepare a spreadsheet that calculates this and present it to team managers as a start." Lisa was trying to draw the discussion to an end. "If it passes their muster, we go forward. Gary?"

Three pairs of eyes fixed on me, expectant. I leaned back. "I agree. But something's missing. What Fabian is suggesting seems too arbitrary. It's like giving a hotel room a rating based on its size. What about the other factors affecting the guests?

"The whole impact of a rating system comes from a cumulative impression generated by repeated reviews. I don't think we've managed to copy that aspect into this idea, which is why I don't think this is a particularly useful avenue. I'm sorry, Fabian. It's a very nice idea but lacks the dynamic component. Does anyone have a thought on addressing that?"

Fabian's body language flipped one hundred and eighty degrees. His face drained of colour and he slumped backwards, as if I'd offended him personally, rather than offered professional critique. I knew exactly how he felt but hoped he could set the childishness in him aside and pull himself together. For now, though, he looked defeated.

"If you're looking for something dynamic," said Laura, "some kind of direct response from people, then let's send a weekly automated message to all activity owners asking them if activities were executed as planned. If they answer yes, we give them a Like. Assurance rises. If they answer no, we give them a Dislike. Assurance drops." Laura was clearly happy with the Facebook-inspired idea she'd proposed.

Fabian was doing something with his head that was neither a nod nor a shake.

"Are you nuts?" Lisa blurted at Laura. "Another automated system messages? People delete those before reading them. What makes you think we could get feedback that way?"

I looked at Fabian, and was again amazed by his ability to turn on a dime. Instead of looking hurt or cowed, he was completely reenergized, and I couldn't wait for him to turn that transformation into a positive for the meeting.

"Now hold on, Lisa," Fabian said in Laura's defense, "maybe the method is problematic, but the idea is good. We just have to think of a way of getting feedback some other way. How about starting the weekly status meeting by asking everyone about their activities?"

"What? All activities? That's too much," I protested.

"Maybe not all. How about two months ahead?"

"Two months ahead?" I mused out loud. "Let's try to imagine it. The project meeting starts. We go over activities scheduled for the next two months and ask activity owners to give a Like or Dislike. If the owner says "Like," everything is hunky-dory, and we can bump the activity assurance a little. If the owner says "Dislike," then..." I was stuck. I didn't know how to continue.

"Then it gets put on the meeting agenda!" Fabian declared. After a beat, he added: "And the task rating goes down."

A satisfied silence filled the room. Through the window to the hallway we saw people milling around Chantal's desk, a signal that our time was almost up. "Lisa – set up a computer spreadsheet that will calculate the new rating system. Fabian – put together an agenda for our next meeting." We summarized the rules for the rating system to make sure we were on the same page. All four of us felt we had something solid to go on.

We left the conference room, passing the stream of entering logistics personnel who, for some reason, smelled of alcohol swabs and Danishes. It reminded me of the meeting with Chris Dumoulin and the challenge he'd posed: "Give me a reason to trust you, Gary." I felt I had a great answer, though it was still hard for me to define it in precise terms. You'll get there, I told myself. Give it another meeting. The right words will come to you soon.

Three months later...

Chapter Seven

Crisis

1

"Staff to antenatal, staff to antenatal!" This seemingly innocuous announcement, made in a soothing female voice, did not generate any particular reaction among the expectant and post-partum mothers and partners on the second floor. It was being broadcast for the whole PA system, though meant only for the staff.

Staff members, however, went on high alert. The announcement meant an emergency was developing in the antenatal ward that local staffers were incapable of handling on their own.

July had been a difficult month for the hospital's maternity wing. Not only were many staff members taking their annual vacations, but it seemed as if more than the normal number of pre-registered women had summertime due dates. The wing was filled to capacity.

The antenatal ward consisted of a hallway with ten rooms off of it for laboring women. Depending on progress, they would be moved either to a delivery room or an operating room.

Emergency calls in this part of the maternity wing were rare. I heard it but didn't respond. I wasn't a medical professional and I assumed that the relevant responders were already on their way. And, in fact, just a few seconds later, I saw several staff members moving rapidly past my office. I was sure that whatever had happened would be dealt with effectively. I certainly felt no particular concern for myself.

But then the PA system sounded the alert two more times.

It was highly unusual to make an emergency announcement more than once. Full response was expected after just one broadcast. So, what was really going on there? Was the whole thing a false alarm? Or a drill? Maybe something *is* terribly wrong, I thought.

While trying to decide what to do, Laura's anxious face appeared in the doorway.

"What's going on, Laura? Are you heading over there?"

Laura rolled her eyes. "Do I have to remind you that I'm not wearing my doctor's hat here? The staffers there will think I'm some kind of impostor."

But before she'd completed the sentence, the PA chimed with its fourth announcement.

"Staff to antenatal, staff to antenatal!" Maybe it was my imagination, but the voice no longer sounded soothing. It was downright scary.

"All right. Let's go see what's happening," I said to Laura, worried.

We headed for the second floor using the staff stairwell. Our offices were located on the first floor, together with all the other non-medical services and public spaces, and the stairs to the second floor were the shortest route.

We opened the stairwell door to the second floor and it was immediately clear that something unusual was happening. The place was crowded with staffers in scrubs of many colours, meaning they'd come from different locations. A group, obviously consisting of the partners of the laboring women was crowded into the waiting area near reception; I assumed they'd been asked to stay there until the incident was resolved. But what incident was happening?

"Are you going in to check?" I asked Laura. "Let me know what's going on. I'll be waiting here, by the door. I don't want to get in the way. I mean, I have no medical training at all."

I remained standing there for several minutes. What was taking Laura so long? And then something else struck me: The lights were off. My disquiet was becoming full-blown anxiety, and I didn't think I could stand around much longer. I had to go in and see for myself. I headed for the nurses' station and sat down in the head nurse's chair. The computer screen was black. What was going on? A power outage? If so, why had the back-up system not kicked in?

Suddenly, leaning over me, I saw Prof. Jeff Thomas's red face. Prof. Thomas was the chief of both the hospital's Fetal Health Department and Antenatal Department, a fundamentally administrative position. It was rare to see him in the antenatal ward or even on the second floor in general. He was a redhead, and his face was perpetually rosy, but now it was almost purple.

"Prof. Thomas! Do you know what's happening?" I asked.

He leaned even closer so that the people around us wouldn't hear, and said: "We're solving the problem on this end, but your problem is only just beginning."

The expression on his face and his tone of voice left no room for doubt. He was furious. I had no idea what he was talking about, but before I had a chance to ask, he answered a call on his cell phone and continued striding down the hall.

My problem was only just beginning? What problem was he talking about?

I left the unpowered nurses' station and went back to where Laura and I parted. I didn't want to annoy her with a phone call, because I wasn't sure whether her help was still needed. Still, I gripped my device and tapped the screen nervously with my index finger.

After another few minutes that felt like an eternity Laura appeared at the end of the hallway. Her hair was a bit mussed, but her expression – like that of someone who'd been running in the rain and just found shelter – told me that the worst was behind us. She beckoned me to follow her.

It wasn't even a question. Something really bad was happening, something that was connected to me, my team, my project.

I followed Laura to the staff lounge, which was completely dark other than the emergency lighting of the EXIT signs. "Are you going to tell me happened or not?" I said impatiently.

Her hands were telling me to calm down. "First of all, it doesn't seem that anything really dreadful happened. Something like this could have ended in death."

Doctors. They have an uncanny ability to put things in perspective, I thought.

"Something like what? You're not telling me anything. And Thomas hinted..."

Laura interrupted me. "Gary, the electricity in the antenatal ward went off half an hour ago. The backup system failed. The staff had to hook up the secondary backup system, but it can only supply electricity for about an hour.

"There are seven or eight women in various stages of labor, all needing immediate attention. So, they had to be distributed to different locations for further treatment. But there were only four nurses and one doctor. And that's why they made the emergency announcement."

"I still don't get it. Why run the code four times?"

"Listen, I don't know if you've ever been in a similar situation. The antenatal ward has no windows, so there's no light coming in from outside. So, when the backup system fails, and the secondary backup system is only good for emergency systems, it means that, except for emergency lighting, everything is pitch black in there. Only the critical devices are still working. So panic ensued. And it's affected the laboring women and their partners. The staff has to make sure that, in addition to the natural fright in such a situation, no health risks to the women or their unborn babies are emerging."

"You said nothing dreadful happened."

"True. No one died. But there is at least one woman who, because of stress, had to be moved to an OR for a C-section. Under normal circumstances, she would have had a natural delivery. Other than that, a partner of one of the women broke his wrist falling over a chair in the dark, and we have a nurse who sustained an injury to her forehead, knocking into an oxygen tank hanging on a wall."

"So, what might have happened?"

Now it was Laura's turn to be impatient. "Don't ask me to describe every single catastrophic scenario that could have occurred. When a hospital wing loses electricity and has no backup system, lots of awful things could happen. Without a doubt, it poses a risk to patients' lives, and we have to be grateful that this incident ended with relatively minor consequences."

"Fine," I said, "I'll talk to Thomas after he's had a chance to cool off and try to understand what he wants from us."

"Wait. There's more."

"Are you serious? What are you waiting for? Laura – spill it. Now!"

Laura's face took on an odd expression, completely ignoring my abrupt tone. She motioned for me to walk deeper into the lounge: "The power loss is Fabian's fault," she whispered.

For a second, I thought I'd misheard her: "What? Come again?"

Her eyes bored into mine, as if saying: You heard me; I don't really need to repeat myself.

The darkness finally got to me and my senses were overwhelmed. I felt the pit of my stomach dropping and tiny razors cutting my breathing passages. I forced myself to take several deep breaths.

"Are you saying that Fabian and the integration team caused the power to fail?" I, too, was whispering as several staff members were passing by. I thought they were all giving us significant looks.

"Not exactly. They didn't cause the power to fail. They shut it off on purpose," Laura said. "And, as if that weren't enough, they also took the backup system offline. We're lucky there's a secondary backup system that can't be tampered with," Laura answered.

"What the hell were they thinking?" I asked.

Laura shrugged. We were both clueless.

2

Over the past three months, we'd managed to effect a dramatic change in the project. After Michael's visit and the articulation of the new plan, we made a point of basing our work on strict adherence to The Project Map. We used it at all meetings, and had even put enlarged copies of it up on our bulletin boards. The new plan was easy to understand, and everyone was starting to use the new "activity area" terminology. Those defined as owners of particular activities updated progress on the project map. The plan no longer belonged only to Lisa; it was shared by us all.

The project map automatically generated coordination plans based on analysis of the links entered during the planning process. Links between groups and activity areas got special attention and helped us focus on the project's traditional Achilles heels. This coordination plan was our guide at the weekly meetings and became part of the meetings' agendas.

Unlike the past, we were now able to focus on the important coordination steps between areas of activity and avoid endless discussions about things that were in any case happening. We found that following the coordination plan closely was our insurance policy for progress.

The number of unwelcome surprises – is there any other kind? – dropped off steeply, and it seemed that running the project using this method intercepted problems before they could happen. In addition, we saw that people were really grasping the plan, working with it, and most importantly sharing it with a growing number of participants.

One group in particular went above and beyond: It used to print out and post its plans in a prominent location, which automatically improved the level of reporting. Because who would want to become notorious as the person holding everyone else up?

Consequent to Fabian's idea, we decided to hold meetings every other week to summarize the preceding work cycle and discuss the next. The meetings often generated creative ideas, with people showing their growing level of investment in the project and competing for the best ways to optimize activities.

We encouraged the teams to use the project map to hold project discussions that were as open as possible and to redefine our next short-term goals. When an initiative that led to positive change was formulated, we celebrated both its originator and the achievement.

Throughout this period, we calculated the assurance index of the project by hand, using an electronic spreadsheet Lisa had set up, but we decided that as long as we weren't convinced the index was accurately reflecting the state of the project, we would continue to work on improving the parameters used to calculate it and not present it to anyone else.

In the first month, we simply calculated the index using the initial set of rules we'd agreed on. The result was interesting but not dynamic. The rating given to the project was pretty constant and did not reflect the changes we were experiencing all the time.

In the second month, Lisa suggested that she sit in on Fabian's meetings and take notes on the activities and their progress. Any activity that wasn't progressing as expected would then be discussed. As time passed, we realized that the information Lisa was entering was lowering and raising the assurance index in a direct ratio to the discussion in the meeting and was providing a good reflection of our assurance that we'd be able to execute the project.

Subsequent to this success, we planned on building a tool that would allow us to gather the ratings from the team during meetings, and we decided to call it the Status Meeting Manager, or SMM, but we had not had the opportunity yet to test the tool with the team before the lights went off in the antenatal ward.

Vis-à-vis George Madison, too, we could safely say we had scored success. He saw a meaningful change compared to the project's meandering over the last two years. Armed with Michael's instructions to avoid the optimism bias, we left our much misleading data from our presentations. We spoke very little about theoretical plans, focusing instead on activity as it was being carried out. We alternated good news with bad news, and the overall impression created was that we were once again in control.

George seemed pleased. Thanks to the new presentation method, he understood, for the first time, how complex the project really was. He was no longer threatening to withdraw his donation. He made no explicit promise, of course, but for now the threat seemed to be off the table.

On one occasion, I screwed up my courage and presented the project's assurance index, which then stood at seventy-eight percent, giving a brief overview of the calculation method we'd devised. One of our bright-eyed and bushy-tailed consultants even gave his blessing: "Good for you! A project assurance index is something I've never seen." I knew the consultant would pass the same comment on to George, and I was filled with pride by what we'd created.

The short-term goals I asked everyone to prepare after the gathering that were met were presented as successes, indicating proven progress. Every such success was matched with the challenges left in every activity area to avoid the asymmetry bias. The difference was striking.

There was no doubt about it. The atmosphere around the project had changed significantly. By the end of May, people were already looking back with satisfaction and optimistic about the future.

One evening on a trip to the West Coast, I made time to have dinner with Michael to thank him again and update him on the way in which we were applying our methods. Michael was happy for the positive feedback and encouraged us to stay the course.

Was all of this now going down the tubes?

Was the darkness in the ward prophetic?

What the hell was I supposed to do now?

What would happen to the project?

What would I tell Chris? Jeff? George? And what was I going to do with Fabian?

Laura, looking pensive, stood in a corner of the lobby. The electricity wasn't back. I looked around in despair, but tried to appear as focused and sensible as possible.

"Do you know what Prof. Thomas wants from us?" I asked her.

"I assume he'll want to hear explanations for this snafu, suspend work on the project until you can prove beyond a shadow of a doubt it will never happen again, and make sure the whole hospital sees your panties."

I'd known exactly what she would say, but hearing it was chilling. The line about the panties was a reference to an inside team joke. We always said that the project manager is at the top of the pyramid and where it's cold and everybody can see up your skirt. I peered into the gloom and, despite the dark, felt completely exposed.

"What can I say? If it's really Fabian's team, then Jeff Thomas is right."

Laura shrugged. "OK. Now what?"

"Let's go back to the office. There's nothing we can do here."

Back on the first floor, I closed the office door behind us and dropped into my chair. Now was the time to consider my moves. "Regardless of the reason from this blunder, we need time to figure it out," I told Laura. "I'll try talking to Jeff, but can you make plans to stay late? Best case scenario, they'll give us until tomorrow before holding the initial probe."

Laura nodded and left. I sent a short text message to Fabian and Lisa asking them to do the same. I knew Fabian was now at the eye of the storm and I wanted to give him some time to decompress. I dialed Jeff's number, but changed my mind before he picked up. It was best to do this face-to-face.

I left for the annex where his office was located. The Imaging and Fetal Health Departments were housed on the other side of the road, a five-minute walk away. When I walked in, Jeff was in his office and talking to someone on the phone about the incident. I heard only the tail end of the conversation: "Yes, of course, we'll make sure it's documented. No, I can't say right now. I assume most of the patients and partners who were there were unaware of the seriousness of the incident. They just thought the lights went out." After a brief pause, he added: "All right. Let me do my part. If you're not happy, we'll discuss this further."

He ended the call and looked at me wearily. His forehead was creased with worry, his hair standing at odd angles. Jeff Thomas, true to the cliché about red-heads, was temperamental. He was at the pinnacle of his profession, a doctor who didn't need to prove anything to anyone anymore, someone for whom nothing ever went wrong. He wasn't a particularly talented administrator, someone who applied varying degrees of bullying to get things done.

"Gary, you know that I like you."

I took a deep breath to prepare myself for a verbal drubbing, though it's never really fully effective. A dressing down is always painful and, no matter how much you psyche yourself up, the blow always hurts. And the blows were raining down hard and fast.

Now, I've been yelled at before. I've often told my own team members that a good boxer has to be able to take a punch. But this was over the top, even for him, certainly for me.

As he raged on, I felt my cell phone vibrating in my hand. Surreptitiously, I glanced at the screen. It was Fabian; he would have to wait. I told myself that it was pointless to try to argue with Jeff, given the state he was in. In any case, all I wanted was a little time before being drawn and quartered in the town square.

I allowed him to wear himself out. When he was done, all I said was: "I understand the severity of the mishap, but I need time to figure out what went wrong. Let me investigate this with my team. I haven't even had a chance to talk to Fabian."

"What's Fabian got to do with it?"

I'd made a serious error. Jeff had no idea Fabian was involved.

"I'm not saying he has anything to do with it. I meant that I have to talk to him to decide how to get to the bottom of this. I've already spoken with my other team members."

"You have till tomorrow noon. It's your lucky day. The CEO is returning from a trip tomorrow afternoon, which is when I'm seeing him. You'd better have a really good explanation, not to mention a crystal-clear plan to prevent anything like this from ever happening again. Till then, the project is on hold."

Walking back to my office, I started a group chat for my team labeled Risk Management. My first message read: "'Only those who dare to fail greatly can ever achieve greatly.' Robert F. Kennedy." I assumed Lisa had already learned what had happened. I then added: "We have to stay late to understand what happened and decide what we're telling Jeff tomorrow. Till then, all project activity is suspended."

I was just about to put my phone back in my pocket when Fabian called again. This time, I picked up.

3

"Bottom line, it was a simple glitch, even if the results were complex. What else do you want me to say?" It wasn't clear if Fabian was on the defense or the offense. His distress was evident, his voice growing louder with each word. He ended with a loud groan.

We were in my office, which only has three chairs as I don't like using it as a conference room. I was behind my desk; Laura, still upset by the stress of the medical personnel in the antenatal ward, and Fabian were across from me, while Lisa was leaning against the door. All of us were trying to get to the bottom of the incident.

Fabian was telling us what he'd learned from the electrical team. He was doing his best to stay calm and explain, with only partial success.

Two hours had passed since we'd completed all steps needed to bring everything back to normal. For now, there was no fear the problem would recur because all work on the project had stopped and all the workers dismissed for the day. Lucky for us, it was close to the end of the day, so not many work hours were lost.

"We're simply trying to understand what happened and how to ensure it never happens again," I tried to sound reasonable.

Laura added: "Please, Fabian, relax. Really. Nobody died."

Fabian rolled his eyes, stung by the implication – and realization – that somebody might, in fact, have died.

"It could have ended in disaster, true, but for us it's disastrous enough," I corrected.

Fabian tried to breathe calmly, but soft groans escaped him with every exhalation. He stood up suddenly, then sat back down again, clearly unable to find a comfortable position. "In the last three months, the contractor in charge of wiring, finishing the electrical outlets, and hooking everything up to the main electrical panel has had a team of electricians working on the second floor. Because they're in an extension of an existing floor, the team has been working on the new part behind a temporary wall. On the other side of that wall, in the old part of the hospital, normal activity has continued as usual.

"The team cuts off electricity in the new wing periodically, or tests the ground fault interrupter on the floor. As a result, they intentionally cut the electricity there two or three times a day."

Fabian continued to explain that a hospital team was concurrently working to connect the new systems to the existing ones. This team works at night to avoid interfering with activity during peak daytime hours, when the scheduled operations are done; at night, only emergency surgery takes place.

"OK. So where did the glitch come from?" I asked.

The luster was gone from Fabian's eyes. He leaned forward, resting the palms of his hands on my desk, took another deep breath, and continued. "Last night – and this was scheduled six months ago – the hospital team hooked up the systems in the new part of the second floor to those in the old part. And the contractor was told. But, for some reason, he did not pass the information on to his own team working on the second floor during the day. In the afternoon, that team, which does this as a matter of routine, cut off electricity and took the backup system offline to test the secondary backup system. And that immediately resulted in the emergency in the antenatal ward."

The electricians, who work behind the temporary wall, built to separate the old from the new wing, could not see what happened as a result of their action. It took the medical personal fifteen or twenty minutes to figure out what had happened, whereupon the electricians were alerted to turn the electricity back on again.

Unfortunately, the electricians also have their procedures and cannot simply flip a switch. They have to make sure no one is working on the assumption the switch is off. That's why the outage lasted for close to half an hour, leading to a serious safety incident.

Coordination between electrical and installation teams appeared in our links. Furthermore, connecting the electrical systems was listed in our plans as a critical task. But we had done nothing proactive to prevent this breakdown.

I looked at Fabian, and for a moment didn't know what to say to him. Everything he said was reasonable, but at the same time unacceptable. On the one hand, he felt bad enough already, and there was little point in heaping it on. On the other hand, it didn't seem to matter what I said; he was going to keep feeling awful. "Bad day at the office" was a gross understatement.

"I think you don't understand just how complex this incident was," Laura started. I wondered where she was going. "With a little less luck, we'd be facing outside investigation, including but not limited to the police. I'm outraged by your description of it as a 'simple glitch.' What's next? Suggesting we don't look into it?"

I stood up to try to keep this from turning into a shouting match, but Fabian was quicker.

"You arrogant quack! I understand the complexity no less than you do. The way you tell it it's as if I could have done something to prevent this. The contractor forgot to inform his team! What do you want me to tell Prof. Thomas? That, next time, *I* will make the phone call?"

Now he whirled on me. "As far as I'm concerned, you can tell the good professor and all the gods above him that you found the culprit and that his name is Fabian, and that he is currently looking for another job. But, before you do, think long and hard what you'll tell him the next time something like this happens. Because what happened today can definitely happen early tomorrow in ten other locations."

I again tried to get a word in edgewise, but Fabian was on a roll. "We're starting three months of integration work, connecting new and old systems, doing Alpha testing and then Beta testing. We haven't yet connected anything and already come close to killing someone. Pardon me, but if anybody isn't taking this seriously it's you." He stood up. Laura, exaggeratedly, shifted her knees to let him pass as he moved towards the door. "Sorry, but I'm leaving. I can't sit here anymore."

Lisa, who'd been leaning against the door this whole time, blocked the way. "Excuse me, but where does His Highness think he's going?" Fabian looked at her with surprise. He couldn't leave without physically pushing her out of the way. "And, you too," she said, pointing first at Laura and then at me. "I've been managing projects for fifteen years and been involved in this project for five, longer even than you!" With a thrust of her chin, she directed her last words at me. "What did you think? That everything would fall into place without a hitch? Look at ourselves! A team of four professionals in a hospital is about to collapse, because of an incident with virtually no casualties? What will you do when a Beta testing fails?"

Lisa turned back to Fabian. "You can leave if you want, though I don't exactly understand how that will help anyone. Forget Prof. Thomas. He's only looking for a way to cover his ass. Two days from now and he won't remember this ever happened. But there are dozens of project members outside that door waiting for us, in here, to show some leadership.

"In the last three months, we've proven to them that it's possible to take a failing project and make it a flagship, a star! But now we're under the magnifying glass. They'll want to see how we cope with a crisis. And, mark my words, this will not be the worst one we'll have to handle!"

Fabian looked at her, then looked at the door. He remained in place.

Lisa was undoubtedly the most experienced project leader among the four of us and she was again demonstrating her ability to relate to project management as a profession, even at this low point. We all knew she was right.

Still, I felt I had to take back the reins.

"All of you – take a deep breath. Fabian, have a seat. Lisa, come sit down too," I said, indicating my own chair. "Lisa is absolutely right. At this moment, though, I have no magic bullet, and I assume that neither do you. I have to think about this long and hard."

Lisa sat down immediately. Fabian took another moment to make up his mind, but finally returned to his seat.

"It would seem I owe you all an apology. Especially to Fabian," I began, "and I want to thank Lisa for putting this in perspective for us. What happened today was a failure of management. I agree with Fabian that we don't know its essence and that we don't know how to keep it from happening again.

"Fabian, I apologize if the discussion began the wrong way, because there was no intention to blame you for anything. Again, I agree with Lisa that everyone is expecting us to handle this situation professionally. If we succeed, maybe we can learn something from this incident and use it to prevent similar incidents in the future.

"But, for now, I can't say that I know how. Let's gather in the conference room in fifteen minutes to continue the discussion. Try to think of practical ways to cope with the situation we're in. From my perspective, the most urgent item on the agenda is to convince everyone – not only Prof. Thomas – that we know how to prevent a recurrence."

"Fine," said Lisa and Laura, though Fabian still looked undecided.

I went to the bathroom, which was mercifully empty. I entered a stall and looked out through the tiny little window. The lid covered the toilet. I sat down and forced myself to calm down. Outwardly, I'd seemed collected, but inside I was roiling. My head was spinning with images of Chris, Jeff, and George, yet I knew I had to get all three to stop distracting me, so I could come up with the best professional solution. The feeling of razor blades cutting into my throat had abated, but physically I was far from being in great shape.

I got up and walked over to the handicapped stall, where I could wash my face in private. I opened the cold-water faucet and stuck my whole head under it, letting the water flow until I lost all sensation of cold. I grabbed a goodly handful of paper towels and stood under the warm air hand dryer to get the worst of the damp out of my hair.

I started to feel refreshed.

I made sure my face was completely dry, went into the hallway, and made a point of walking with my shoulders back and head held high. Nearing the conference room, I worried that Fabian might have left, but when I opened the door I saw him there, still looking upset. I took a sheet of paper and, with a marker, wrote "Please do not disturb" on it, and stuck it to the outside of the door. Just like at a hotel. I closed the door and took my seat. My team sat ready and expectant.

4

I looked at each of my three team members in turn to make sure I'd succeeded, at least temporarily, in calming everyone down. We had to find a way out of this crisis.

Should I call Michael? I dismissed the idea. Maybe later, I told myself.

The details of the incident, as Fabian described them, were fairly simple: If the contractor had informed his people, we wouldn't be where we were. But was this to be our only conclusion? I didn't think so. We could certainly frighten the contractor by piling on doomsday scenarios that might have happened, to the point he would never again forget to keep his workers in the loop. But this was just the electrical contractor. Who's to say this would help us get through the coming months without mishaps?

The insight that we were failing to manage the inherent risk of the project started taking hold and I therefore tried to steer the renewed discussion in that direction.

Despite the closed door, I felt that we were completely exposed. I tried hard to ignore that sensation.

I realized that the previous session had been badly handled. My desk had separated me from my team; Fabian and Laura, seated side by side, were at daggers with one another, while Lisa, who was standing because there wasn't a fourth chair in the room, was left out of the discussion altogether, though, in the end, it also allowed her to bring us all to our senses.

A discussion held at a round table is a discussion of equals, just like King Arthur's knights. The round table allows the discourse to develop according to its content without a predetermination of who explains, leads, observes, or dominates. I promised myself; no more discussions in my office, certainly not discussions that fraught.

Fabian still looked upset; in particular, Laura's presence seemed to be stressing him out.

"All right," I began, "although we marked many risks in the project map, we haven't yet made any use of the automatic table the tool generates, and that is why we're not really managing risks very effectively. Considering the activity we may expect from now on, this is a very disturbing thought."

My team members nodded. We seemed to be in agreement.

"If so, let's try to list the things we agree on based on what we said earlier. But I insist we conduct this discussion differently. Lisa – you managed to stop the previous round, and just in time! – so I'd like you to start this one. What's the first thing we must agree on to be able to provide risk management solutions for the future?

"We are responsible for this breakdown," she shot back without hesitating.

"Fine," I said. "Are we all in agreement?"

Fabian and Laura nodded.

I took a deep breath and walked over to the whiteboard. I wrote "Risk Management" across the top. The first point I added beneath the heading was:

Risk management is the project manager's responsibility.

"OK, what else?" This time, I was addressing everybody.

"I'll tell you what else," said Fabian. His voice sounded as if he'd spent the last fifteen minutes chain-smoking. "But before I do, I want to remind you that we have had a risk management chart since the project's early days, before Michael's visit even. Obviously, this specific glitch wasn't on it. I mean, who could have anticipated it?"

Laura gave him a look as if saying, *You* should have anticipated it. He, in turn, glowered at her. "Get off my back already" was his unspoken message.

Instead of answering Fabian, I turned back to the whiteboard and wrote:

The attempt to foresee all risks is doomed to failure.

"Agreed?" I asked.

"Absolutely," Fabian answered. "The fact of the matter is that we talked the process through but didn't catch this eventuality."

"Great," I said. "Let's go on."

"Hang on. We have a problem here," said Laura suddenly. "As a surgeon, everything that happens in an operation is my responsibility, and there are risks. But when a risk materializes, it's considered to be part of one's professional life. Doctors are supposed to know what could happen and try to keep it from happening, but also learn from events in which they failed to avoid the risk. In any case, the responsibility is professional, not criminal, and that's an important distinction."

"All right," I said, "but what's your point?"

Fabian's eyes darkened. The word "criminal" had entered the room and seemed to have settled on his brow. He glanced sideways and seemed to be trying to control a tremor in his right hand.

"My point," Laura continued, "is that mishaps happen and will continue to happen as a function of the complexity of the process. In other words, if a project is very complex, it will be difficult to avoid glitches altogether. I'm trying to say that the project manager's job isn't to try to foresee all risks, but to know the risks to the extent possible and create a process of learning for the risks that were not anticipated."

I again turned to the whiteboard and added:

Strive to define risks as much as possible, and to define a learning process from risks that materialized and were not anticipated.

"Did I get that right?" I asked.

"Exactly," said Laura. "For example, promote a process of learning from almost-disasters. That type of incident can also be considered an unforeseen risk. Our test lies in our ability to learn from it and adopt the learning process to as many similar situations are possible."

On the board, I added:

Promote a process of learning from almost-disasters.

"Great," I said. "So now we have a general definition of risk, but what about risk management?"

"There are very many methods of risk management," Lisa began, "and I've used some of them. Generally speaking, the method is to generate a list of possible risks and note the possible effect on the project as well as the timeframe within which the risk exists. Then, two plans are created for every risk; a prevention plan and a containment plan.

"In general, the prevention plan is supposed to keep the risk from materializing, and the containment plan is supposed to create the conditions making it possible for the project to proceed properly even if the risk materializes."

Sometimes Lisa's knowledge stunned me. She was the most professional person I knew, and I don't know what I'd have done without her. Were it up to me, I'd have given her a raise a long time ago.

She broke the silence: "But here's the thing: We are conflating project management risks, which generally cause a delay in schedules, with safety risks."

"So what?" Fabian asked too loudly. "In either case, we're talking about the project proceeding properly. Why do we have to separate the two?"

"I'm not saying to separate. I'm just pointing out a fact. Don't you agree that even if we decide not to separate them, we still have to sort the risks by category? A safety risk has to be handled differently, because we can't afford to have it materialize. By contrast, a schedule risk is something we may agree to be exposed to, no?"

Fabian shrugged. Laura looked at him with a mixture of disgust and pity, whereas he made a point of not looking at Laura at all. I noted to myself that I had to tell Laura later to ease up on him. Her attitude wasn't helpful in the least.

I felt this was another point that warranted noting, so I again wrote on the board:

Risk management requires a prevention plan, a containment plan, a risk level rating, and an exposure feasibility rating.

In any case, when I turned back to face my colleagues, it was clear that Laura had lobbed another grenade at Fabian. I didn't know what it consisted of, but he suddenly stood up, dramatically swept the papers on the table to the floor, and hissed: "You know what? Leave me alone. I've had it up to here. It's been very nice working with you, but I'm out of here."

"What the hell happened?" I demanded.

Lisa leapt to bar the door again, but Fabian was quick this time and got there first.

"Leave me the hell alone!" he shouted, and stormed into the hallway.

Laura sat as if frozen. Lisa looked at me. I didn't hesitate. "Do me a favor, Lisa. Get him back in here." She nodded and hurried out.

Laura looked at me in embarrassment.

"What did you say to him now?" I asked.

She had tears in her eyes. "Now? I only asked him if he was OK. And I put my hand on his."

"So why the outburst?"

She looked at me pleadingly. "I don't know... He was completely wound up even before we sat down." She shook her head.

"Listen, don't take this the wrong way, but I think you've been way too harsh with him."

She nodded, the tears spilling down her cheeks.

"All right, let's not make this any worse. I'm sure Lisa will bring him back."

"I actually think I should do that."

"I disagree."

Laura nodded morosely.

Was Fabian serious about quitting? I asked myself, or was it just an understandable outburst of anger? That's all I needed, I thought. I texted Lisa: "Update me ASAP." She didn't answer.

"Do you think he means it?" Laura whispered.

"I hope not. He's very upset. He has to calm down and I hope reason will prevail when he does," I said. But, for just a second, it occurred to me I might be wrong, that he would really walk out, leaving a huge gaping hole behind him, which I'd have to fill as soon as yesterday. The very thought of it made me nauseous.

"Listen, I'm going to the bathroom. I'll be right back," I said to Laura, intending to drench my head in cold water yet again.

5

I took my time, occasionally glancing at my cell phone display, wondering whether to bug Lisa again. Laura was all alone in the conference room. I walked towards my office, then turned around, not knowing where to put myself. When I couldn't bear it anymore, I called Lisa.

"Is he with you?"

"Yes."

"What's happening?"

"Wait a minute."

"Why?"

"Give me another minute."

"Should I bring Laura over?"

"God, no! Just give me another minute."

It was a very long minute. I headed back to the conference room. Laura's face was swollen. "I'm really sorry," she said. Now I had to calm her down. "It's OK. They'll be back any second." I felt I had to keep Laura in check, though, honestly, I had no clue how.

After what seemed like a very long time, I saw Lisa, followed by Fabian, through the window. Fabian looked much calmer. He came into the room and sat down without saying a word. Laura, however, couldn't help herself, and threw herself into his arms: "I'm so sorry!"

Fabian looked embarrassed but calm. Lisa defused the awkward moment by joking: "Hey – no public displays of affection. It's against the rules. And we still have a lot of work to do here."

Laura let go. Fabian seemed to want to speak. He looked at me with questioning eyes, as if most of his self-confidence had fled. I was sure it would come back in due course.

"I have to tell you, Lisa," he said in a relaxed voice, "that, with all due respect to risk management charts, I have never yet seen one that does the job. People always end up defining the risks everyone already knows how to prevent.

"As for other risks, sometimes it's possible to define them, but in many cases the 'containment plan' you referred to is simply the project plan in practice. In other words, if it happens, we'll know how to handle it."

Lisa was happy to see that Fabian was back in the discussions and answered: "Well, if the risk can be handled, let's define it as a risk to which we can afford exposure. That's exactly what Gary wrote in point number five. But if the risk is too great, the prevention plan has to be detailed."

This was an excellent opportunity to continue from where I'd stopped. Suddenly, everything that had happened earlier seemed like ancient history, and I again found myself facing the whiteboard writing another point:

The prevention plan and containment plan defined for every risk must be doable and certain to prevent or contain the risk.

I immediately felt the need to explain: "I'm insisting on the word 'certain' because defining plans that don't eliminate the risk are a risk in and of themselves, and that puts risk management into an endless closed loop. The criterion for a defined plan is the certainty that it can neutralize the relevant risk."

"What about risks that can neither be neutralized nor contained?" Laura wanted to know.

"What do you mean?"

"I gave you an example before – the risk entailed in an operation. There are operations in which the chances of survival stand at fifty percent or even less."

"That, too, is covered by existing methods," Lisa asserted. "A risk that cannot be prevented or contained ends up in the category of risks that must be justified. In other words, it is necessary to list them and explain why we can't function without them.

"For example, in the case of an operation, the patient might die unless he undergoes the risky procedure. That's the ultimate justification. But a normal project may also have risks in place because of the high costs involved in preventing them or in order to allow the project to proceed normally. For example, it's impossible to stop all activity in the maternity wing, even though that would certainly remove many of the risks."

"Again, Lisa, thank you for that explanation," I said and turned back to the board. "I think that requires another point."

A risk that cannot be prevented or contained must be justified and essential to the project. Furthermore, it is necessary to note the significance of the risk should it materialize.

I looked at all the points and felt we were actually getting something out of what had happened. Taking that awful lemon and trying as hard as possible to turn it into lemonade. How would it affect Chris and Jeff, and even George? It was too soon to guess, but we were going in the right direction.

"Are we done?" I asked.

"I don't know," Fabian sighed, "but even if we are, we haven't made a lot of progress. So, we know how to create risk management charts and define plans. You could say we also did in the past by marking critical tasks on the project map. Now we'll add plans to handle risks. Super! But let me ask you honestly – and I'm asking myself too – would any of this have prevented what happened today? If you ask me, the answer is no."

Fabian spoke simply and to the point. What's more, he was right. So where was the solution? All over the world, risks were managed exactly like this, and the seven points on the board weren't exactly the invention of the wheel. On the contrary. Our discussion was the result of common sense and the experience of anyone who'd experienced risks being realized in the past.

Where was Michael Hamilton when we needed him? But the tight schedule didn't allow me to call him. And, besides, I wasn't sure he could help us this time.

I sat down again and Fabian continued: "Lisa raised a point just a while ago. If we define risk management and then have another incident like this one, we'll lose any credit we have. It's better to admit that we don't know how to manage the risks in the situation that was created and shift the responsibility to someone who does."

"Hold it for a second!" Laura, who'd been quiet for a while, seemed as if she'd had a eureka moment. "We're going backwards but we can't afford to. I don't buy this 'we don't know how to manage the risks.' We live in a world where, every day, people climb up on roofs to fix them, mix volatile materials in labs to do groundbreaking research, and treat communicable diseases face-to-face with real live patients. There has to be a way to manage this."

"Laura," I said, "I think we all agree that, theoretically, the way to manage risk is on this board, but we all have the sense that none of it would have helped in this case. I think you feel the same way. So, what are you suggesting?"

"I'm suggesting going to someone who does know what to do in such cases. As far as I'm concerned, that person can be found in a hospital or anywhere else where risk is routine. I promise you that such a person can show us something we don't know. And I agree with Fabian on one point: What you've written on the whiteboard is fine and there's no doubt that we have to follow through, but it's not enough."

"You know what?" said Fabian after a long, profound silence. "I think I have an idea. My brother-in-law works in a warehouse that stores gases for industrial use. It's on the other side of town. The gases there are so hazardous that factories can't store them on their own premises.

"One time, I went to see him at work. I have to say, safety is their business. I'm sure they have risk management procedures and I know they manage projects because the warehouse almost doubled in size in the last two years."

"Great," I said, "but how does that help us now? We need an answer by tomorrow."

"The warehouse works around the clock, just like the factories whose gases they store. If you want, we can head out there now. Even if my brother-in-law isn't there, he can arrange a meeting with the on-duty supervisor."

"What do you say?" I asked Lisa and Laura. "Feel like a field trip? Some fresh air in a toxic gas warehouse?"

The two women smiled. Fabian was already on the phone. All the vitality that had seeped out of him earlier was flowing back. Fabian was back. If he never brought up the scene of storming out of the room, I wouldn't either.

"Come on! It won't hurt to get out of here for a bit."

"All right," said Laura. "Besides, I'm hungry. I need some carbs."

We left the conference room and the whiteboard with the seven insights we'd generated:

Risk management is the project manager's responsibility.

The attempt to foresee all risks is doomed to failure.

Strive to define risks as much as possible, and to define a process from risks that materialize and were not anticipated.

Promote a process of learning from almost-disasters.

Risk management requires a prevention plan, a containment plan, a risk level rating, and an exposure feasibility rating.

The prevention plan and containment plan defined for every risk must be doable and certain to prevent or contain the risk.

A risk that cannot be prevented or contained must be justified and essential to the project. Furthermore, it is necessary to note the significance of the risk should it materialize.

Chapter Eight

Preventive Risk Management

1

The drive to the warehouse took about an hour. We were all in the same car and Fabian was driving. The ride was unexpectedly pleasant. While we spent a lot of time together, we'd never all been in the same vehicle, and somehow this expedition to the warehouse (and the restaurant where Laura sated her craving for carbs, as did the rest of us too) filled us with peace, though at some point Laura and Fabian backslid to their old pattern and bickered over the radio station.

Until, oddly, one of them again hit a station playing "Lithium" from *Nevermind*. It reminded me of Michael and our initial meeting. I told them that, by virtue of the authority vested in me as project manager, I could decide on the station and that was it.

There was no objection. Lisa merely said that Nirvana was like a sleeping pill; Laura said the band reminded her of a depressing period in her life; and Fabian said they reminded him of goats.

Fabian's brother-in-law was not at the warehouse when we got there but Alberto, the shift supervisor, was expecting us. He was a pudgy fellow dressed to the nines, looking more like an investment banker than a warehouse supervisor. After introductions, he said he was here to help us in any way he could.

I checked my cell phone and saw several missed calls. I recognized one of the numbers as coming from the hospital. I didn't want to think who was looking for me at this hour. Jeff? Chris?

As Fabian had said, the concern with safety was felt already at the warehouse's threshold. At the guard post, we were given a thorough safety briefing, including pointers on evacuation in case that became necessary. We were asked not to operate any electrical devices outside the office building and were issued guest passes in neon green.

The path from the entrance to the office building was marked off by two bright yellow stripes painted on the floor and, even though no one else was around, we were told to walk only between them. At the bottom of the stairs leading up to the offices, Alberto told us to hold onto the railing. He glanced behind him to make sure we were all lined up, right hands out.

Once inside, Alberto offered us coffee and took us to a conference room built as a gallery above the main storage area. Alberto told us the room, with its two rows of seating facing the glass, was used every day for training sessions. In case of a leak, it was supposed to serve as command center. The room allowed a clear view of the entire warehouse floor and the sightlines were rigidly maintained so that, in time of need, the room could fulfill its function.

Alberto then launched into a short explanation about the warehouse, noting that he'd worked there for more than a decade. According to him, the warehouse stores hazardous gases and issues them to factories according to demand, either daily or weekly.

I was eager to get to the reason we'd come, and therefore used Alberto's next pause to give him a brief overview of ourselves and our project. He listened politely to my description of the day's events and my conclusion that we were hoping to learn something about risk management from him.

"You've certainly come to the right place, but don't expect any magical solutions. Risk management is hard work and involves a high degree of meticulousness."

"Oh, I know. I stopped believing in magical solutions long ago," I said. "So what kind of risks do you face here?"

Alberto was ready for that question. In fact, he could have answered it in his sleep. He categorized the gases on site into several groups according to the type of danger each group posed. There were odorless gases that were toxic on inhalation, volatile gases that could explode on contact with air, gases needing very particular handling, gases needing constant temperatures, and so on.

Storage required special structures, ventilation systems, isolation, insulation, separation, and signage. Almost any violation of the rules could result in a severe safety breach.

"It sounds as if we're sitting on top of a keg of dynamite," said Laura, with more than a trace of fear in her eyes.

"To an extent," said Alberto sincerely, "but this is also the safest place in the neighborhood. Given all the methods and procedures we have developed and implemented over the years, the risk is greater at the furniture shop across the street, and I say this with utter seriousness. There's no reason to be afraid."

"BOOM!" Fabian shouted, startling her.

"That's just great, Fabian," Laura said, using the tone of a teacher scolding her pupil.

Alberto, shaking his head, looked at Fabian. "Your brother-in-law told me to keep you on a tight leash."

"Unfortunately, that won't help much," Laura noted.

I decided to jump into the deep end. I brought up the photo of the seven points on the whiteboard I'd snapped before leaving the hospital and showed it to Alberto. I told him that this was how we were trying to manage risks and asked him what he thought. As he was looking intently at my phone, Fabian spoke to me: "Gary, it seems they don't have anything resembling a containment plan. Here, they can't afford any risk to materialize."

Alberto looked up from the screen: "That's not exactly true. We have risks that are defined as preventing other risks. For example, there isn't a single thing here that, if ignored, can create a mishap by itself. Everything has its own containment plan, so that a blunder in obeying one thing is corrected by a different thing. So, we too have containment plans. Many, in fact. I'll show you one in a moment. But first let me finish reading this."

After peering at my phone another minute, he looked up. Addressing all of us, he said: "This looks like a very good foundation. There's nothing new here; it's implemented here as well. But I think you're forgetting something important and it's what we call

Preliminary Risk Prevention. We deal not only with preventing the risk itself, but also with preventing an event that might lead to a risk and takes place beforehand."

"Preliminary Risk Prevention?" asked Lisa. "Interesting concept."

Alberto looked around as if trying locate something, finally saying: "Look, I could give you examples related to gas storage, but it would take too long to explain. Maybe I'll resort to it later, but first I want to ask you something. Let's say you wanted to walk a tightrope strung between two tall buildings, three hundred feet up in the air. What would you do to prevent risk?"

We all had something to say, but Alberto didn't pause.

"You'd hang a safety net at two hundred fifty feet, right? That's a classic containment plan. If the risk materializes, the safety net will stop the fall and you'll stay safe. The containment plan has saved your life.

"To create a prevention plan, you'd invest a lot in training. You'd try to overcome your fear. You'd practice losing your balance and trying to recover it. Eventually you'd feel that you'd done all you could in terms of prevention.

"So, now you've completed all the preparations and are on the tightrope three hundred feet in the air. Masse of people below are clapping and shouting encouragement.

"Now, let's assume for a moment that the rope has actually been strung three feet above the ground. You'll agree that the prevention plan would have stayed the same. You'd train, practice, work on recovering balance. But what about the containment plan?"

This time, Alberto did expect an answer, but we were clueless.

"You don't need a containment plan," Lisa tried. "Worst case, you jump and land on the floor in one piece, no?"

"Great," said Alberto, "but not necessarily true. In the first scenario, I intentionally left out a piece of information that has a decisive effect on the containment plan. Note that I didn't say what exactly we were trying to prevent, right?

"So now let's think together," said Alberto, and for a moment I thought he was speaking in Michael's voice. "If we're trying to keep the tightrope walker alive, the containment plan at three hundred feet is a safety net, while at three feet a containment plan is totally unnecessary. And in that case, you're absolutely right.

"But what if the point of the exercise is to safeguard the integrity of the mission? In this case, the safety net thirty feet below the tightrope walker has safeguarded him but not the mission. At the end of the day, the containment plan hasn't helped and we've failed.

"Similarly, if the tightrope is strung at three feet, the tightrope walker may not get hurt but we've again failed to complete the mission. Can someone here think of a containment plan that also helps safeguard the mission?"

Alberto looked very pleased with himself and with our puzzlement.

"I dropped you a clue," he said. "I said that in order to practice, you would have to..."

"...lose the fear," Lisa completed the sentence.

"Exactly. What else?"

"Practice losing your balance and recovering it." Lisa was again at the head of the class.

Sometimes, I envy people with Lisa's capacity for retention. She heard him say it only once, yet had no trouble reciting the right answer, while I was still trying to figure out the question.

"Well done," said Alberto, approvingly. "So, you've lost your fear of falling and practiced losing and recovering your balance. So, what then is the containment plan?"

The room was again silent. I was starting to wonder whether this outing had been a crazy idea. I thought about my cell phone and the unanswered calls and voice messages that were undoubtedly piling up.

Laura finally saved the day: "Recovering one's balance, no?"

Alberto nodded, but the rest of us still didn't get it.

Laura continued: "You can think about losing one's balance as a risk, so that all preliminary training can be considered a preventive plan. But the training aimed specifically at recovering balance is actually the containment plan. If the tightrope walker loses his balance, the risk materializes and recovering his balance is the containment plan."

"Excellent! Well done," said Alberto and started clapping his hands.

Laura blushed.

"She's also a board certified surgeon," Fabian added with a wink.

"I should tell you," Alberto said with satisfaction, "that I run this exercise in my training sessions, including actual tightrope walking. Sometimes two hours can pass before someone grasps the point."

We looked at Laura with pride, and Alberto continued: "This is an extremely important idea, because someone who understands this in-depth, understands how to roll back the risk factors and slowly focus work on the area closest to the sources of the risk, not just its results.

"Note that, instead of relating to the risk of falling off the rope, we've been talking about the risk of losing balance. Later on, we may be able to talk about insufficient preparation and prepare a containment plan for that too. I hope you're starting to understand what a preliminary risk management plan is.

"You know what?" he interrupted himself. "Take this problem home and try to think about the tightrope walker at three hundred feet. Would you prefer a safety net thirty feet underneath or doing without one altogether? For most people the instinctive answer is a safety net. I mean, only a madman would try a stunt like that without one, right?

"But for someone for whom tightrope walking is a profession or even a way of life, the very idea that there is something that can handle the risk at the expense of completing the mission might hurt confidence and increase the risk of falling. That's why some tightrope walkers, especially in dangerous situations, insist on walking without a safety net and claim that it's actually safer. But don't try this at home!"

I leaned back in my seat to stretch and saw Fabian doing the same. I glanced at my watch, trying to calculate how many hours we had left, how many hours we still had to work, and what exactly those hours had in store for us.

Alberto went on: "Now try to think how all of that relates to this warehouse. I can define a risk according to which a certain gas cannot come into contact with air. My prevention plan would include definitions for the particular valve at the top of the tank, the procedures to prevent it being opened, what to do in case we discover damage to the tank, and so on.

"My containment plan is very complex, consisting mostly of operating an emergency procedure and evacuating the premises. Only luck can save someone who's there when that gas comes in contact with air.

"Of course, I can't afford not to do more. Were I to remain at that level of risk management, my workers would constantly have their lives put at risk, and statistically speaking would experience serious incidents every so often. We have to think differently than the tightrope walker, OK?"

We all nodded. Things were starting to make sense.

"Let's get back to the gas that explodes upon contact with the air," Alberto suggested. "After a long process of thinking, we decided that any activity involving the tank would occur in a sealed, oxygen-free room. The workers in that room would work with oxygen tanks in a closed system, like firemen.

"In such a case, leaking gas can't result in fire because the oxygen isn't there. We also decided to have our workers wear fire resistant suits that provide protection for about ten seconds, enough time to leave the room and shut the door. That way, there are no casualties and the incident is contained inside a safe space.

"Our new containment plan is no longer based on luck. We have three circles of protection and casualties can occur only if all three are breached. Proper handling of the tank is supposed to prevent a leak; an oxygen-free environment is supposed to prevent a fire; and even if fire breaks out, the workers are protected, and the incident is contained in a sealed room. Compare that to the previous protection model with its one protective circle and no containment plan. You're following me, right? Well, say something!"

"We get it," I said. That seemed to be enough for Alberto who went on: "Now, let's try to take an in-depth look at the process of preliminary risk management. At the start of the process, I referred to the basic risk of fire resulting from the gas coming into contact with air. Later on in the process, I defined two additional, preliminary risks, creating another layer for the materialization of the basic risk. I defined the first preliminary risk as the presence of oxygen near the gas. I defined the second preliminary risk as the presence of workers without fire-protective gear near the gas. So far, so good, right?

"Now, if I manage to define a separate prevention plan and containment plan for each of these risks, the chances that a fire will start as the result of gas coming into contact with air, thereby causing a safety hazard, drops off steeply.

"This process repeats itself and gradually tweaks risk prevention at this warehouse. And this was just a single example. For this specific gas, there is risk management in at least ten different shapes, from operating the valve by a system of meters sending a warning signal for any change, to means preventing physical damage to the tank.

"At the end of the day, ten different unrelated processes would first have to fail for us to have a gas leak that would cause a fire and casualties. Statistically, the risk is lowered, and we continue to lower it all the time."

Fabian cleared his throat. "I think I'm starting to understand this. It's like an enormous spider web."

Alberto laughed. "That's an interesting metaphor. If you prefer to think of it that way, but here spiders arouse different associations."

"Please don't talk about spiders," said Laura, "I suffer from full-blown arachnophobia."

"Including Spiderman?" Fabian teased.

She looked at him and contracted her eyebrows: "Yes, including Spiderman."

"OK, my friends," said Alberto, "spider web or not, Spiderman or not, this is preliminary risk prevention. We preempt handling the risk using two main tools. The first is making the risk as inclusive as possible; that is, we don't handle just the isolated risk, but also all risks having the same characteristics.

"And the second is rolling the risk back to its sources. We don't handle just the risk itself, but relate to earlier stages as a risk and deal with them as well.

"So before going back to your situation, note that we have already rolled the risk back to places that sometimes seem ludicrous. We make sure that we hold the railing on the stairs, because our prevention plan includes safety awareness of everyone who enters the gates of this warehouse. That's how far we've gone.

"We also debrief every worker who is cut by a kitchen knife while slicing a cucumber. My position is that a worker who is not hurt by a kitchen knife will also not pose a danger to the gas tank we spoke of earlier. It may sound bizarre, but you can't argue with results."

"It's truly impressive," I said, "but I assume that you would also agree that, in our environment, it's impossible to invest that much in risk prevention. Were we to try, it would come at the expense of other things. How would you propose to translate that to our risk management?"

"What you've started to do is excellent," said Alberto, "but in addition to a prevention plan and a containment plan, you must also protect every risk by defining another risk, more generalized and/or earlier than it. This may be done in several layers, but even a single layer is very significant.

"What do I mean by that? For example, in your case, the electricity was cut without prior coordination. Obviously, you're not going to define the risk as 'the contractor must remember to tell his workers,' right? Even in the initial definition there will be a certain level of generalization. For example, you may define the risk as 'flawed coordination of power cut among different groups.' That's a

190

good definition and it may be that you won't have more mishaps of that kind.

"But the process layer you're missing is around the word 'coordination.' As I explained to you, if you want to get close to the locus of the risk, you have to generalize it and take a step back towards its sources.

"Now, without even knowing the contractors involved, I can tell you that your problem isn't this specific contractor who forgot to inform his workers. I'm telling you that in order to handle risk you have to assume that there is no coordination whatsoever between the various people working on the electrical systems.

"But if you invest in four or five aspects of coordination, not necessarily connected to the mishap that has you all hot and bothered now, you will prevent a much broader range of problems. Clearly, the problem isn't limited just to your electrical contractor. Similar glitches are inevitable in other places too."

It was already eight o'clock, and we were reaching the limit of our ability to take in new information. Alberto's approach sounded promising, but I couldn't yet imagine what our preliminary risk management chart would look like. It was clear that my team was also trying to understand the value of what Alberto was saying, but none of us tried arguing. It was obvious he was speaking from experience.

Alberto, of course, read our expressions, and immediately proposed a tour of the floor. "Theory is all well and good, but there's nothing like seeing for yourself," he said, as we found ourselves following him like ducklings to an area that smelled weirdly like cough syrup.

It seemed that, here, there was no scenario that didn't have safety procedures. We again walked between yellow stripes, and I tried to imagine how many times Alberto leafed through his risk charts before deciding that people must walk only between the lines.

Alberto finally led us to the receiving dock where the trucks unload the gas tanks they've picked up at the port.

"Look," he resumed, "we have a type of gas tank that mustn't be laid on its side. If it's not upright, an explosion could happen at any moment. For years, we had many procedures in place to prevent a situation in which it would be laid down; we even had a special, secure cage that made it possible to put the tank upright, in case it tipped over or was laid down contrary to procedure.

"In other words, we had a prevention plan and a containment plan, and we supported these plans process-wise as I explained. But nothing prepared us for the day when a truck entered the receiving dock right here."

Alberto pointed to the end of the ramp on which we were standing. "The on-duty supervisor opened the truck and, to his horror, discovered not one but twenty gas tanks lying on their side!"

"Wow," said Fabian, "I think my brother-in-law told me this story."

"I'm not surprised," said Alberto. "Speaking of hospitals, that day I was ready to sign myself into your trauma unit."

"Anyway," Alberto continued, "although we were acquainted the particular risks posed by that type of tank, we never imagined a situation in which someone else would make it materialize. The supervisor applied our emergency procedure, but it was pointless. The tanks were still lying there, and the vicinity was full of people and other gas tanks."

"So, what did you do?" I asked, remembering standing in the dark waiting for any scrap of information to tell me what was going on.

"We started evacuating the building, because that's part of the emergency procedure, but it didn't solve the problem. The whole warehouse was liable to blow up. We couldn't lift the tanks because our facility was designed for a single one that had tipped onto the floor, not for twenty tanks coming off a truck.

"But leaving them where they were wasn't an option either. The supervisor and the driver kept their cool, though. They closed the door and drove the truck out of the compound. This was a really gutsy move; as far as they knew, the truck could go sky-high at any second. Anyhow, once they reached a safe zone, they stopped, ran like hell, and alerted the authorities to close the area to traffic. This is an example of a simple glitch that could have led to horrific results.

"Later on, the investigation showed that the cold snap that morning prevented the tanks from blowing up in the truck. Now, the weather can't be considered a safety measure; that was pure luck. Of course, the driver and supervisor were praised for their courage and quick thinking, but we realized that we were *this* close to catastrophic consequences.

"When we analyzed the incident, we didn't try to provide a solution just for this type of gas. That specific problem was actually solved rather easily by one of our engineers. The tank was about seven feet long, and the engineer constructed transportation cages to be only four feet long. Since then, it's been physically impossible to lay the tanks on their side without them significantly sticking out the back of the truck, even preventing the doors from closing.

"Our most important addition to risk management was generalization: analyzing dozens of cases where errors by external parties are liable to cause safety incidents here. When I presented the issue to management, I didn't say 'We have made sure no more Type X tanks will arrive on their side,' but rather presented a generalization of all cases that might occur as the result of a safety violation committed by someone external to the warehouse.

"In addition, we started adding processes that would precede the risk and bring us closer to the risk's sources to serve as another layer of prevention. Currently, all suppliers are obligated to participate in safety trainings we hold here periodically. I can confidently say that our storage method is enforced not only from the loading ramp inwards, but also at all our suppliers and transporters. And, obviously, this has greatly reduced the chances of a whole range of mishaps with the same basic outline happening."

"Wow, to think what might have happened..." said Lisa.

I looked at all the objects and tanks around me and thought that we had to expand our list. In addition to the seven points, we also had to include every defined risk, and for every defined risk we also had to include a prevention plan and a containment plan. It was also necessary to try to precede the risk towards its sources, at least by one degree, and define prevention and containment plans for the new risk as well.

"I don't know how to thank you," I said to Alberto, "you've been tremendously helpful. That's my sense, anyway."

"Me too," said Laura, "and hats off to Fabian for thinking of coming out here."

From Fabian's face, it was obvious how much he needed to hear a kind word from her. "Just don't hug me again, OK?"

She laughed. "I'll do my best."

2

I slept badly that night, my back to Anna, my mind churning over the day's events again and again. I would occasionally get up to pace, trying not to wake my wife. In that, at least, I was successful. Less successful was my attempt to visualize our risk management plan. How would we translate Alberto's experience into the realm of our new maternity wing?

By sunrise, I still had no clear-cut answers.

But I seemed to have dozed off. I croaked out a request asking Anna to let me sleep in and get the kids ready for school by herself. She wasn't happy about it, but realized how beat I was.

It was nine thirty before I got into the car, a cup of coffee in one hand, putting the car in Drive with the other. It took a bit of jogging the car back and forth to get it out of its tight city space. Then I heard a thump. I freaked out; clearly, I'd hit something behind me. Great, I thought, that's all I needed today. I moved ahead a bit and got out to see what happened.

I heaved a huge sigh of relief when I realized that all I'd hit was an empty carton, the type our local grocery store uses for deliveries. It must have been left on the sidewalk and somehow, with the help of the wind or a playful kid, wedged itself behind my car. I pulled out the carton's tattered remains and tossed them next to the garbage cans.

I got back in the car and finally pulled out of the space, but only a few feet farther on, heard a soft knock on the roof followed by another noise. Now what? A check of the rearview mirror showed my coffee cup behind me in the street. I must have put it on the roof before getting out to check the first thump.

What a start to a morning of risk management. All I needed now was a bird to poop on my head in the hospital parking lot.

On the drive to work, I wondered if Alberto, the risk expert, would have backed into a grocery carton or let his coffee cup fly off his roof, or if his car was as safety-enhanced as a Space Shuttle. Houston, we have a problem; coffee cup hurtling towards planet Earth's solar orbit.

Ah! I should have first walked around the car! That would have been the prevention plan. I was pleased with my ability to apply a lesson of yesterday's discussion.

But what would have been a containment plan? As in the case of the tightrope walker, once the carton was crushed there was nothing one could do. It was necessary to precede the risk by one step as Alberto had instructed.

And what was the preceding risk? I shouldn't have gotten into the car with a cup of coffee. Well, that was again a prevention plan, and one I would never succeed in sticking to.

All right, then. The preceding risk was shifting the gear into reverse without a means of observation. And a prevention plan? Installing an observation system that is automatically operated when putting the car in reverse to shoo away a stray puppy or remove a carton.

What about the cup of coffee? Thinking about anticipating the risk was too much for me. All I could think of was the old cliché: It never rains but it pours. What was there about a risk, once realized, that brought other misfortunes in its wake? Maybe disrupting a routine was itself a risk? On a normal morning, I would never have put my cup on the roof of the car.

Thinking about risks is what created other risks, I laughed to myself with bitter irony.

Still, risk management is not a chart of prevention and containment plans. In fact, every hour of the day and every little mishap can be analyzed in terms of prevention and containment, including preliminary risk management. It's a way of thinking, capable of neutralizing "surprises" in a project even in general, and not only preventing risks. I suddenly understood the centrality of risk management in the project's plan.

A project plan is an attempt to define what is going to happen.

Risk management is an attempt to define what is not going to happen.

Either way, the first thing I did when I entered the hospital was buy an extra-large coffee and drink it in peace, standing up, risk-free.

My three team members were already waiting in the conference room, fresh, ready to work, and smiling.

"Hah! Got coffee only for himself!" Fabian greeted me.

He was right. I should have brought cups for everyone, but I excused my behavior: "Sorry, but I lost my earlier cup in traffic."

Three pairs of eyebrows were lifted in my direction. "Really. I'm not kidding. And there isn't even a good story to go with it. But it is related to risk management."

"In that case, do tell," Laura prompted.

"Maybe later."

She dropped it for now.

"So, what's happening?" I asked.

Lisa decided to seize the reins and said she wanted to share some insights from some working methods she knows so that we'd be starting from a better point. I was happy for her initiative. Lisa took her spot near the whiteboard and started to sketch a chart.

"OK, I think we should start from the risk sources," she said. "I propose we divide it in this way." She turned to write on the board:

Past experience

Activities defined as a risk

Safety

Mishaps

I looked at Fabian. He had clearly put yesterday's events behind him, but I still felt a need to support him, tell him how much I valued him, and promised myself I'd do so as soon as possible, because he may have been expecting such a talk. Were our places reversed, I would be expecting one too.

"Past experience includes **the risks we know of from the cumulative knowledge of the organization and project team**," Lisa continued. "These are usually risks we can anticipate and to which we can adapt prevention and containment plans. I would add problematic suppliers to the list, the ones that, based on past experience, cannot be relied on to meet the goals defined for them.

"**Activities defined as a risk** are already marked on the project map. A glitch in these activities is a problem and a risk to the project as a whole, and we therefore have to arrange a risk prevention plan for them.

"When it comes to safety, I would list **safety risks resulting from running the project**. We have no intention of managing professional risks for everyone; that's impossible. What happened yesterday is an example of flawed project coordination. Safety related to testing on the ground should also be included."

Suddenly, some of yesterday's bad feelings were back, as I remembered that I still had to report to Jeff and Chris. But it didn't make me despair. I was sure that the approach we were taking was useful and that it gave me something concrete to take back to them.

"Glitches are **risks that have materialized**," Lisa went on. "We're exposed to a risk and then try to prevent its recurrence. An investigation of glitches that almost happened, the almost-disasters, is an attempt to create a constant process of learning from small mishaps we failed to anticipate."

"It's interesting," I said, "just this morning I realized – because of a string of random accidents – that risk management includes all project components not defined in the plan, in other words, everything we would want not to happen. When I look at the whiteboard, I see many aspects that, in practice, cover all our preliminary knowledge about risks in the project."

"So, what happened to you this morning?" Laura was asking again.

"I forgot my coffee on the roof of the car."

"For real?" Fabian started laughing.

"Thank you, Fabian," I said, cracking a smile, "but let's keep going. My coffee is really not the point, and the next time it happens, I promise I'll bring everybody a cup from the machine."

"Forget it! I'd rather drink rainwater from the downspout!" Fabian shot back, then turned serious. "The truth is that I left yesterday's meeting a little confused, but if there's one thing I got it's this: It's possible to create a glitch-free environment with a high degree of probability."

That last sentence was like a ray of light suddenly illuminating a gloomy, musty room.

"But," he continued, turning now to Lisa, "when I look at the board, I imagine an enormous chart that will enable us to encompass all the points we've mentioned. Scout's honor, I could add a hundred lines just under the 'past experience' point and I'm sure each of you could do the same. Do you suggest a chart with hundreds of lines? And that's before adding what Alberto proposed yesterday – a preliminary risk for every basic risk we defined..."

Lisa seemed to take the criticism in stride. But Fabian wasn't finished: "I think we have to find a way to shorten the risk documentation. A giant chart may please the management, but won't be useful."

"Don't discount things that please the management," said Laura, looking me in the eye.

But I didn't want to go there. At least, not yet.

I got up, finished my coffee, threw the disposable cup in the wastebasket, and remained standing in a sort of Churchillian pose, minus the belly and the cigar, and said: "Remember what Alberto said about our mishap? He talked about coordination between groups. If we define coordination as a risk, we can skip the risks related to coordination glitches, and assume it will contain other risks with similar characterization. Will we then get a chart we like?"

"It's doable," said Laura, "but how do we adapt a prevention and containment plan to coordination?"

"Great question," I said. "Now, if it also has a great answer, we're on track to shortening the chart."

I went back to my chair. The bitter taste of the machine coffee was still in my mouth. Maybe rainwater from the downspout did taste better. I had no idea how to get out of the dead end we seemed to have hit. Then, out of nowhere, Fabian's face lit up: "That's brilliant, Lisa! I'm realizing only now the significance of what that investment banker at the warehouse was saying."

Both Laura and I were clueless. Fabian stared into space another couple of seconds, and then addressed all of us: "Listen. Let's assume that our chart defined 'coordination between groups working concurrently' as a risk and we attached a prevention plan to it. As part of the plan, we'd define a daily stand-up meeting at the start of every workday, right?

"The meeting would last fifteen minutes and require the participation of a representative of every group scheduled to work on the floor over the next twenty-four hours. During the meeting, every rep would give a short description of the work planned for his group.

"Now, let's go back to yesterday. The electrical contractor's rep and the integration group's rep both come to the stand-up meeting. The electrical contractor's rep, or the contractor himself, says that the day's plan includes testing the ground fault circuit interrupter and that, as a result, the electricity will be cut on purpose several times.

The integration group's rep reports that during the night the new electrical network was hooked up to the existing network. Bingo!"

Fabian's eyes glittered as though he had just discovered the secret of life. We were still looking at him skeptically, not understanding how his excitement related to what he had just said.

"Listen! I'm serious! Not only does this resolve the problem we had yesterday, it resolves all sorts of possible problems we can't even anticipate. If this stand-up is managed right, all sorts of coordination glitches will come to light. And this is only a single layer of prevention. We can define more, and that's long before we've discussed a containment plan that provides even more protection. Do you understand the potential of this process?"

I wasn't sure. I wasn't sure Lisa and Laura understood either. But Fabian did. And how. His realization seemed to fill the room with a glow. He opened the project map and pointed to the next critical activities:

Connecting the old wing to the new

Integrating all systems

Software provider handing over the system

Beta testing

Alpha testing

"Do you miss the Gantt?" Laura suddenly asked Lisa.

Lisa snorted. "As much as I miss my ex."

"Now, look at this list," Fabian pleaded. His body seemed to be quivering. "I'm not sure I marked it properly. It's possible that we have to add another activity or two. Still, for every activity defined as critical, we'll adjust prevention and containment mechanisms and get a broad spectrum of communications and activities designed to lower risk in the project.

"By the end, we'll have a risk management chart of less than ten lines but with much more added value. It will be way more efficient than an attempt to detail hundreds of risks and handle them!"

Something was starting to click in our heads. Had Fabian really hit on a solution?

"And, this way, Alberto's method becomes much more applicable," he went on, "and the chart doesn't go on forever. We can precede risk for every area and create additional layers to reduce the probability of glitches. What do you say, Gary?"

By now, I was able to nod wholeheartedly. I again scanned the activities Fabian defined as critical on the project map. Documenting the risks this way and defining prevention and containment activities suitable to a wide range of possible incidents might make a real change. This was precisely the generalization of which Alberto had spoken.

For example, in the past, the risk of "Software provider handing over the system," was attributed to the slowness of the information system. Rethinking it now, I understood that the risk of the system's slowness was no different from the risk of the system's stability. And neither differed from the risk of the system being available for use. The system features were missing or different from what had been defined. In all of these cases, the generalized risk was that the software provider would not be able to meet the system's many requirements.

I looked at Fabian, who was still waiting for me to say something. "I'm trying to think, as you present your ideas. The more this discussion progresses, I'm realizing that the risk is located in places we haven't gotten to yet.

"Yesterday's glitch is making us look for answers only in the most obvious places, like looking for the car keys you dropped only under the streetlight. But while we're defining necessary, desirable coordination plans, we must not set aside other, no less important threats that haven't been realized yet."

Fabian looked like he'd expected something else entirely, but was still full of vitality. The Fabian of yesterday, of storming out, was gone like a puff of smoke. In fact, the Fabian of the last weeks and months was gone. This was a different Fabian – new and focused, as if the crisis had caused him to sprout a pair of wings.

I took a moment to look at my team members and imagined the hospital as an endless line of streetlights underneath each of which lay a car key. I took a deep breath and approached the whiteboard.

"This board has gone through a lot," Fabian said.

"And who knows what else it'll go through," Laura added.

Ignoring them, I wrote:

A project plan is an attempt to define what is going to happen.

Risk management is an attempt to define what is not going to happen.

"Great, Gary. That was short," said Fabian jokingly, which momentarily reminded me of the old, cynical Fabian.

"Remember Michael's sagas?" Laura asked.

"We haven't seen him in a while," Lisa noted. "Is he supposed to arrive soon, Gary?"

"He'll come when we need him."

"I sometimes feel we need him much more than we think," Laura said.

"And sometimes not," Fabian concluded. "He's just a consultant. He's not part of the team. We're supposed to be able to solve our own problems."

Laura looked at him with wonder.

"All right," I said, "let's move this to more practical realms. I want to define what isn't going to happen during the project's future. For example, I want to define how the risk of not meeting the system requirements will not materialize. I know it's problematic; the provider has already completed his work and we still haven't Beta tested it.

"But now that I understand the notion of risk management, I'm no longer willing to wait three more months to realize that we have an unstable system. I have to define an earlier, preliminary risk and neutralize it, just as Alberto suggested."

As I was speaking, I was becoming more and more convinced we had hit on a direction worth pursuing. I left the whiteboard and instead hooked my laptop up to the projector so that we could construct a chart together within the project map.

We started with Fabian's list. After about an hour and a half of work, we had a risk management chart! I felt this chart had the potential to change our way of managing risk from the bottom up, and move us to broader risk management beyond our own group through prevention and containment plans we would dictate to other teams.

Suddenly, I couldn't wait to present the plan to the hospital chief.

Suddenly, I was no longer worried about my meeting with him.

I realized I could take the challenge and turn it into an opportunity and seize the lead we'd wanted.

For every prevention and containment plan, we defined an owner and agreed that we'd follow the implementation of these plans until we got to a point where they were applied in every activity area.

"All right," said Fabian, "now what? Can we start working already?"

We all laughed. As we got up to leave the conference room, Chantal came in. "Somebody's birthday? A surprise party?" Fabian joked in her direction. She smiled automatically, busy putting the chairs back in place. Fabian, realizing his words had fallen flat, let it go, and turned to me instead. "So, Gary, are you taking me out for coffee?"

"Are you kidding me?"

"I never kid when it comes to food or drink."

"Later then. Let's get some work done first."

"You're absolutely right."

3

I knew I had to have a one-on-one with Fabian, but I couldn't decide on the right time. Sometimes it's best to let one's team member calm down a bit and then speak, when there is less adrenaline in the blood and logic is in control. His asking me to take him out for coffee almost certainly meant that he felt he needed to talk to me, perhaps even more than I needed to talk to him.

The café in the hospital was oddly relaxing. Seeing so many people in hospital robes, many hooked up to IV poles or beeping machinery, placed our problems in their rightful proportions. Almost every single person around us was suffering so much worse.

"'Failures are finger posts on the road to achievement.' Know who said that? C.S. Lewis, the novelist." I answered my own questions, before giving Fabian a chance to guess.

"So, you're saying I failed," he answered. "If that's what you truly think, then, as a project manager, you're supposed to know what to do."

"I'm not saying you failed overall. I'm saying that this experience of failure will lead you to greater achievement! People love to learn from successes, remember them, relive them. But failures garner just as much knowledge that can be exploited for future success."

I gave Fabian the short version of how I changed my approach to work at the hospital as the result of the advice I received from my forum of buddies. I think I managed to win his attention back.

"A project manager has overall responsibility for the project," I said. "It makes no sense for us to take credit for a successful project if we're not prepared to be accountable for failures. You're responsible for a glitch in a project you manage. And I, as your manager, am also responsible. But it's a professional responsibility," I continued. "A professional failure doesn't make you into some kind of criminal. In fact, it's up to you to decide the direction in which the failure will take you. If you hunker down in self-pity, it will mar your career. But if you decide to learn from it, it will make you a better professional."

It was the furthest I could go with Fabian without getting into aspects of personality that were beyond my scope. In general, the line dividing professional feedback from personal criticism could be very fine. I had learned the hard way that managers can't forget they're not psychologists and that their employees have never asked to be clients. Focusing on the professional side becomes even more critical if the employee is older and more experienced than the manager. In such situations, personal feedback can be seen as arrogant.

"There's something you're not taking into consideration," said Fabian. "You've put all operational areas under my responsibility. In terms of the workload, it's fine; everyone is more or less as busy as everyone else. But in terms of responsibility for such events – handling the electricity, and so on – chances that something like this would happen to Lisa are close to zero. She's not involved in that at all. The riskiest thing that could happen among her software suppliers is a keyboard accident!"

"Don't underestimate the impact of keyboard accidents!" I tried joking. Then, turning serious, I said: "Look, I don't believe in homogeneous teams. In every team, someone will have more operational responsibility and someone else will have more financial responsibility, like Laura, for instance."

I was touching a point I knew Fabian didn't want to deal with. The invoices Laura had to sign involved six-figure sums, as did the errors for which she might be held liable. Nobody, including Fabian, wanted to trade places with her.

"I would think you felt comfortable with your realm of responsibility. I mean, it's directly related to your strengths. You're the master of operations. Isn't that what you told Michael?"

"Fine," he said, "but I want credit."

"I don't give you credit?"

"No."

Fabian's answer was short, blunt, and unequivocal. I focused on his face and realized he hadn't gotten everything off his chest. Our coffee was almost gone. Fabian was nibbling on a slice of chocolate cake.

"Look, Gary," he said, wiping his lips with a paper napkin, "when I was a kid, my dad taught me how to ride a bike. He told me that, with his beer-gut, he couldn't run with me holding onto the bike the way all the other dads did.

"Instead, he said: 'Look ahead at a distant point in the road, and that will help you keep your balance.' I did what my dad said, because, with my dad, there was no other way. I picked a spot in the distance and rode. From behind, I heard him yelling 'Atta boy!' and 'Way to go!' but the sounds faded until, at some point, I realized I was riding completely on my own."

I nodded, trying to understand the analogy.

"That was also the point where my gaze fell to the handlebars and my face met the asphalt."

I laughed out loud. Fabian was a great storyteller, whether the subject was learning how to ride a bike or dealing with a goat who'd inhaled a wasp. But I still didn't get his point.

"When I came home covered in blood, my mom almost had a heart attack, but my dad was thrilled. He wiped cleaned my face and said, 'As long as you looked ahead, you didn't fall. Now that you looked down and crashed, don't forget you know how to ride. Just remember to keep looking ahead.'"

"All right, Fabian. What are you trying to say?" The long, drawn-out parable was making me uncomfortable.

"I'm saying you're a great manager. I really like working with you, and I hope you like working with me. But when someone looks down and crashes, you still have to be there. And being there means not talking about the crash but about the need to look up and keep going."

"OK. I've got to get going," Fabian said suddenly, and stacked the empty cups and saucers to return them to the counter.

"Hey, wait a second," I said.

He stopped and looked at me.

It was hard for me to say, but I forced myself. "I just wanted to tell you that you are a great colleague and that I don't regret having you on my team for as much as a second."

He looked at me quizzically. A strange smile spread over his features.

"And most importantly, I'm glad you didn't walk away."

He nodded and went on his way, but not before saying, "Finish my cake. Don't let it go to waste."

Obediently, I picked up a fork and did as I was told.

4

I sat alone in my office, preparing for my meeting with Prof. Jeff Thomas and Chris Dumoulin where I would have to explain the actions we'd taken since the power cut. While working with the project map and the risk management chart, I suddenly had a strong sense of the change my process and way of thinking had undergone as a result of the use of The Project Map. In our effort to define the risk management chart, we'd had to think a great deal, as not every activity could be considered a risk. Marking too many activities resulted in a chart that was too big. Marking too few activities made us think we were missing key risks. The Project Map mechanism was a kind of catch; the only way out was to think in depth and define the risks we should and could handle.

The realization about risk management that just hit me was equally relevant to the coordination plan. There, too, marking too many links resulted in an overly long coordination plan, while marking too few links made us think we were missing important junctures. An informed process of working on a coordination plan created focus on the links and junctures that were truly critical to the project's success.

In fact, there was no way to complete The Project Map, the coordination plans, and risk management chart without in-depth thinking about implementation and possible failures. Consequently, completing the process would ensure that the people planning the project had actually undergone the process necessary to implement the plans.

I realized that this insight was critical for the project manager himself and was an excellent indicator for senior managers needing proof that planning was completed to its necessary level of assurance.

This insight hit me like a ton of bricks. I realized that I had the key for this afternoon's presentation.

Yes. I could prove to the hospital administration that we were really doing what we were supposed to be doing. All I needed was an indicator that would show that the coordination and risk management plans were complete. I had often been in a situation where I had to prove to managers that a lot of thinking had gone into working plans we had created, but I never had the tools to demonstrate it that simply.

Suddenly, I felt buzzed with energy. I closed my office door, drew the blinds across the window to the hallway, ignored the phones, and immersed myself in planning virtually every word I would say. I tried to think of all the counterarguments, put-downs, and distracted and angry faces I'd be facing, until I felt I had an answer to every objection.

By mid-afternoon, I even had a short presentation of several slides.

I illustrated the first slide with a picture of Philippe Petit pulling his famous stunt in 1974 – tightrope-walking between the Twin Towers in New York – planning to explain in general terms what a prevention plan and a containment plan were, and how one can identify preliminary risks to improve these plans.

The second slide included a short explanation of the project map and the way it generates coordination and risk prevention plans.

The third slide consisted only of a title: "The project plan defines what is going to happen and a good risk management plan defines what isn't going to happen." Here, too, I planned on listing the insights at which I'd arrived.

In the fourth slide, I presented all the activities for which we'd defined prevention and containment plans on the project map.

The fifth slide consisted of our requirements of the other groups, an attempt to get the management's support for a series of steps I thought might give rise to objections.

The sixth slide showed some of the actual plans. I didn't want to go over all the plans with management, only assure them we were managing things right from now on.

On the seventh slide I created a dashboard that presented an indicator for the completeness of the coordination and risk management plans as well as some statistical data about our plans. To my mind, this was proof of the process we had undergone.

The messages I planned on transmitting through these slides were these:

My group understands risk management.

The risk management plan was constructed on the basis of an informed process rather than being the outcome of chance.

The plan encompasses all important areas.

Everybody involved in the project must help make it a success.

"Good luck," said Lisa and Laura whom I bumped into on my way to see Jeff and Chris.

"I'll be fine," I promised, looking at their expressions of pity and concern.

"Still, best of luck," Lisa said again. "Are you sure you don't want me at the meeting?"

"Positive. You have plenty of work to keep you busy, no?"

"As always."

"Maybe you should have done a dress rehearsal in front of us," said Laura.

"Isn't it a little late for that?" Lisa turned on her, annoyed.

"Really, it's fine. There wasn't enough time in any case," I said, glancing at my watch. "Speaking of time, they're waiting for me. I'll see you later. And do me a favor, eh? Stop looking so glum. I'm not about to be crucified and this hallway is not the Via Dolorosa, all right?"

The hospital's top management was waiting in the CEO's expansive office, which also served as the boardroom. There was easily room for ten around the heavy wooden table, and there was additional seating along the wall for guests. All eight senior hospital directors, including Prof. Thomas, were present.

It was evident they had all been informed of yesterday's glitch; their angry stares signaled that they had come here to lace into me. But I was ready for them.

I assumed that, given the rumors about the mishap, they all expected the discussion to focus on the incident's details and its severity, and that they all planned on participating in the semi-public flogging that was about to take place.

The CEO opened the meeting. With a grim expression, he began describing yesterday's power cut, saying the situation created was "but an inch away from disaster." A few sentences later, he gave Prof. Thomas the floor, who immediately handed it off to me.

I began with a dry description of the facts, trying to race through them, while urging the men and women around the table to focus on the first slide showing Philippe Petit crossing the two hundred feet, from the South to the North Tower one-quarter of a mile up in the air. Despite my attempt to keep it brief, I was interrupted by nitpicking questions and by barbs shot alternately at Prof. Thomas and at my group.

But Petit had the directors' attention, and gradually the discussion went from being a blame-game to a survey of professional project management in complex environments. The dry facts of the incident were all but forgotten. At that point, everything was going according to plan. I even imagined Michael sitting at the far end of the table, silent, smiling, encouraging me with his mere presence.

Not only that: At a certain stage I even dared tell the esteemed directors that their questions on specific issues indicated a lack of understanding about project management as a comprehensive approach. I sensed how the attack Dobermans were morphing into obedient poodles.

I used Fabian's example to explain how a coordination meeting would prevent similar mishaps in the future, but in the same breath said that the probability of a similar glitch was close to zero. The electrical contractor knew he'd messed up and would, from now on be walking on eggshells. Far greater risks would come from other contractors who had not experienced a glitch of that magnitude, and for them we were constructing prevention and containment plans.

I obviously skipped over our trip to the hazardous gas facility and Alberto's contribution or the fact that, as of yesterday, we had no risk management to speak of. But Alberto was in my mind the whole time, as I felt myself anticipating the hospital directors on every aspect of project management, activity coordination, and risk analysis. They were not expecting this. Some of them looked positively disappointed to have been denied a chance to berate me. But, I reminded myself, it was too soon for me to get cocky.

At the end of the presentation, the CEO addressed the directors again. This time, his tone of voice was completely different. He started giving instructions directed not only at Prof. Thomas. After stressing some points that had been brought up in the discussion, the CEO made it clear he would have little tolerance for anyone not cooperating with the plans I had presented.

Normally, I would have expected him to reprimand me for yesterday, but after the discussion he seemed not to feel any need to do so. Instead, he put all of his weight into ensuring the cooperation of everyone involved.

At that moment, I savored the sweet taste of victory. True, I didn't have a reason to celebrate. I was facing mounds of work. But I had walked into the eye of the storm and come out unscathed, feeling stronger than ever.

Leaving the room on my heels, Prof. Thomas leaned over my shoulder and whispered in my ear: "What did you have for breakfast this morning?" I gave him an enigmatic smile in return.

"You do understand that, yesterday, he wanted your head on a platter, right?" he continued.

I shook my head. I hadn't known what a close call this had been. And maybe that was all to the good.

"Yesterday, he wanted to fire you," Thomas went on. "It was all I could do to convince him to wait for this discussion. What you did in there was the equivalent of disarming a land mine you were standing on. I told you that I really like you, Gary!"

Thomas thumped me on my shoulder and disappeared down the hallway. Left alone, I started to wonder if he'd been telling me the truth. I knew him to be not only short-tempered but also sneaky, and I preferred not to pay too much attention either to his attacks or his compliments. Though what he said wasn't particularly far-fetched. So, I'd been saved from getting the axe. This just meant that, from now on, I had zero margin for error.

I suddenly felt completely drained. The thought process and the workload of the last twenty-four hours had made me walk into that meeting like a coiled spring. The energy had been let loose into the atmosphere, only to disappear without a trace.

I turned my cellphone back on and sent a text message to the team: "Just wanted to thank you for the excellent prep for the meeting with the CEO. Prof. Thomas left smiling. That says it all. Our plan has been approved without reservations and the CEO backs us a hundred percent. He's instructed all the directors to give us their fullest cooperation."

Then I added: "Meet me in the office at five. We have one last thing to discuss."

On the way from the CEO's office to the maternity wing building, I stopped in at one of the gift shops to buy a bottle of wine and some top-quality chocolate. This, I decided, required a team celebration. My people had earned it. And so had I.

Chapter Nine

Change as Working Method

1

A few days before my next meeting with George, Fabian entered my office looking worried, saying he'd just come back from his bimonthly meeting. These meetings, which had been his idea, were run with great focus, something that all participants appreciated very much.

"So, what happened?"

Fabian sank into a chair and said: "Everything went fine. It's just that I feel that these meetings, which were so useful three months ago, aren't doing the job anymore."

"What do you mean? Is this related to something that wasn't done at a previous stage? Or something that was badly planned for the next?"

"No, not at all," said Fabian. "It's a feeling I have. They're not working any longer. Three months ago, these meetings generated brilliant, creative ideas. People spent time thinking about things before showing up. I felt that the meetings had added value and were actually guiding the project along. But now... I don't know, but something's missing."

By now it was mid-August. I was feeling optimistic about my next meeting with George. The project was looking great, no doubt about it. And our high spirits were a direct consequence of our high degree of assurance of completion.

The processes we'd established in every area to improve coordination and prevent large-scale mishaps had also prevented a range of smaller problems, so in addition to improved safety and risk prevention, we'd ended up with significantly better operational outcomes. Not only that, but I could actually see the project becoming an essence, just as Michael had described.

Our activity was notable, mostly for its high level of control and stability. The operational side grew increasingly complex the closer we came to testing on the ground, but the number of surprises decreased, and out working methods served as a kind of sifter catching much of the uncertainty.

The hospital had many other projects going on simultaneously. Though there was no formal competition, it was clear to everyone that we were the hospital leaders in project management. We knew that most of the project team provided services to other projects and could compare projects on a daily basis. Often, managers, and even external providers, would tell me how much they enjoyed working on this project compared to others. According to them, our management system saved them time, generated less friction among teams, and was simply more pleasant.

And now Fabian was telling me something was wrong.

I turned my computer screen to the side and, sighing loudly, said: "I never take your intuition lightly. But aren't you being just a little tough on yourself? I mean, if everything is working well, then everything is fine, no?"

"It's more than that," Fabian retorted. "It's not just that there's no enthusiasm or no new ideas. No. People are coming to the meetings with new problems instead of ideas and solutions."

"What kind of problems?"

"Here's an example. The group in charge of preparing Beta testing is suddenly asking questions about the experimental operation. We have to come up with test subjects – women, obviously – to use the systems and provide feedback. There are plenty of solutions, like the medical school and the nursing school next door.

"Medical and nursing students have to serve as test subjects for a certain number of hours in order to graduate. And we have faculty members who'd be happy to participate. Even some members of the steering committee have volunteered. But instead of solving the problem, my people are presenting it as an issue for open discussion. I don't get it. A few months ago that would never have happened."

I looked at Fabian not knowing how to respond. He was describing a certain kind of fatigue, or at least that was my impression, not having been to the meeting. I didn't attribute much importance to this, but Fabian looked deeply concerned, as if having concluded that this trend would only grow worse unless nipped in the bud.

"Do you want me to sit in on the next meeting?" I asked.

I normally didn't participate in meetings my team members ran, assuming that in most cases my presence would have a negative impact. My being there would invariably undercut my team members' leadership, casting them as people needing supervision or help in steering a debate.

Nonetheless, situations would sometimes crop up in which I was asked to intervene. In those cases, I used my presence to communicate to participants that something was happening. It occurred to me that Fabian may need a little push in that direction.

But Fabian politely rejected my offer. He said that, in this case, he didn't think it would help. After a brief pause, he asked: "Do you mind calling Michael?"

"Michael? Are you sure?"

He nodded. For a second I was almost insulted that he wanted Michael instead of me, but I rejected the thought immediately. If he needed Michael, I had no objections. Why should I?

"Don't misunderstand me," Fabian went on, "I have no problem having this conversation with you, and maybe with Lisa and Laura as well. Both of them were in the room and came away with the same feeling. That's why I think Michael can help. At the meeting back in April he said something to me about changing working methods, but I don't think I fully grasped the meaning. What do you think? Should we talk to him?"

"Sure. I can see when he's available later today. From my experience, he'll find it easier to help if you come up with some concrete examples. A general statement that 'something's missing' will make it hard for him to get to the bottom of whatever this is."

Fabian agreed. I sent a brief message to Michael who, true to form, answered me almost immediately. The truth was that I missed him too. While we felt we were managing fine without him, there was something about his presence that always filled us with positive energy. We decided to hold a conference call precisely an hour later. I informed Lisa and Laura, both of whom were excited by the prospect.

2

"How are you all? I'm so happy to be talking with you. It feels like forever since our last conversation," said Michael, his face beaming at us on the computer screen. It is so much easier to listen to someone when you can also see the speaker's body language. Some things can't be communicated only by voice, which is why I prefer video chats whenever possible.

"We're really glad you could make time for us," I said. "We miss you here."

"Are you managing without me?" he asked with a wink.

"Most of the time," Lisa answered with a smile.

"That makes me happy," he said. "So, what's up? I assume you're calling not only to ask how I am, right?"

I started describing my earlier conversation with Fabian and asked Fabian to provide some examples. He repeated the example of the Beta testing and added another example from the already problematic integration team.

According to him, the integration team collects all problems that crop up during the two weeks between meetings and then proceeds to toss them into meetings like so many hot potatoes.

Fabian was speaking earnestly and openly, saying he had no solution for the situation and that his guess was that the situation would only worsen. According to him, he was thinking of canceling the meetings, but was afraid of a negative backlash if he didn't come up with an appropriate replacement.

Michael listened in silence, interrupting only to ask for a few clarifications. After Fabian had presented his example, Michael asked me what I thought. I said, simply, that I don't sit in on those meetings but understand Fabian's dilemma. These meetings had become one of the cornerstones of our management method, and there was something worrisome about the fact that they were turning less effective.

It suddenly occurred to me that we'd never told him about the snafu with the electricity, our visit to the gas storage facility, and all the subsequent changes we'd made.

Michael remained silent for a beat, then asked: "Fabian, do you know Allen Iverson?"

"Not personally," smiled Fabian. "You mean the guy who plays for the New York Knicks, right?"

We'd become accustomed to Michael's way of imparting information. We knew the likelihood of hearing about random events – such as parents' day at his daughter's school – and getting assigned arbitrary tasks was high. Michael had no magic answers that he plucked out of thin air; everything he taught came from real life situations.

"The Knicks player?" Michael's laughter boomed through the computer speakers. "If he was here now, he'd be pretty upset with you. No, Allen Iverson was a Philadelphia 76er. He's been retired for a while. Great player, but he never played for the Knicks."

"OK," Fabian cleared his throat, "basketball isn't really my thing. And what does he have to do with me? Want to send me to a basketball game? Hey, if it's instead of working, then – you know me!"

"He has everything to do with you," Michael said insistently. "He's a player, you're a player. Despite the fact that you don't play the same game. You said that your meetings aren't working anymore, right? Well, Allen Iverson has a solution for you."

"All right, I'm listening," said Fabian, his hands miming the shooting of a lazy basket.

"Wait, is this going to be a boys-only example?" Laura wanted to know.

"Why?" Lisa interrupted. "I played basketball in high school. Varsity, as a matter of fact."

"Really?" Laura seemed amused. "I have a hard time imagining you dunking."

"I was a great point guard. Averaged twenty points a game," Lisa said, pretending to be miffed.

"OK. So, it's like this," Michael wrested control of the conversation. "Iverson played in the NBA. His story starts in 1996, when he was the 76ers' first round draft pick, after having had two excellent years in college ball. Georgetown. But, unlike other basketball stars, Iverson never had the option of being like everyone else.

"He was born to a fifteen-year-old single mom and grew up poor in Hampton, Virginia. As a teen, he got mixed up in a fight triggered by racism, and sat in prison for a few months. After his release, he turned into a kind of community hero, but the experience did not help him become an outstanding athlete.

"He came to college only after successfully completing high school, a court-mandated condition of release. At only six foot and one hundred and sixty-five pounds, it seemed that a basketball career was doomed before starting. Not unlike your project. Still with me?"

"Yes," we answered in unison.

"So far, so good," Fabian added.

"In any case," Michael continued, "all this changed when he entered college and met an experienced coach who allowed him to realize his tremendous potential. Iverson exploded on the court, excelling in every aspect of the game. Two years of unbroken success made him the most sought-after draft pick, hands down the best college ball player."

"Suddenly, I feel like shooting some hoops," Fabian joked.

"Yeah, me too," said Lisa, though she was serious. "Did you know there's a court near here, next to the rehab wing?"

Fabian gave her a puzzled look. Michael ignored them and went on: "Iverson's first few years in the world's top basketball league were amazing. In his first season alone, he averaged four rebounds per game, even though he was consistently the shortest man on the boards. His speed, peak physical form, and control of the ball made him unstoppable. The points he scored steadily increased and guards, taller than Iverson by a head, were helpless to stop him."

"I averaged two rebounds a game," Lisa said wistfully.

Michael nodded and went on to say that, in his first year, Iverson's success did not translate into wins for the team. Despite his extraordinary achievements, the 76ers usually lost. But after a while this changed, and the team made the playoffs several times.

However, none of this helped him shed the image of being a problematic player, a stigma that had stuck to him since his teens. He refused to become another star. Off court, he continued doing what he wanted. This led to friction with the team and negative coverage in the press. His relationship with Coach Larry Brown, an interesting, brilliant person in his own right, and the 76ers' management eventually soured. Before the 2000-01 season, the team tried to trade him, despite his capabilities.

Michael paused, then resumed the narrative. "This has all been background. Now we've gotten to the year I really wanted to talk about. Are you all hanging in there?"

"Yes, we're still here," I answered for the group.

"I guess I'm Iverson in this analogy," Fabian piped up.

"Not exactly," Michael smiled. "Back to the story. The attempt to trade Iverson failed. Before the season started, in the summer of 2000, Iverson had a meeting with Coach Brown and told him something I want you to remember."

Michael, eyes gleaming, took a deep breath and quoted: "Coach, I can change."

"Nice," said Fabian. "So? Did he change?

"He didn't merely change. This attitude turned him from someone about to be traded to team captain. But before I go on," Michael said,

"I'd like to ask you, Fabian, why do you think the willingness and ability to change were so important to Larry Brown, Iverson's coach?"

Fabian didn't answer right away. I could almost see the wheels in his mind turning.

"Change enriches capabilities and makes it possible to realize inherent talent in new ways," I said. My attempt to provide the conversation with a direction fell flat.

"Variety, more options for action," Fabian tried.

"It's true," said Michael, "but I have something different in mind. What happens to people who don't make a change?"

"They become predictable," I said.

"They're like standing water," said Lisa, "they start to grow microbes."

Michael laughed. "It's a great image, Lisa. But so what?"

"It's easier to play against them," said Fabian, returning to the basketball court.

"Precisely!" said Michael. "That's exactly what happened to Allen Iverson. In my opinion, he was the best basketball player in history. I know many disagree with me, but if you factor in his background and physical limitations and consider his achievements, he is by far the greatest ever. He was a superstar."

"Better than Michael Jordan?" asked Lisa. "I find that hard to believe."

"In my opinion, yes."

"Nobody's better than Jordan."

Michael shook his head and said that, despite Iverson's abilities, other teams learned how to play against him and limited his capacity to succeed. Two or three players were always assigned to guard him, committing fouls on him all the time and keeping him away from the basket by brute force.

"As I said, it got to the point where the team stopped believing in his ability to continue making future contributions, even though at the time he was one of the best players in the world. Maybe Jordan was the only one even greater. Happy now, Lisa?"

Michael continued to say that Larry Brown knew that unless Iverson learned how to change he would hit a glass ceiling he could never crack. He was the best shooter in the league, but couldn't do the really big thing; take his team to the championship.

It was precisely why Iverson's statement about making a change was so powerful and the reason an experienced coach like Larry Brown seized the opportunity with both hands.

"The moment Iverson decided to change, success followed suit. I won't bore you with the minutiae of the 2000-01 season, but I will tell you that Iverson scored over thirty points a game on average.

"On average, he stole three balls a game and caught four rebounds, despite his height and weight. And, unlike previous years, this time he brought his team to early the second-best win-loss record in the league.

"But the most important thing was the ongoing change. Iverson learned to pay attention to his coach. He forced rival teams to contend with new situations every game, even after every timeout. By the end of the season, he was named Most Valuable Player, the highest individual honor in basketball. The ability to change made a huge talent into the greatest basketball player ever. Except for Michael Jordan. Maybe."

Fabian sighed and asked: "So I'm supposed to change? Is that what you're getting at?"

Michael smiled but wasn't ready yet to deliver the bottom line. He was still in the grip of the story. "The best example of Iverson's commitment to change occurred during the playoffs. The Philadelphia 76ers were playing the Toronto Raptors, a legendary team in its own right, with its own superstar in the form of Vince Carter. Ever hear of him? No? Doesn't matter.

"Carter was exactly the kind of star everyone loves to love, a star of the type Iverson never was. This only honed the rivalry between the teams. Both Iverson and Carter met everyone's expectations, scoring about fifty points per game. In one game, Iverson scored the last nineteen points of his team consecutively!

"You can only imagine the Raptors trying to guard him. In a best-of-seven series, the teams clashed like titans, and were tied at three games all before the clincher, which was going to be played in Philly. The city's excitement was unprecedented."

"I remember it," Lisa said.

"No spoilers!" Laura warned. "So, what happened?"

"Before the last game, Toronto understood there was no way to stop Iverson and so they made him their target. They double-guarded him from the jump-ball and aggressively brought him to the boards at every opportunity. Iverson had a hard time shooting. The beating he took threatened to take him out of the game altogether.

"Brown saw what was going on and realized that victory was slipping away. He asked for a timeout and aimed a single sentence at Iverson. He simply told him what everyone was seeing from the bench: **When they're double-guarding you, the ball has to go to someone else.**"

"OK," said Fabian, "so I have the ball? Should I pass it to Gary? Lisa? Laura?"

Michael ignored him and went on: "It was so simple. It seemed terribly obvious, but when you're playing right, in a way that has already brought you so much success, somebody else has to tell you that it's time to change. For Iverson in 2001, that sentence was enough. He went back onto the court a different player.

"In every situation of double-guarding, Iverson found the open player and passed him the ball. When the game was over, with the 76ers' victory, Iverson was credited with sixteen assists, compared to five assists on average during the season. The highest of any game in his entire career.

"His ability to change as a player won the game and brought Iverson to places in which his talent alone wasn't enough – the Atlantic Division and Eastern Conference titles and a shot at the NBA championship."

"OK, I'm off to get you all to the championship game," Fabian quipped.

"The question is whether you'll win for us too," said Lisa.

"Of course!" he answered.

Michael sipped from a bottle of water, sighed, and continued: "Let's get back to Fabian. The situation created in the project arena is very similar to the situation on the basketball court. You're an excellent player; you've played right and scored successes, but the people in your meetings have learned your way of playing. The moment that happens, none of your talent and ability can help. You have to change."

Fabian crumpled a piece of paper lying on the conference table into a ball and shot it at the garbage can. It bounced off the rim and fell to the floor.

"When you began your bimonthly meetings," Michael went on, "you drew everyone in your wake. You made them finish tasks early, take on more, think, be proactive and creative, and so on. Your success made you continue exactly the same way, but this did not ensure the game would stay as it was.

"The other participants learned that their good ideas generated more work. They learned that cooperating with you, helped you more than it helped them. It was too soon for you to notice a change. It was only once they started using your method against you that you started feeling that something was off.

"You can't complain that someone presents a problem during a coordination meeting. You created a game in which you present the problems and get updates. At the start, this worked unilaterally. But, after a long time in which you changed nothing, the other players simply learned to exploit the game for their own benefit. They, too, have problems they'd be happy to pass onto someone else."

"So do I," muttered Laura.

Michael took a deep breath. He said that Iverson, as an example, demonstrated that, at some point, things will start to work against you. "Toronto's aggressive double-guarding stemmed from their

223

inability to control Iverson any other way. The problems of your Beta testers stem from their inability to deal differently with the pressure that you, as project manager, exert on them. Just like Iverson, this is the point at which you have to make a change."

Fabian nodded, wadding another piece of paper into a ball.

"Fortunately," Michael continued, "it doesn't really matter what you change. Change the meeting's format, forum, or location, the speakers, the way of presentation. But don't give up on the essence. You still want to promote the project, exactly as Larry Brown asked Iverson to do when he told him to stop throwing the ball but still aim to win.

"The ability to make a change requires a more realistic attitude to your methods. Don't fall in love with it, don't think there is only one way to attain results. A project manager who manages to generate frequent change in how he works, overcomes opposition with greater ease and succeeds in meeting the project goals better. It makes for a better player."

"I think I understand," said Fabian, "and I still want to know what you think I should change, but first – what happened in the end?"

"What happens at the end of the process?" Michael misunderstood the question.

"No, no," Fabian clarified, "what happened in the end with Iverson?"

Michael smiled. "Of course! How could I forget? Well, Iverson went on to the Eastern Conference series, excelled, and won it in seven games. It was the 76ers' first championship in eighteen years, and it turned Iverson into the audience and city mascot.

"Later on, Philadelphia met with Los Angeles for the NBA championship game. Iverson was brilliant in the first game; in hindsight, it was probably the peak of his career. The 76ers won. But as the series progressed, the team succumbed to fatigue and the Lakers' greater experience."

"You mean he lost," Laura said, disappointed.

"It was a fantastic game," Lisa reminisced.

"I'm sorry it wasn't the classical happy end," Michael laughed, "but I think that Iverson's story is one of the great dramas of modern sports and is greatly under-appreciated. It is so instructive. Any other Iverson-related questions?"

"All right. Our project isn't exactly a championship series. On second thought, though, I can imagine us as a team, and I have a pretty good idea of who the rival team is, but I'm not going to give it away," said Lisa.

"Since when did you become so sarcastic?" Laura inquired.

"Sarcastic? Me?"

"I hope we have a happy end," said Fabian. "As for my meetings, what would you propose I change?"

Michael thought for a moment and said: "Why don't you move the meetings?"

"Move?" asked Fabian. "Like to the basketball court?"

"No, just move out of the conference room. You can say that, as the project has progressed, it's necessary to observe things first-hand, which you can't do in the conference room. You can also use this as a way of reducing the number of participants to the ones you really want, because you can't walk around the hallways with fifteen people trailing you.

"You can also ask that every group send only a single representative. Carry these tours out in a structured way and try to achieve the same goal you defined at the beginning of the process, only using a slightly different method. Summarize each of these tours in writing and forward the summary to everyone.

"I think you'll see that the change turns the clock back and you'll see more enthusiasm and greater willingness to present successes and new ideas. What do you think?"

"It sounds interesting," Fabian replied. "I'll have to try it out."

"Obviously," said Michael. "By the way, do you know Allen Iverson's nickname?"

"Not a clue."

"His nickname was The Answer."

"The answer?" Laura asked.

"The Answer," Michael.

"Excellent," said Lisa, "you had a question and now you have The Answer!"

"Exactly!" said Michael. "All right, my friends. Keep in touch. Oh – Gary? Can I have a few more minutes of your time?"

"Sure, Michael," I said, and looked at Fabian. He was still crumpling that second piece of paper. He stood up against the wall and shot. This time he also scored.

Chapter Ten

Dealing with Resistance

1

Everyone left the conference room feeling good. For a second, I thought Fabian and Lisa would actually go outdoors and shoot some hoops. Had they done so, I'm pretty sure I'd have joined them. But, instead, each headed for their offices. We were still facing another long day of work, and Michael was still on the line.

"So, how are you doing, Gary?"

"All right, I suppose. If you'd asked me this morning, I'd have said everything was great. But then Fabian showed up. I have to say that Fabian's request today surprised me. If this is how he was feeling during meetings, maybe I've been overconfident. We have to make sure not to lose control of the project just as it's coming to its conclusion."

"Do you have a reason to think that you're losing control? Is something going on that didn't happen in the last couple of months?"

"Nothing special, but there's more pressure. Most of the time I tell myself that the increased pressure is directly correlated to progress. We're doing Beta testing and there are different glitches, some of which are a little worrisome, at least until solutions are found.

"But, who knows? Maybe I'm missing something, and it's more than just pressure. There is a general sense that we're facing more resistance, as if there's a rival team playing against us on the court, to continue the basketball analogy."

"For your sake, I hope it's not the Lakers," Michael said. Suddenly it hit me: Most of the resistance was coming from managers and senior personnel not directly connected to the project at all. Among the project personnel, the atmosphere was good; people responded favorably to most of our initiatives.

Michael was still talking, but this insight came at the expense of hearing him. "Michael? I'm sorry, but I drifted off. What you said about the Lakers made me notice something I'd missed till now. There is more than a little resistance to our way of working, but it's coming, oddly enough, from managers and personnel who aren't connected to the project."

"For example?" Michael queried.

"For example, in recent weeks, some parties have been refusing to work according to the stages we defined or to keep abreast through the project map. They're insisting we use their forms and a bunch of methods from the previous century to coordinate work.

"For example, to place new equipment on the floor, we have to provide the guy in charge of hospital equipment with Beta test results. We suggested that the conclusion be updated online, but he refuses to go along."

"Have you tried to talk to him?" Michael wanted to know.

"Of course I have. Look, it's obvious that the methods we're using are better. We're doing all coordination using an intranet page accessible to every hospital employee. The page also shows the project map, Fabian's meeting summaries, system demands, glitch lists, and Beta test results.

"Instead, they want us to show up in person and fill out a form by hand. What is there to talk about? If they haven't figured out that these methods are passé, I'm not sure I can help."

Michael sighed and then said: "I knew this would happen."

"You knew what would happen?"

"Success."

"Success?"

"Yes, success. Succeeding is dangerous. Didn't you know? When you succeed, you make other people look bad. They're using older methods, insufficient explanations to management, and at some point a senior manager says to them, 'Why don't you present your plan like Gary does?'

"Nobody likes looking bad. Therefore, some have decided to join your success, even if this automatically makes them second fiddle. Others have decided to make your life miserable. Unfortunately, the more you succeed, the greater the resistance will grow.

"To a certain extent, resistance is one of the hallmarks of success. If you have no opponents, you haven't made anyone squirm with discomfort, and that's worrisome for someone whose main work is to push the organization in a certain direction. These people from equipment are fighting for their handwritten forms because they know that the second they give up one of them, people will begin to question the need for all the others.

"Perhaps shifting everything to the intranet means somebody will lose their job. The fear of jobs being cut is terrible. I'm only guessing here, but it's the type of thing that forms the underpinning to organizational resistance to success."

I thought about what he said, and, as always, it sounded absolutely logical. The price of success wasn't just an empty slogan. While I thought that the definition of success was completing the project, it wasn't just that. Success also lay in the smallest details, in the process, in every stage.

"So, what do I do?" I asked.

"There are many things that can be done, and I'm sure you're already doing some of them. You argue with your opponents, persuade them, try to show them how your requests help them too. When it doesn't work, you apply pressure through managers – your own and theirs – or through project goals, in effect forcing them to fall into line. Right?"

"Generally speaking, sure. I'm doing all that, and sometimes it works. But not always."

"Great," said Michael, "but here's the problem. Turning to management is like drawing from a savings account. You accrue credit with your methods and successes and the progress of the project. This credit registers in the management's consciousness and you can use it to your benefit as needed.

"But, as with all credit, it diminishes with use. If you appeal to management too often, they stop noticing you. This means you have to develop alternate methods for facing resistance, so that you'll be able to draw on your credit when you really must, rather than waste it on bureau-rats. In general, these methods cannot be built on you forcing your opinion on others."

I laughed: "'Bureau-rats.' Brilliant! I'll have to remember that," I said. "Sometimes I really do feel as if I have rodents all around me… But what methods are you talking about?"

Suddenly, I heard a knock at the door. Chantal poked her head in. As if conjured up by the magic of our words, she was flanked on either side by a bureau-rat. Using hand signals, I indicated I was on an important call and would soon be available. She wrinkled her nose. One of the bureau-rats squeaked something in her ear. I looked at him. For a second, he didn't look quite human. The three trooped away with huffy expressions.

"I just shooed away two bureau-rats and a secretary," I reported to Michael.

Michael snorted. "I'm glad to hear it. Don't waste any expensive cheese on them. But seriously, my impression is that you're doing a great job on the project. You turned things around one hundred eighty degrees, and I think that the failure you described almost half a year ago doesn't exist anymore. Am I right?"

"I think so."

"Wonderful!" Michael went on. "As far as I'm concerned, yours is a great case study from which I've learned a great deal. I think you're ready for the next stage and I wanted to invite you and your team here for a couple of days to talk it through. I especially want to discuss organizational resistance, the very topic you just raised. But it can't be done over the phone. Do you think you can set it up? This time, you'll be my guests."

"Thank you so much!" I answered. "We'd be thrilled."

In the last six months, I had come to appreciate how lucky I'd been back then in the bar. Michael had an articulated method of project management and his guidance and the tools he had developed put us on track towards the success of which he spoke.

Furthermore, in the last six months, Michael had become a phone pal. I would call him every week or two to keep him informed of our progress. This time, I used the opportunity to tell him about the electricity cut and the visit to the gas warehouse. "Amazing idea! Kudos to Fabian," he said.

Virtually every conversation honed my understanding in some way or provided me with another tool for the project. I was sure that we had a lot to gain from another meeting and I was curious about the topic he had defined as organizational resistance. Besides, getting out of the office and breathing different air was always nice, even that of a hazardous gas warehouse.

"Next week, we're busy with George, but the following week I think we can clear the decks for two days. I'm guessing you want my whole team at this meeting."

"That's right."

"OK. Let me check with everyone and get back to you."

I walked out of my office. I stopped at Lisa's room, but it was empty. I then peeked into Fabian's space; also empty. Then I heard Laura's voice from someplace, and, like Hercule Poirot, I tracked her down to the copy machine niche.

"Do you know where Lisa and Fabian are?" I asked.

"And what am I? Chopped liver?" she asked with mock anger.

I smiled. "I have to set something up with all three of you."

She still wouldn't answer. This was suspicious.

"Laura, where are they?"

She smiled mischievously. "I feel bad ratting them out, but..."

"But what, Laura?" My patience was stretching thin.

"They went to shoot hoops."

"You're kidding me!"

She shook her head. "Nope. They took a ball from Steve in Equipment and said that instead of lunch they would play for half an hour and then come back. Fabian left his suit jacket here. As for Lisa – I have no idea. I assume she keeps a spare set of clothes in her office, just like I do."

"Fine. Do me a favor, OK? When they get back, I want all three of you in my office. I have to coordinate something."

"Is something the matter?" she asked, suddenly full of concern.

"On the contrary," I said and smiled.

2

Two weeks later, we met at the airport to fly to Michael's hometown. My team were happy for the break in routine and happier for taking the trip together. "Laura wanted to bring her husband, but he said no," Fabian joked.

Laura rolled her eyes. "As if!"

"And what's with the luggage? You know that we're only going for two days, right?"

Indeed, Laura's bag was enormous, and she was forced to confess that she didn't know any other way of traveling. She needed several sets of clothing plus shoes because she never knew what she'd want to wear, especially when she wasn't just going to work.

"You too, Lisa?" Fabian asked.

"No," Lisa answered, "I know what I'm wearing every day of the week, regardless of location. I don't have the time to worry about it."

It wasn't long after takeoff that my team members started asking me what we were in for. The truth was that I didn't really know. I simply said I was sure it would be interesting and unusual. "Knowing Michael, we won't be stuck in an office for two full days," I added.

"How ever did you find him?" Fabian wanted to know. "In the Yellow Pages? Through friends?"

Lisa and Laura also sent me questioning looks. The flight attendants were just starting to hand out peanuts and soft drinks.

"In a bar," I answered.

"What?" Laura said.

"OK, that's it. Out with it!" Fabian ordered.

And I realized that I owed them the story.

I told them everything, including the drive to Eric's Place and the manager asking me if I was the electrician. Fabian burst out laughing, startling a good number of passengers on the plane.

"I would have stayed till they opened," he added.

"Oh, I'm sure," said Laura, filling her mouth with peanuts.

"Seriously, I'd have stayed to see the show and drawn conclusions, which I would then have shared with you," Fabian said with a self-satisfied smirk.

"I can only imagine what sort of conclusions you'd have drawn," I said. "All right. How long is the flight? I need a nap."

"Me too," said Lisa, sinking into her seat.

"What about you?" Laura asked Fabian.

"I'm going to read for a while," he answered.

"Read?" she asked, surprised.

He pulled a book out of his carry-on and showed it around: a biography of Allen Iverson.

It was still morning when we landed. Michael said he would pick us up. And, in fact, his huge grin underneath the gleaming dome of his head greeted us at the bottom of the escalator outside the baggage claim carousels. After quick hugs and handshakes, we quickly found ourselves on the highway towards town, Michael asking us how we were doing.

"So, what are your plans for us?" I asked, noticing we were not heading for the hotel.

"A basketball game?" Laura wanted to know, letting go of a yawn she seemed to have held in for the duration of the flight.

"A strip club?" Fabian leered.

"No, to see a tightrope walker," Lisa said.

Michael laughed. "You know, I'm really going to miss you all once the project is complete. I mean it." Then he added: "We're going to the movies. There's plenty of time before check-in at the hotel. My favorite movie of all time is being screened in about an hour, and I wanted to see it with you people."

"I'm so tired from the flight. I hope I won't fall asleep," said Laura.

"Which movie?" asked Lisa, half-curious, half-scared.

"This movie theater specializes in eighties and nineties films. I'm sure you'll have a good time," Michael answered without disclosing any more information.

"All right," Lisa shrugged.

"I need coffee," Laura added.

"And popcorn," Fabian said helpfully.

As it turns out, the movie was *Under Siege*, a Steven Seagal movie. Fabian was amused. Laura struggled to stay awake, while Lisa stared open-mouthed at the screen. I'd seen it and its sequel when I was a kid, and had loved the action, but now it seemed slow, outdated, and faintly ridiculous. In the film, Seagal plays a cook whose ship is seized by mercenaries. The plot is really unimportant and can be summarized by Seagal's character stabbing, breaking, throwing, smashing, and punching the dozens of bad guys crawling on and below deck. He also saves the beauty-du-jour from certain death and she, of course, becomes the inevitable love interest of the cook, who, to begin with, came on board only to flip hamburgers.

What are we doing here? I asked myself. But I remained patient. Lisa and Laura, on the other hand, were losing it. Every time another body flew through the air, they got a fit of the giggles, which grew steadily worse with every blow. Eventually, their loud laughter began turning heads.

"If you behave yourselves, I'll let you leave at intermission," Michael stage-whispered with a wink, "but till then, you have to watch. It's a great flick!"

"I'm not leaving," said Fabian, "I have to know how it ends."

"You want to know how it ends? He kills everybody and lives happily ever after," sneered Lisa.

Fabian tossed a few popcorn kernels at her.

At intermission, Laura said: "Guys, I've had enough. I'm exhausted. Can we please go?"

"Don't be such a wet blanket," Fabian complained.

But Michael nodded. "Have a heart, Fabian."

On our way back to Michael's car, we wondered about the point of the movie and if Steven Seagal would have made a good project manager. We concluded that he was definitely assertive enough, but had to get over his habit of pummelling anyone who didn't agree with him. Although, as Fabian pointed out, the method worked.

"Sure," said Lisa, "it's a terrifically effective way to eliminate risk."

When we were back on the road, Michael told us that Seagal had actually started out as an Aikido master before going into the movies. Michael thought that the method could also be applied to project management, but was having trouble articulating this into a structured methodology and therefore wanted to brainstorm it with us.

"It wouldn't hurt Chris Dumoulin to be on the receiving end of a swift kick in the pants or two," Fabian snorted.

"Never mind Jeff Thomas," Lisa added.

"All right," said Michael, interrupting my colleagues' fantasies. "We're having lunch at this diner. Laura, I apologize, but it'll be a while before we get to the hotel."

Laura yawned again, rolled her eyes, but was a good sport: "That's fine. I'm quite curious to see what else you have in store for us."

After lunch, Michael brought us to the local university where he'd reserved a small meeting room, usually used for academic working groups. The walls were covered with appreciation plaques, faculty awards, and photographs of various university functions. The room was small and comfortable, and the fact that it was located at the university lent it an atmosphere of openness, a wise decision on Michael's part. A conference room in an office building would not have generated the same ambience. We sipped at our coffees while waiting for Michael to begin.

"Well, here we are. As you've probably guessed, this movie as well as similar Steven Seagal epics gave me an idea and I wonder if it can be applied to project management. I mean something not essentially connected to the project itself, but rather to communication around it and cooperation, or the lack of cooperation you've been experiencing. When it comes to the examples you selected, I want to know more about what happened and, perhaps more importantly, why it annoyed or bothered you."

"Listen," Laura began, "this is a little awkward, but this coffee is dreadful."

Fabian barked a laugh. "You took the words out of my mouth. It tastes like stale oregano."

Michael smiled ruefully. "You're absolutely right. Why don't you go to the kitchenette? Take a left at the end of the corridor. But think about what I said in the meantime."

"Sure, as long as the coffee there isn't subpar," Fabian said.

"I hope not."

"Well, it can't be worse than this," Laura said decisively.

I used my team members' temporary absence to update Michael and warn him that, after the intensive months we'd just had, latent tensions might bubble to the surface. Michael wasn't fazed; in fact, he seemed happy about it. "Just what I wanted to hear," he said enigmatically.

The three were back a few minutes later with fresh coffee that seemed passable. We started the discussion, Fabian as usual volunteering to go first.

"My problem," he began, "it that the integration team manager keeps going above my head and complaining to *my* manager" – Fabian pointed at me – "and other managers. This is particularly maddening because he – how do I say this politely? – does not cooperate with us and never has. It seems that he pays more attention to organizational politics than to his job."

"OK," said Michael, "that's an excellent example. What about you?" he asked Laura.

"What about me?" she repeated, sipping coffee. "My problem isn't really connected to the project itself. We're installing medical equipment and the hospital's overall safety department, which isn't involved in the project at all, insists on being present to approve every installation."

"What's wrong with that?" I asked. "That's their job, isn't it?"

"Sure it is," Laura replied, "but may I remind you that you sent me to take a safety supervision course that cost almost five thousand dollars to qualify me to sign off on everything? Not to mention the fact that I'm a medical doctor by training, which nobody else in the safety department can say. It's demeaning to be told I'm not trusted."

Laura was speaking with uncharacteristic vehemence, clearly communicating the insult she felt, though she had never mentioned it before.

"Let me understand," Michael said softly, "they insist on checking something you are authorized to check yourself?"

"Precisely. And they also issue a report so that everyone will know that they're looking over my shoulder. I'm sorry if I sound harsh, but it's obnoxious," she concluded, but then added, "though not anything a kick or a fist from Steven Seagal couldn't fix."

Michael chuckled. "Thank you. That's a second great example. And you?"

Lisa sighed, leaned forward, and said: "I'm not sure this is what you meant but my problem is the negative feedback from system testing. I'm getting terrible responses, such as 'this is an awful system,' and the like, even though the glitches are pretty much what you'd expect at this stage. I don't seem to be able to create a calm, sensible process of testing, fixing, testing, and so on. I'm getting into a lot of power struggles over it."

"OK," said Michael. "So, we have Fabian with teams escalating issues and not being cooperative; we have Laura with unnecessary checking; and we have Lisa who can't stabilize a testing routine without power struggles. I think it's exactly what I needed. Let me tell you a little bit about Aikido," he said in a seeming non-sequitur.

"Be careful or Fabian will be ordering a book on Aikido any second now," said Laura.

Fabian snorted at her. "Are you trying to be funny?"

"Not at all."

Still, Michael laughed and said: "Have I told you I'm going to miss you?" His reminder put everyone back on track as he launched into a short introduction about the Japanese martial art and its key principles. Aikido, we learned, was relatively new, having been developed only after World War II.

It contains elements of other martial arts, but unlike them it is considered an art of peace, a technique to create harmony rather than competition and a way to prevent conflict and war. Odd for a method that, at least in *Under Siege*, seems pretty aggressive.

"Aikido" consists of three words: *ai* meaning harmony, *ki* meaning energy, and *do* meaning way. It can be considered a form of self-defense, but its essence is deeper: resolving conflicts by peaceful means, letting go of fear so it doesn't dictate action, and combining physical and mental strength. The notion of positive conflict resolution in project management sounded promising, but how? It seemed that this was precisely what Michael wanted to investigate with us.

"So, when it doesn't work you start hitting?" Laura wanted to know. She was bothered that she hadn't figured out where Michael was going, but Michael only shook his head and instructed us to crowd around his laptop. He now proceeded to show us several video clips of Aikido masters demonstrating their techniques while providing a running commentary that consisted of the following points:

Unlike other martial arts, Aikido practitioners don't block their opponents' attacks. Instead of blocking or resisting force others use, there is a "flow" and a kind of merger of the force coming from the other with the force needed to execute a countermove. Aikido teaches you to go with the direction of the flow of force and exploit this force instead of resisting it.

Aikido practitioners aren't passive. They respond fast and with finesse. But they're not aggressive either, and the response is not calculated to inflict immediate damage to the other. The response can be described as assertive because it shows self-confidence and awareness of the force being used, but there is an avoidance of aggression.

The outcome of Aikido isn't win-win, because one side does "lose." On the other hand, the result isn't necessarily zero sum either, because the "loser" is only temporarily neutralized rather than hurt.

To avoid blocking, which is an instinctive response, it is necessary to let go of fear. To hold back from beating the opponent and harming him, it is necessary to strive for a non-violent form of conflict resolution.

Without Steven Seagal portraying a ship's cook and bodies flying all over the screen, it was easier to see the flow and the principle of exploiting the opponent's force for defense.

But why was it so important to avoid blocking one's opponent? And how would you apply this to project management? Michael insisted that Aikido's principles were perfectly aligned with the principles of good organizational conduct of project managers and others.

Newton's third law states that for every action, there is an equal and opposite reaction, meaning that in every interaction, there is a pair of forces acting on the two interacting objects. The size of the forces on the first object equals the size of the force on the second object. When translated into Aikido, it means that every action causes a reaction of similar or greater force. Therefore, anyone who wants to stop the use of force must refrain from blocking, because blocking creates a situation of force-versus-force wherein the greater force wins.

"But is that a win?" Michael asked with urgency. "Not if you take into account the loser's determination to return with even greater force and seek revenge. Do you follow?"

We all nodded, but I wasn't sure we all fully grasped what he meant.

As if reading my mind, Michael continued: "Look, in organizational conflicts, we can think of Side A's claims against Side B as an attack. What is Side B's instinctive reaction? Blocking, of course, preferably with greater force, which is manifested in directing even harsher claims against Side A. If the reaction deters Side A and forces it to retreat, Side B feels it's won.

"But, in the long run, Side A knows that next time it will have to be even tougher in its claims against Side B to emerge victorious. And that's how you arrive at an ongoing organizational conflict.

"If Side B succeeds in responding the Aikido way, however, the conflict will dissipate. Avoiding blocks and counterattacks helps eluding the force being operated. It allows absorbing the other side's force and even using it to stop the aggressive behavior.

"Aikido doesn't espouse avoiding engagement or fleeing. It favors leading the other side to a path of no conflict in two stages. The first actually involves engagement, which allows the second stage of leading the opponent to where we want him. Following?"

"I think so," said Fabian, sending questioning glances all around.

"Great. Anyway," Michael went on, "another important principle in Aikido is calm. Not as a response to pressure or nerves, but in the sense of lowering the body's tension. A body that is free of tension, a little loose, weighs more. Think of how much harder it is to lift an unconscious person than a conscious one. The concept of 'dead weight.'

"When we're calm, we have a weight that, passively, makes it more difficult for our opponent to move us. When this is translated into an organizational environment, a situation of calm makes it tough for our opponent to begin a conflict and find a way to change our minds or force us to concede on something that's important to us.

"In Aikido, the center of gravity comes from the fighter's calm and lies in the lower abdomen. This also applies to your opponent, so that you must try to move his center of gravity away from his lower abdomen."

"I need more coffee," Laura interjected.

"Me too," said Lisa.

"Bring me one too, please," added Fabian.

"All right, I'll wait," Michael said, adding, "but don't worry. My lecture is over. Aikido is much more sophisticated than that, but these principles are enough for our purposes. OK?"

Fabian nodded, rubbed his hands together, then asked: "So why are we on campus?"

Michael smiled. "It seemed like a good place for learning stuff."

When Laura and Lisa were back with coffee, Fabian resumed the discussion by saying: "I still don't understand how to deal with the problem I presented. How do I absorb my opponent's force and use it to my own ends?"

"I don't have clear-cut answers," Michael confessed, "and that's why I wanted you all here. There are obvious implications for organizations, so the question becomes: Can we together come up with better solutions for current conflicts? What is your instinctive reaction to the escalation you described before?"

"To do a Steven Seagal and retaliate, no doubt about it," Fabian answered. "He's complaining about me? Bring it on, because I have a ton of complaints about him. He'd better watch out."

"But you said it's not working," Michael countered.

"Right, but what else am I supposed to do? Use my fists? Once, I tried ignoring it. I was summoned to a meeting because of the crap he'd said about me and I decided not to go. Well, they went ahead with the meeting anyway, where he managed to convince management that we had to change our working procedures when dealing with him."

"According to Aikido, you shouldn't have avoided the engagement. You should have gone to the meeting," said Laura, ever didactic.

Fabian stared hard at her. "You've really fallen for this, haven't you?"

Laura didn't answer, only smiled a little Cheshire-cat grin.

"You should avoid an aggressive countermove, not block the punch, go to the meeting, and then lead it in a different direction," I explained, but added, "though I'm not sure how."

"Neither am I," said a pensive Michael, "but I can tell you about the principle of leading; using the opponent's flow of force to steer him. What's the flow of force in this case? I think it's the escalation itself."

Fabian seemed to be thinking hard. His shoulders hunched forwards, but then he straightened up.

"Hang on. I'm trying to understand. Let's say I go to the meeting, greet everyone nicely, project business as usual. Tell them I'm happy to have been invited even. And then, when they start to discuss the escalation, I say, 'Yup, he's right.' Now there's an energy in the room he now expects to use to his own advantage, but instead of allowing the discussion to go the anticipated route, I suggest an alternate solution to the situation, one that is less advantageous to him."

"Clever, but what good does that do? He'll say no," Lisa argued.

"Yes, but he asked for the meeting," Fabian answered. "He raised the issue, I agreed with him, so I've banked some credit and I have the ball. Now I offer a solution. It won't be so easy for him to reject it. I'm using his own momentum against him here."

The intensity that Fabian brought to this exercise was infectious. Suddenly, all of us started to think Aikido and toss out examples, scenarios, and solutions. I looked at Michael and thought: How does he do it? How does he manage to take something seemingly unrelated to our project and make it pertinent to the situation? And how, damn it, does he make it work, every time?

I was used to looking for solutions in the arena of work itself, but with Michael it seemed to be the opposite: Every problem dredged up associations to other places, whether it was a navigation app, a basketball player, a parents' day at school, or Steven Seagal. Everything was connected to everything else.

At a certain point, Laura said: "I'm sorry we walked out on *Under Siege* at intermission."

Fabian snorted and said: "Don't worry. Michael has planned a Seagal marathon for tomorrow, am I right, Michael?"

But Michael just smiled and stayed silent.

"All right. In the conflict I presented," Laura was thinking out loud, "my opponent's energy is the insistence on doing safety inspections. How do I exploit this energy to resolve the conflict?"

"I know, I know, I know," Lisa cried like an excited sixth-grader.

"Really?" I said, lifting an eyebrow.

"Yes, I do, and I want you to do it right now! Let's see if it works. Send them an email saying that, next week, there are three safety tests a day and you are therefore asking for a safety department representative to be assigned to you full-time for the whole week."

"There's no way they'll assign me somebody for the week," Laura replied.

"Exactly!" Lisa laughed. We realized she understood what would happen but wanted to make sure we arrived at the same conclusion.

"We can reasonably assume they'll email Laura back saying they can't do it," I said. "In which case, if they're not willing to assign an employee, they'll be forced to skip the whole thing and tell Laura she'll have to manage on her own. Or she'll suggest that she can manage by herself. Either way, from that point onward, I think the entire double inspection thing will simply evaporate. Fascinating."

"It's not only fascinating, I'm sure it'll be effective too. However, my problem is a little tougher," Lisa said.

It seemed that Michael had bowed out of the discussion, preferring to observe rather than participate. He really wanted to see what we had to say about the application of Aikido principles and was happy to see the discussion develop without him.

"In my case, the conflict isn't between me and someone else, but between two parties I oversee. The one who carries out quality testing claims the system is bad and the other counterattacks by saying the testing is wrong. It's a vicious cycle," Lisa explained.

"I know, I know, I know!" Laura, who had just finished emailing the hospital's safety department, was subconsciously mimicking Lisa.

The rest of us broke up. "Well, maybe I don't *know*, but I think that something in the working method isn't allowing the conflict to flow or letting the cycle weaken."

"That much is obvious," I said, "that's precisely the problem. But if we think along the principles we learned today, the development group must be persuaded to avoid blocking and instead flow with the feedback from the testing group. But how?"

"Maybe, if the development group is made to feel that it's to its advantage, it'll adopt this approach. Lisa should make sure of it," Laura said, thinking hard. She continued: "For example, as of now, the number of glitches is presented in reports that go to management. Obviously, this makes the development group unhappy. But what would happen if, instead of a list of glitches, the development group were to be given full credit – in front of management – for resolving problems the testing group identifies? Suddenly, instead of resisting, they'll want as many glitches as possible, so they can look really good for fixing them."

"Laura, are you saying that if I follow up on glitches that are fixed instead of the glitches themselves I'll have united the interests of the two groups?" Lisa asked. "Wow. One group earns credit for finding the problems and the other group earns credit for solving them. This is the language of shared achievement instead of conflict, even though in essence nothing has changed."

"This is amazing!" Michael was truly excited. "Simply wonderful. I've been thinking about this for months and you have now managed to apply the principles to three organizational problems of distinct and separate natures in a single afternoon! It really works. I can't tell you how happy I am!"

It seemed as if Michael wanted to envelop each one of us in a bear hug. His eyes shining, he went on: "The truth is that the part I love most about Aikido is the calm and how it affects the opponent's ability to change your mind.

"Try it the next time you attend a meeting where there's conflict. Sink into your chair, slow your responses, and make yourselves as heavy as you can."

"Can we continue thinking about it over dinner?" Laura wanted to know. "I'm sorry, but this flight left me starving. My body is craving carbs."

* * *

We had dinner at a restaurant just off campus. Nobody had the energy to go into town. We were all tired. I was sure Michael had plans for us for the next day too, but I was wrong. During dinner, he asked if he could see me privately in the morning, and then suggested I use the rest of the day to have fun with my team and build team spirit.

I immediately knew where I'd take them; the bar where it all started, though not to Eric's Place, even if Fabian begged me to take him.

And, so, we found ourselves back where it all began. I felt a wave of nostalgia washing over me as soon as I saw the bar's front door. So much had happened since then, I thought. So much had depended on random luck. What would have happened had I chosen not to go into this bar and not met Michael? Would I have been in the same place and the same situation? Would all of us have been?

But bars have a pulse of their own and the place was exactly as I remembered it. This time, though, instead of sitting at the bar, we took a table for four and intended to make a meal out of it, even though Laura said she was feeling nauseous and wasn't sure she could eat. She looked exhausted and I suspected she wanted to be home already.

We didn't talk about work. The distance from the hospital and relative peace and quiet we'd achieved thanks to better progress in the project allowed us to take a timeout with a clear conscience. On the table were triangles of garlic toast, toppings, and a little dish of olive oil.

"So, what are you going to do when it's all over?" Fabian suddenly asked Laura.

The question seemed to take her aback. "I haven't thought it through altogether, but if you're asking me if I'm going back to

245

practicing medicine or staying in project management, then the answer is pretty straightforward. I never thought of this as a career change. I've learned a great deal, but I don't see myself leaving medicine. I assume I'll go back to doctoring as soon as the project makes that possible."

Laura was looking around for the barman, who was also the bouncer and waiter and maybe the cook as well, but he was nowhere to be seen. "This garlic bread just made me feel sicker. I need some water."

"I'll get it," I said. "In medicine, there is something beyond the profession. I don't think I could be a doctor, but I can understand a medical person not finding other work satisfying."

"Personally, I love our profession," said Lisa. "At one point, I was a product manager – an unhappy product manager. I mean, I thought I'd like it, and at first the conferences, marketing efforts, and product definitions seemed interesting, but I found myself going back to project management. I realized I had treated product management just like project management, so I decided that that's where I belong. Project management involves leadership and being in the eye of the storm. And I'm not ashamed to say that, often, it boosts my ego."

"For me, it either boosts my ego or kicks it to pieces, depending on when you ask," Fabian said ruefully.

"I think my ego needs to throw up," Laura whispered. "I think I've got some kind of bug."

"End-of-project bug," said Fabian, "it's a well-known phenomenon."

"I like the challenge," I said. "The tougher the project, the sweeter the process of beating the obstacles. And that goes not only for the operational aspect. The people around you want to see you as self-confident, even – or especially – when there are problems. So your challenge is twofold: to resolve the problems themselves and to help the project team deal with them. When I was here last year, I felt that maybe the challenge was too great, but that's all history now," I smiled, again glancing at the bar and the seat I'd occupied in my first conversation with Michael.

"Speaking of challenges, what's next for you?" Lisa asked, catching me unawares.

That morning, I'd had a very interesting talk with Michael involving a fascinating offer. I felt it would be wrong to hide it from the team.

"You have no idea how timely that question is," I began. "I spoke with Michael this morning. I'm sure you realized he wanted to meet with me in private. He thinks that the method he developed can replace existing management methods. We need no convincing, but that's just us. What about every other project manager? Anyway, he wants to start a company that will apply his methods and develop the relevant tools."

"Wow," said Fabian, "and he wants you!"

"Yes, he wants me to join him. How and in what capacity precisely? No idea. First I have to be sure that it's something I want to do."

"That's amazing," Lisa was delighted for me. "I mean, I hate the idea of not working with you anymore, but it's a great opportunity. I hope he's willing to wait until the end of the project."

"Of course. Besides, right now, the idea has just been floated; I haven't had a chance to consider it seriously. But I wanted to share because you've been a part of the process and I didn't think it would be right to keep it from you."

I felt our time together needed an injection of energy, given the surprise I'd just sprung, but I didn't know what direction to take. Instead, the table went quiet. Maybe my team members were wondering how this would affect them. The silence grew longer and turned awkward. In such situations, Fabian could usually be relied on to make some flippant remark, but not this time. What is there about silence that can make you feel so uncomfortable?

"I hope this wasn't a bombshell. It's not something that's happening tomorrow or the day after."

"No, no, we're fine," said Fabian.

Silence descended once more. The background music playing in the bar resolved itself into a piece I knew – "Misfit" by Curiosity Killed the Cat. I started laughing, eliciting questioning looks from my tablemates.

The silence reminded me of a senior manager meeting my fellow students and I attended in the last year of our MBA program. Each senior manager was asked to give the soon-to-be-graduates a tip. The one I remembered best was "Speak less, be quiet more." Seriously? the MC of that event asked that senior manager. That's your tip for new managers? Yes, he insisted. This tip is especially important for young managers like these. When you're quiet, several processes occur around you.

First, the level of expectation from you drops. Everyone is thinking, oh, he's quiet because he doesn't have anything to say. So, later, after you do say something clever, you sound much more intelligent because the level of expectation from you is lower. Furthermore, when you are silent more, you disclose less information and focus on the things you really want to express, the things that serve your goals the best.

During a discussion, the information you provide immediately fuels talk, and in many cases it can and is used against you. If you share less, it's harder to argue with you. It's no coincidence that people who are quiet are often considered more ruthless, more calculated, and more cerebral. Talkative people, on the other hand, quickly lose respect.

The students, who at first considered the tip a joke, were suddenly more attentive and quiet.

The MC, however, wasn't done. Why, he asked, is this important specifically for new managers?

In response, the senior manager said that, as new managers, we would often find ourselves having to deal with stronger, more senior, and obviously more experienced managers. Quite naturally, we would prepare lots of talking points for meetings with them, points we would want to deliver with a flourish. But, he said, it wouldn't necessarily work in our favor. Therefore, he concluded, don't feel obligated to plan speeches or fill a silence with another argument. Simply focus on your position and frame it in brief. If necessary, repeat it several times. Remember that sometimes the senior manager you're dealing with has little time or is weary and therefore impatient. If you take your time don't try to push the conversation forward, you have a better chance that he will lose his patience before you, and this gives you a slight edge against him.

And I'm not only talking about face-to-face meetings or formal discussions. It's OK to keep quiet also when using digital communication systems – email, text messages, and organizational chats. The patience to allow things to happen in their own good time, the ability to provide your employees with room for maneuvering, and the capacity to wait for the other side to blink first in a negotiation all depend on self-control, on silence.

* * *

"What are you laughing at?" Fabian finally broke the silence.

I took a deep breath and spoke about the advantages of quiet I'd learned about almost twenty years earlier.

"I actually don't have a problem with silence," Lisa said.

"I'm never silent," Fabian stated the obvious. "It's not good for me. If I think too much about what to say and when to say it, it feels... Well, it makes me feel constipated."

"Ugh, Fabian." Laura had come back from the restroom just into time to hear Fabian. She crinkled her nose. "You're making me even queasier with your imagery."

"Are you OK?" Lisa inquired.

"Yeah, I'll be fine."

"So, do you apply all of that?" Lisa stared at me, clearly wanting to know. "Because you're not exactly a Trappist monk..."

"You're right. But I get it, and sometimes it affects my behavior. I told you, it's more an issue of control and self-discipline than some kind of vow of silence. Managers aren't supposed to be quiet. They're supposed to communicate things that matter. But, sometimes, to get there, you have to stop en route as an exercise."

249

We had finished lunch and had our coffee. Nobody wanted dessert, especially not Laura who expressed her objection quite vehemently. I think she expected the rest of us to abstain too.

The way back passed in silence. Perhaps my words had had an effect, or maybe it was because we were driving along back roads and the scenery was spectacular. But, in my mind, I was already back at the hospital. Over the next three months, we expected to see our baby start taking its first steps. The many systems were supposed to start functioning in real time.

As for Michael's proposal, I intended to shelve it for now, at least until I felt that I could once again go to the top of the Jenga tower.

Chapter Eleven

Not the Movies

The audience in the hall roared with laughter. The main screen showed a clip in which Laura, a huge pillow stuffed under her clothes, and an unshaven, stressed-out Fabian are driving fast to the hospital.

It may have been the surprise of seeing my team members playing roles or the mental acrobatics necessary to imagine Fabian and Laura as a couple (though, in a certain sense, it wasn't all that bizarre, perhaps even natural). Either way, the walls all but shook with the viewers' merriment.

In honor of the opening of the new wing, and knowing that George Madison would honor us with his presence, the hospital's management decided to contact a PR firm to produce a video clip to introduce the refurbished maternity ward.

The PR people's production company suggested "before" and "after" clips to show the dramatic change in the experience of expectant mothers and their loved ones. But while all of us were trying to imagine the glowing "after" video, Fabian's cheeky brain was busy with the "before" clip and casting the four of us in it. He kept badgering us until we agreed, which resulted in Fabian and Laura playing the expectant parents, Lisa the receptionist, and I – despite my protestation – the role of the OB-GYN.

I allowed one eye to follow the action on the screen, but my other eye was fixed on George and his team. The satisfaction on their faces made my heart soar. Hats off to Fabian, I thought, and hats off to all of us for pulling this off.

The atmosphere, as befits an opening event, was festive. Nobody remembered – or mentioned – the almost-disaster, the power cut in the antenatal ward, the thousand and one big and small conflicts along the way. And although the event wasn't designed to honor our team, we strutted around like peacocks.

At the pre-screening reception, George signaled that he wanted to speak to me alone. He then told me how close he had come to stopping the funding of the project a year ago. "I'd lost faith it would succeed," he said, "and I'd already instructed my people to look into withdrawing the investment according to the terms of the contract."

This, of course, wasn't really news, but I hadn't known how serious he'd been.

"May I ask why you decided to give us another chance?"

He smiled and explained in his typically blunt fashion: "The day I threatened you with a doomsday scenario, I didn't expect you to come back. I expected the hospital to fire you in a desperate attempt to salvage the situation. When you returned with a new plan, I realized you were more determined than I'd thought.

"I realized you managed to convince the hospital's management to continue to believe in you. I decided to give you another chance, but, as I said, I had no faith it would do any good. The fact that, today, we're celebrating here is your success, my young man, so go have fun!"

I lifted my wineglass in George's direction and said: "Thank you. That means a lot to me. Yes, it's my personal success, but also the success of my entire team."

George nodded. For a second, I felt like adding, "and Michael's too."

I considered the process we'd experienced since that meeting with George, in which he threatened to withdraw his investment. That crisis had erupted a year ago and the recovery had lasted six months. The main difficulty occurred in the first few months when we changed the way we worked, presented the project in a different way, and started using different indexes than those the project team was used to. Six months later we all felt we were in a different place altogether.

The visual tools, the involvement of our personnel, shifting the weight of responsibility to activity area managers, and measuring progress in the project by that cross-section – all of these were factors in our success. The electricity cut crisis was a setback, but in the long run it strengthened us and added an important dimension of risk prevention.

In the second half of the year, we benefitted from a well-oiled system, a high level of team involvement, and activities that came together to show real progress. But, after the initial enthusiasm generated by the changes and the new tools, came to a plunge. In hindsight, I realize that the process was perfectly natural to situations of change in general. Suddenly, the lacunae in the new method come to light, people are forced out of their comfort zone; some feel their toes are being stepped on or are put in situations where they must step into other people's comfort zones.

It is a refining process. It ensures that problems are aired, that working methods are tweaked, and that fields of responsibility are redefined. Only from the nadir is it possible to rise to the level of performance that characterized us in the second half of the year. To a certain extent, an organization that undergoes a change without a bit of a storm suffers from apathy and can never demonstrate truly excellent performance.

My mind was still flashing on events and situations from the last year. I again glanced at the screen where Laura, pillow and all, and a worried Fabian approach the hospital entrance where everything goes wrong; a traffic jam outside the parking lot, a wrong turn trying to find the maternity ward, and – the icing on the cake – a locked entrance door.

Several other amusing situations later, they come face-to-face with Lisa, the bored receptionist, chewing exaggeratedly on a huge wad of gum and chatting on her cellphone.

"Hey, darling, there's a woman about to pop here…" and, to Fabian, "Why are you so stressed out? Look at your wife and how nicely she's behaving. Forget to shave? She wake you up in the middle of the night? Or – wait – were you watching the game with your buddies?"

Lisa blithely continues her monolog as Laura doubles over in pain, panting and sweaty, and then I enter the frame in scrubs and reading glasses that enlarge my eyes to triple their real size. My bumbling appearance draws another gale of laughter from the audience.

The part where I approach Laura to examine her pillow – well, we must have shot it at least twenty times. I couldn't keep a straight face and Fabian's antics didn't help.

When the clip ended, the audience composed itself once more and straightened up in their seats to watch the more professional clip of the current situation; the early involvement of the expectant mother, the identification on entrance, the accompaniment into the department, the transmission of the information, and the navigation app inside the hospital – everything looked perfect.

The production team had been careful to record feedback from the trial subjects involved in the Alpha testing, so we had descriptions of the experience from the users' point of view as well. The PR campaign was capped by a member of the state legislature giving the keynote speech in which she said she would work to make what we achieved into a model for the other hospitals in the state, just as George had hoped. I stole a glance at him; he was glowing, maybe also a little tipsy.

The four of us ended the night at another of Fabian's must-try restaurants. Everything had already been said but we wanted to savor our success a little longer. We ordered virtually everything on the menu; I told them to go to town because George was footing the bill. Fabian was totally plastered and funnier than ever, and even Laura seemed high, even though she drank only water. However, she grew giddy over the array of desserts.

"That's the movie star in her," Lisa laughed, "they know no bounds!"

As Fabian launched into a description of a scene from a Steven Seagal epic, I leaned back and looked at my people with a great sense of satisfaction. The difference between the self-doubting, insecure team that had met Michael on his first visit and the confident group before me was startling.

I took credit for some of the success. I allowed myself this immodesty because we had taken the project, not just beyond our own limits but also beyond the limits of anything we'd ever heard about. As manager, my gut instinct told me that not only would the hospital's new technology serve as a model for others, but the way in which we managed the project would too. We had created something of intrinsic value.

At some point, I headed for the bar and talked to Anna on the phone. I told her about the laughing audience, the conversation with George, the general mood, and the celebration with my team; I also told her that, next week, come hell or high water, we were finally going away on a family vacation, damned the expense. She reminded me that she had never been to Paris. I said: "I'll see to it, *madame. Je t'aime!*" Maybe I, too, was just a wee bit drunk.

Just before midnight, I had to help Fabian to his feet. Laura was nowhere to be seen.

"What happened to her?" I asked Lisa. She looked around while Fabian giggled quietly to himself. Just as we were about to give up, we found Laura outside, speaking sweetly on her cellphone with her husband.

"Is everything all right?" we all wanted to know.

"Everything is more than all right," she answered, beaming. "How do I register on the new system? You know the pillow? It wasn't just playacting; I'm pregnant for real!"

Afterword

The maternity wing expansion at this fictional hospital is no different from any project you manage daily. Everything is based on true events. Projects may differ in their duration and complexity, the professional challenge they pose, the number of people involved, and other details, but all share the same characteristics that make it possible to improve how they are managed.

It is always necessary to think of a project as, first and foremost, a social event. It is impossible to overstate the importance of the project team's connection to the plan and its manner of execution. A wonderful, detailed plan that is intelligible only to the project manager will lead to disaster. By contrast, a clear, simple plan that is understood by all participants and encourages their involvement will lead to success.

I cannot tell you if the hospital project was a success, because it is a product of my imagination and its relationship with a real-world project is coincidental at best. But what is absolutely not fictional are the challenges and solutions described in this book. All are completely realistic and borrowed from real projects I managed or got to know in the course of my career.

The message of this book is that project management is a profession. Successful project management depends on consistent use of the right methods and appropriate tools. These help us, the project managers, document the project clearly and according to activity areas, and then analyze the project to arrive at a plan having a high probability of implementation. Such a plan can be tracked and measured not only so we can report to managers, but, more importantly, to serve as a tool for continually improving the way the project team works and behaves.

Leonardo da Vinci once said, "Simplicity is the ultimate sophistication." This saying encapsulates my philosophy of management; finding the simplest way to allow a complex sequence of actions to occur without mishap. Like other management challenges, it is easy to define simplicity but very difficult to execute. I hope that the methods described in this book will help you simplify the challenge of project management and enjoy the fruits of the sophistication that springs from it.

Appendix

Project Management: Background

What is a project?

A project is an activity that is not part of the routine of a company or organization. It has a start and finish date, resources, and contents, as well as a manager and a team. A project is planned and timed to achieve a particular goal.

Projects can be almost anything; planning an event, moving to new premises, developing a new product, construction, a marketing campaign, and so on.

When we speak of project management we usually refer to projects lasting a month or more. Shorter recurring projects may be considered part of an organization's routine and are therefore not projects in the sense we are discussing here.

Who leads projects?

Everyone! At work, at home, and in life.

Project managers can be professionals who do this for a living, but can also be regular employees appointed ad hoc. Project managers can also be self-appointed to head a project they have defined for themselves.

The more complex the world around us becomes, the need for inclusive, effective project management grows greater. Large and medium-sized organizations therefore tend to appoint professional project managers to head important projects and provide them with sophisticated tools and the full backing of management.

Why are projects so complicated?

That's a great question, because projects fail even in smart, highly-experienced organizations. One explanation for the difficulty of project management lies in the definition of a project; a break in the routine. The interruption of routines raises all sorts of questions that do not come up when organizations operate along established routines; blurred lines of responsibility, the sense there isn't enough time to complete the project, unfamiliar schedules, and the uncertainty stemming from inexperience and/or insufficient knowledge.

Some organizations and companies have no routines and handle only projects. Even those find themselves in quandaries with every complex project as every project poses its own new and unique challenge.

What are the major challenges in a project?

There are many challenges, and one could try to list some of them, but at the end of the day every project, by virtue of its own special nature, raises new problems.

In terms of planning; allocating resources, creating schedules, constructing a budget, defining the criteria of success, attempting to predict risks, and managing testing and certifications.

In terms of execution; planning versus performance, getting the team on board to make the required effort, communicating organizationally about the project, coordinating different parties, solving problems, and tracking the implementation of decisions.

During and after the project; analysis, identifying weaknesses, correct allocation of resources, managing necessary meetings, effective status discussions, learning, and creating a knowledge base for future use.

The history of project management

One of the outcomes of the industrial revolution was the increased need for project management, which in turn sparked the development of several methods of operation that, surprisingly, are still in use, first and foremost the Gantt chart, named for its creator, Henry L. Gantt (1861-1919). This chart is a visual depiction of a hierarchy of assignment on a timeline, and is similar to the way production lines and sequential machines in industry were described and visualized at the beginning of the twentieth century.

The computerization revolution of the 1950s, followed by the personal computer revolution of the 1970s and 1980s, added the ability to effortlessly incorporate tremendous amount of data, further refining project management tools.

What project management tools exist at present?

The available tools may be divided into three main types:

Project portfolio management tools; tools showing all projects being carried out by the organization, allowing management to see project progress in a very general way and make decisions on priorities, resource allocation, justification, and financing.

Project management tools; tools for planning, tracking, and presenting project activities on a timetable. Diagrams created by these tools allow the graphic representation of progress and a schedule of inter-connected tasks.

Task management tools; tools focused on lists of tasks that sort them into tasks awaiting execution, tasks being executed, and completely executed tasks. A table of this sort gives the project manager a good idea of the progress of the work.

This book deals mainly with the second category of tools, and here and there alludes to the third.

What is the common way to present a project visually?

The way projects are usually presented, which was introduced at the beginning of the last century, is still being used to present projects in the 2000s, that is the Gantt chart.

This diagram was originally created to describe production lines. It made its way into the world of project management only in the 1980s, and since then it has become the standard working method in the field. This book demonstrates that the method's industrial roots affect its every aspect, making it problematic for project management.

Below is an example of a typical Gantt chart applied to a project:

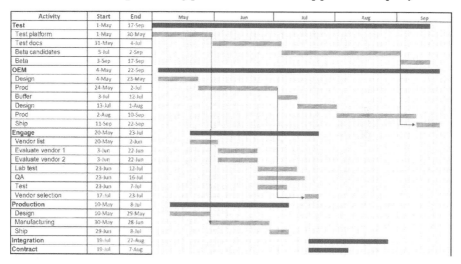

Activity	Start	End	May	Jun	Jul	Aug	Sep
Test	1-May	17-Sep					
Test platform	1-May	30-May					
Test docs	31-May	4-Jul					
Beta candidates	5-Jul	2-Sep					
Beta	3-Sep	17-Sep					
OEM	4-May	22-Sep					
Design	4-May	23-May					
Prod	24-May	2-Jul					
Buffer	3-Jul	12-Jul					
Design	13-Jul	1-Aug					
Prod	2-Aug	10-Sep					
Ship	11-Sep	22-Sep					
Engage	20-May	23-Jul					
Vendor list	20-May	2-Jun					
Evaluate vendor 1	3-Jun	22-Jun					
Evaluate vendor 2	3-Jun	22-Jun					
Lab test	23-Jun	12-Jul					
QA	23-Jun	16-Jul					
Test	23-Jun	7-Jul					
Vendor selection	17-Jul	23-Jul					
Production	10-May	8-Jul					
Design	10-May	29-May					
Manufacturing	30-May	28-Jun					
Ship	29-Jun	8-Jul					
Integration	19-Jul	27-Aug					
Contract	19-Jul	7-Aug					

This type of presentation is rife with drawbacks described in the book, but to date there has been no real alternative. As a result, even those who understand its problematic nature and would prefer not to use it are forced to do so in the absence of a better choice.

One of the Gantt chart's main disadvantages is that it relates to projects as though they were problems of engineering, even though a project is, above all, a gathering of people who have to work together to achieve a common goal. Gantt results in project engineering rather than project management. In today's social, sharing, dynamic, decentralized world, it simply doesn't work.

What is the Critical Chain?

The Critical Chain is the longest chain of links in the project's plan. In fact, shortening any task in the Critical Chain will shorten the duration of the project as a whole. By contrast, tasks that are not in the Critical Chain can be shortened or lengthened (up to a point) without affecting the total duration of the project.

The idea of focusing on the Critical Chain is also to be found in the production line, and its analogy is the longest sequence of the production line's machines. If the capacity or capability of a machine in the Critical Chain is enhanced (e.g. it attains greater speed), the total production time will be reduced.

At first glance, this insight seems like pure genius, and the ramifications of the method have led to great success. The world of project management received this method with open arms and shifted to Critical Chain analysis. This came with a veiled working assumption, namely that the project's weak spots and the risks of execution were hiding within the Critical Chain.

But, years later, that which had seemed so right on paper turns out to have been inadequate in the modern reality of project management. Many attempts to use the methods ended in failure, trailed by frustrated managers and an aversion to Gantt and related analytical methods.

Just as Gantt survived thanks to the absence of an alternative, so did the Critical Chain, because they were looking for the answers in all the wrong places. Here, too, the book presents a completely fresh take, explains the drawbacks in working with the Critical Chain methods, and offers alternatives to finding the project's weaknesses.

What is the Theory of Constraints?

This is a completely developed doctrine and can therefore not be presented here in full, but in very brief form, TOC is borrowed from the world of manufacturing and insists on carefully analyzing the production line to determine the plant's bottleneck, focusing on relieving it using the organization's resources. This is done over and over again, in a sort of wash, rinse, repeat cycle.

As applied to project management, TOC adds another layer, creating a parallel between the management of a factory's inventory and the management of a project's surplus time. Just as sufficient inventory is placed next to the machine creating the bottleneck on the factory floor so that it is possible to load it efficiently, so, in project management, it should be possible to manage surplus time in a more centralized and efficient fashion when it comes to the project's bottleneck.

A project manager using TOC will try to elicit the minimal implementation time from every task manager and promise to "save" the surplus time to the end of the project. The project manager is then supposed to be able to direct this time to tasks running behind schedule.

The method's operating assumption is that managing surplus time in a centralized way and tracking it as a function of progress may lead to raising the level of plan's certainty and the ability to carry it out in time.

The method has been roundly criticized. The ability to carry it off effectively in project management is in doubt. It is enough to mention the infinite changes typical of modern projects that pull the rug out from under any attempt to manage surplus time this way. Profound organizational education is needed to persuade task managers to report precise surplus time data to project manager. In every organization, it is only natural that people try to cling to whatever breathing room they have, and this consistently undermines the method.

What is the traveling salesman problem?

The classic traveling salesman problem tries to find the shortest route among a network of nodes. Given a list of cities and the distances between each pair of cities, the traveling salesman must calculate the shortest possible route that visits each city exactly once. The problem serves as a basic explanation for concepts dealing with optimizing possible paths through a project, but it requires a link of all tasks to one another and the assumption that the other factors remain static.

What alternative does the book offer?

The book proposes a different working method at all levels; communication about a project, its planning, presentation, risk management, change management, and more. One of the components of the new working method is a graphic alternative to the Gantt chart – The Project Map.

Where can one read more on the topic?

We recommend starting with this book and visiting the www.projectmap.solutions website related to the book. The website contains articles and more information on specific issues mentioned in the book and also refers you to the appropriate tools, templates, and suggestions for the proper use of the method.

New essays and tips are regularly posted on Facebook and Twitter @The_Bald_One. You're invited to follow!

Made in the USA
San Bernardino, CA
23 February 2019